SELECTED PAPERS OF J. R. FIRTH 1952–59

INDIANA UNIVERSITY STUDIES IN THE HISTORY AND THEORY OF
LINGUISTICS

Selected Papers of
J. R. Firth
1952-59

Edited by F. R. Palmer
Professor of Linguistic Science
University of Reading

INDIANA UNIVERSITY PRESS
Bloomington & London

Printed in Great Britain

Contents

Acknowledgments

For permission to reproduce the following papers by the late Professor J. R. Firth, we are grateful to:

Messrs. Baillière, Tindall & Cassell Ltd for 'The treatment of language in general linguistics' published in *The medical press*, 19th August 1959; Mouton & Co. n.v. for 'Linguistic analysis and translation' published in *For Roman Jakobson: Essays on the occasion of his sixtieth birthday*, and Routledge & Kegan Paul Ltd for 'Ethnographic analysis and language with reference to Malinowski's views' published in *Man and culture: An evaluation of the work of Bronislaw Malinowski*, edited by R. W. Firth.

Publications by J. R. Firth

In the list below items with a single asterisk were reprinted in *Papers in linguistics* (1957). Items marked with a double asterisk are reprinted in this volume.

1929   *Pioneers: being selected prose for language study*, compiled and edited with notes, glossary and exercises by J. R. Firth and M. G. Singh, ix, 259. London.

1930   *Speech*, 80. London: Benn's Sixpenny Library, No. 121.[1]

1933   'Notes on the transcription of Burmese', *BSOS* 7.137–40.

1934   'Linguistics and the functional point of view', *English studies* 16.2–8.

       *'The principles of phonetic notation in descriptive grammar', *Congrès international des sciences anthropologiques et ethnologiques: compte rendu de la première session à Londres* 325–8.

       Sectional proceedings of the International Congress of Anthropological and Ethnological Sciences, first session (in) London: Section H, 'Languages and writing', *Man* 34.150–2.

       'A short outline of Tamil pronunciation', appendix xxxiv to A. H. Arden, *A progressive grammar of Tamil*. Madras.

       *'The word "phoneme"', *Maître phonétique* 46.44–6.

1935   *'The technique of semantics', *TPS* 36–72.

       *'The use and distribution of certain English sounds: Phonetics from a functional point of view', *English studies* 17.2–12.

1936   *'Alphabets and phonology in India and Burma', *BSOS* 8.517–46.

       *'Phonological features of some Indian languages', *Proceedings of the Second International Congress of Phonetic Sciences held at London in 1935* 176–82. Cambridge.

1937   *'The structure of the Chinese monosyllable in a Hunanese dialect (Changsha)' [with B. B. Rogers], *BSOS* 8.1055–74.

       The tongues of men, vii, 160. London.[1]

1938   'A practical script for India', *Indian listener* 3.356–7.

1939   Specimen: 'Kashmiri', *Maître phonétique* 68.67–8.

---

[1] *Speech* and *The Tongues of Men* were reissued in a single volume in 1964 as Number 2 in the Oxford series *Language and language learning*.

1941 'Speech in fellowship and community', *The new era in home and school* 22.185–9.

1942 'Alphabets for Indian languages', in Daniel Jones, *The problem of a national script for India*, 12–17. Hertford.

1944 'Introduction [on pronunciation and the alphabet]', in A. H. Harley, *Colloquial Hindustani*, ix–xxx. London.

1945 'Wartime experiences in linguistic training', *Modern languages* 26.38–45.

1946 *'The English school of phonetics', *TPS* 92–132.

1947 'The place of the spoken language and the use of technical aids in language teaching', *Proceedings of the Sir William Jones Bicentenary Conference, Oxford 1946*, 30–33, 59. London.

1948 *'The semantics of linguistic science', *Lingua* 1.393–404.
      *'Sounds and prosodies', *TPS* 127–52.
      *'Word palatograms and articulation', *BSOAS* 12.857–64.

1949 *'Atlantic linguistics', *Archivum linguisticum* 1.95–116.

1950 *'Improved techniques in palatography and kymography' [with H. J. F. Adam], *BSOAS* 13.771–4.
      'Introduction [on spelling and pronunciation]', in T. Grahame Bailey, *Teach yourself Hindustani* xi–xli. London.
      *'Personality and language in society', *Sociological review* 42.37–52.

1951 *'General linguistics and descriptive grammar', *TPS* 69–87.
      *'Modes of meaning', *Essays and studies of the English Association*, N.S. 4.118–49.

1955 'Joseph Wright the scholar', *Transactions of the Yorkshire Dialect Society* 9.55.22–33.
      **'Structural linguistics', *TPS* 83–103.

1956 'Indian languages', *Encyclopaedia Britannica* s.v.
      'Introduction [on spelling and pronunciation]', in T. Grahame Bailey, *Teach yourself Urdu* xi–xxxix. London.
      **'Linguistic analysis and translation', in *For Roman Jakobson: Essays on the occasion of his sixtieth birthday* 133–9. The Hague.
      **'Philology in the Philological Society', *TPS* 1–25.
      Plenary Session 1, 'Linguistics and the problem of meaning', Report; Preliminary remarks on the report; Comment at the end of the first session; Concluding remarks at the end of the second session, *Proceedings of the Seventh International Congress of Linguists, London 1952* 6–9, 181–5, 202, 230–33, London.

1957 **'Applications of general linguistics', *TPS* 1–14.

**'Ethnographic analysis and language with reference to Malinowski's views', in R. W. Firth (ed.), *Man and culture: an evaluation of the work of Bronislaw Malinowski* 93–118. London.

'Hindustani language', *Encyclopaedia Britannica* s.v.

Papers in linguistics 1934–1951, xii, 233. London.

'Phonetic observations on Gujarati', *BSOAS* 20.231–41.

**'A synopsis of linguistic theory 1930–55', in *Studies in linguistic analysis* (special volume of the Philological Society), 1–32. Oxford.

1959 **'The treatment of language in general linguistics', *The Medical Press* 242.146–7.

'Linguistics in the laboratory', *Zeitschrift für Phonetik und allgemeine Sprachwissenschaft* 12.27–35.

1960 'The study and teaching of English at home and abroad', in H. G. Wayment (ed.), *English teaching abroad and the British universities* 11–21. London.

(Previously) unpublished papers (in various stages of completion).

**Linguistic analysis as a study of meaning, Nice Colloquium, 1952.

**The languages of linguistics.

An approach to linguistic analysis, Summer School, Oxford, 1955.

**Linguistics and translation, Birkbeck College London, 1956.

**A new approach to grammar, Bedford College London, 1956.

**Descriptive linguistics and the study of English, Berlin, 1956.

Language games: an approach to linguistic analysis, Birkbeck College London, 1956.

The place of grammar in the study of English, Summer School, Oxford, 1956.

The challenge of translation, Broadcast, March 1956.

Linguistic analysis and the study of style, Bedford College London, 1957.

Linguistic analysis in English studies, Institute of Education, London, 1957.

The place of general linguistics in the university curriculum, Belfast.

Statements of meaning by linguistic analysis.

Linguistic analysis and modern English.

Languages of record and statement in history.

Linguistics and language teaching.

Notes on references in the text

1. The convention of marking articles that appeared in *Papers in linguistics* with a single asterisk and those that appear here with a double asterisk, is followed in all references.

2. Page references to all articles are references to the relevant pages in *Papers in linguistics* or this volume.

3. Page references to *Speech* and *The Tongues of men* are to the Oxford University Press reissue (*Language and language learning* series, Number 2, 1964).

4. The following abbreviations are used in referring to journals:
   BSOS   *Bulletin of the School of Oriental Studies.*
   BSOAS *Bulletin of the School of Oriental and African Studies.*
   IJAL   *International journal of American linguistics.*
   TPS   *Transactions of the Philological Society.*

Introduction

This volume contains seven previously published and five as yet unpublished papers written by J. R. Firth in the years 1952–9. The years during which they were prepared were largely co-extensive with those years in which his influence was greatest. He was until his retirement in 1956 the Professor of General Linguistics and the Head of the Department of Phonetics and Linguistics at the School of Oriental and African Studies in the University of London, and was for that time surrounded by a group of young scholars most of whom had joined his department in the years 1948–50, and whose publications together with his own in the fifties, form the bulk of the 'corpus' of 'Firthian' linguistics.

It was a period of consolidation rather than of discovery. The exciting new ideas, context of situation, the spectrum of meaning, prosodic analysis, collocation, had come before. But Firth was not merely prepared to develop his views, but was also turning his attention to their application to new fields and in particular to translation, to the description of English, and to language teaching.

In fact most of the papers were written in two years—1956–7. Firth published nothing in the years 1952–5 for, for most of that time, he was a sick man, though the first of the papers presented here was apparently prepared for publication as a result of the Nice Colloquium in 1952. Upon his recovery, however, during what was roughly his last year as Head of Department and his first year of retirement, he returned to great activity both in publishing and in giving public lectures.

It is not easy to assess Firth's contribution to linguistics except to say that it was enormous. He and he alone pioneered the subject in Britain. For years he was, like Henry Sweet (with whom he loved to be compared), a voice crying in the wilderness. His greatest achievement was perhaps simply that of making people think again and refuse merely to accept traditional approaches to language, by, for instance, questioning the value of normative grammar and the validity for language study of the dualism of mind and body. But he himself did not merely bring linguistics to Britain; he brought his own original brand.

Firth was, as is very well known, misunderstood and largely ignored

I

by almost all his contemporaries except those in his immediate circle, and, alas, he was misunderstood by some of these too. The theories of Hjelmslev were for him mere 'linguistic philosophy',[1] and there was little contact with the American linguists of the forties and fifties for Firth had little time for their 'mechanical procedures' and they were mostly so convinced that there was little more to do than to dot the final i's and cross the final t's of phonemic-morphemic structural linguistics that they had no interest in his theories or in his objections to theirs and largely shook their heads with an unspoken 'poor old Firth, he doesn't understand'.[2]

Firth was himself largely to blame for the fact that he was both during his lifetime and afterwards so misunderstood. For apart from the works on prosodic analysis by his younger colleagues there is little to exemplify the application of his theories. It was believed in his years of retirement that he was busy preparing a book entitled *Principles of linguistics* which was already advertised in the booksellers' catalogues and that he was also thinking about a grammar of English. But among the papers left at his death there was not one sheet that belonged to either of these projects.

Some of the articles published up to the year 1951 were reprinted in *Papers in linguistics*,[3] edited by Firth himself. But at his death he had not only published many more articles but also had left behind no less than seventeen folders containing material in various stages of preparation, most of them texts of public lectures he had given. It seems appropriate then to collect the more complete of these and print them.

The selection of the papers included in this volume was not an easy task. I decided to include all the major published works of the period, but to add only five of the unpublished papers. Since most of these were not intended for publication and were addressed at various audiences, there is a great deal of repetition which would be out of place in a single volume. I have quite deliberately refrained, however, from making many deletions or alterations in the text, even where the manuscript was hand-written and obviously in a very early form. I have omitted only a few small passages that seemed largely irrelevant or obscure. Parts of the previously unpublished papers may appear, therefore, colloquial in style.

'Linguistic analysis as a study of meaning' was written as a result of the 1952 Nice Colloquium on semantics. It was apparently intended for publication and would then have appeared perhaps in 1953, but was probably put aside as a result of Firth's illness. It is one of the more detailed expositions of some aspects of his ideas about meaning and is of particular interest to those of us who were working with him at the time for its discussion of Edith Sitwell's 'Emily-coloured hands'. It also contains a section at the end on the verb *get*. The analysis is not easy to follow but is concerned with establishing collocations and situational meanings which are different from those of the dictionary.

'The languages of linguistics' also seems to have been written (from internal evidence) in 1953. It is, however, in a completely unfinished state and has required considerable editing, especially with regard to decisions about including handwritten emendations and additions. But it has a number of points that Firth does not make elsewhere and I decided therefore, with some misgivings, to include it. But the reader must be warned that it is still very much in the form of an early draft.

'Structural linguistics' is partly a historical account of the subject, partly a survey of the state of the subject in 1955. Firth saw 'several approaches in linguistic analysis, the axiomatic approach, the procedural approach, the theoretical approach and a combination of the theoretical and empirical approaches' (43), the last clearly being the one he favoured. He has a little to say on his distinction between *structuralist* and *structural* linguistics. The former was in his view a very limited approach, the latter 'aims at employing all our technical resources systematically for multiple statements of meaning in the appropriate linguistic terms'. (50)

'Philology in the Philological Society', a Presidential address to the Society, is rather more historical. A small item of interest is its reference to the Unesco Language Commission meeting in 1955.

The next two papers both deal with the subject of translation. 'Linguistic analysis and translation' was already in the press at the time that 'Philology in the Philological Society' was read; 'Linguistics and translation' was read to an audience at Birkbeck College in the University of London in June 1956, and therefore was chronologically the second of the two. But the two papers are so different that they are obviously both worth publishing. Among the other papers there was in fact yet another brief contribution entitled 'The challenge of translation' which was broadcast, but this was on a much more popular level and is not included here.

'Descriptive linguistics and the study of English' and 'A new approach to grammar' give us some inkling of the way in which Firth would probably have tackled his book on the grammar of English. The first of these contains the best account of his treatment of the English verbal system and the second of his handling of negation. 'A new approach to grammar' is unfortunately not complete; the final pages were hand-written and little more than an early draft. It has required considerable editing.

'Applications of general linguistics' shows that Firth in 1957 was turning his interest to yet another field—what is now generally known as applied linguistics. When he died, it was on a morning when he was preparing to attend an important conference on English language teaching.

It was appropriate that one of Firth's last works should be about Malinowski, for he owed to Malinowski his 'context of situation'. 'Ethnographic analysis and language with reference to Malinowski's views' not only discusses the contribution Malinowski made to linguistics, but also indicates quite clearly that while Firth derived his theory of context of situation from Malinowski, he nevertheless developed it upon his own lines and produced what was essentially a quite different theory.

'A synopsis of linguistic theory 1930–55' is the best known and perhaps the most important paper of the period. It is the most complete statement by Firth himself of his theories. Yet it is a most disappointing paper. It is less easy to read than many of his other articles and though Firth himself assured me on one occasion that he had carefully weighed every single sentence in it, it looks today even less coherent and consistent than de Saussure's *Cours de linguistique générale*. It is divided into twelve sections, but (and this is typical of so much of Firth's writings) it is difficult to be quite clear exactly what is the subject of each. My own choice of headings would be: (1) Theory, (2) Levels of meaning, (3) Context of situation, (4) Collocation, (5) Colligation, (6) Exponents, (7) Structure and system, (8) Grammar and phonology, (9) Stylistics, (10) Lexicography, (11) Translation, (12) Conclusions. No single section is devoted to prosodic analysis, one of Firth's major contributions, or to his views on 'restricted languages', though the former is treated in sections 6 and 8 and the latter in 4 and 10.

The last paper is perhaps lightweight but very readable. 'The treatment of language in general linguistics' was written for *The medical press*, but it has perhaps the best account of Firth's ideas on 'restricted languages'.

There are several excellent accounts of Firth's theories by R. H. Robins,[4] but I do not always find myself in agreement with what Robins says. I intend therefore to discuss briefly the chief aspects of Firth's beliefs as I myself understood them with a few comments on their relation to linguistic approaches, both at the time they were written and now. As far as possible I shall attempt to follow the order of the topics in 'A synopsis of linguistic theory 1930–55'.

Theory. Firth insisted on the importance of theory rather than procedures or methods. As I have already suggested, he regarded his own approach as 'a combination of the theoretical and the empirical approaches',[5] and reacted most strongly against the essentially procedural approach of Z. S. Harris' *Methods in structural linguistics.* What he was saying is, I think, almost commonplace today; few linguists believe that linguistics is concerned with 'discovery procedures'.[6] But at the time there were few who even understood, let alone accepted, Firth's view.

Levels of meaning. Firth insisted that levels of analysis were essentially a 'hierarchy of *techniques* [my italics, F.R.P.] for the statement of meanings' since 'a statement of meaning cannot be achieved by one analysis at one level, in one fell swoop'.[7] Meaning, then, was stated at every level. This was the essential characteristic of Firth's 'monistic' approach, monistic in the sense that it rejected the duality of mind and body. It has been thought that Firth's use of the term 'meaning' involved equivocation and that his rejection of the duality depended upon the extended meaning he himself gave to 'meaning', but he was not unaware of the distinction between 'the interior relations within the language and the exterior relations between structures and systems in the language and structures and systems in the situations in which language functions'.[8] These levels were, however, interdependent or mutually congruent.[9] Above all he rejected the current view that the linguist must start at the 'bottom' and work up, from phone to phoneme to morpheme. Phonological analysis especially needs to be undertaken along with all its grammatical correlations.[10] In this respect too he has surely been vindicated. But at the time K. L. Pike was perhaps the only linguist who had any sympathy with his view. 'Pike's heresy' was set out in his 'Grammatical prerequisites for phonemic analysis',[11] but even this, Firth felt, suggested that priority was given to phonology and this he denied.[12] The simile that Firth liked to use in his later years was of the lift that moved freely from one level to another, without giving priority to any one and without proceeding in any one direction.

Context of situation was one of Firth's levels of analysis. In recent years the idea that context can in any way be identified with or even related to meaning has come under attack.[13] Some of the criticism is fair; it is obvious that the statement of Malinowski,[14] from whom Firth took the idea, that 'the meaning of a single utterance . . . can be defined as the change produced by the sound in the behaviour of people' is, as it stands, untrue. Quite clearly utterances with different meanings produce the same change in people's behaviour and utterances with the same meaning produce different changes. But there are four points to be made on Firth's behalf. (1) Whatever practical difficulties there may be in using context of situation for linguistic statement, surely in some sense or other the meaning of an utterance is related to the way in which it is used, and in some way to the contexts in which it is used. Unless this is so, it is difficult, if not impossible, to understand how a child learns his language. (2) Firth's aim was to provide what would now be called an 'integrated theory'.[15] He objected, and quite rightly, to approaches that left meaning in its usual sense out of account. (3) He insisted that for him context of situation involved abstraction and was not, as it had been for Malinowski, 'in rebus'.[16] His theory is not open to the objections made above to the Malinowski quotation. (4) Firth held that context of situation could demonstrably be used for the statement of meaning in 'restricted languages'. He would discuss the meaning of *Tickets please* and *leg before wicket* in situational terms. And (see below) he held that 'descriptive linguistics is at its best when it concentrates on what I call "restricted languages"'.[17]

Collocation is concerned with the company that words keep. Firth seems, however, to have restricted his interest to specialized collocations —to *silly* with *ass*, to *cow* with *milk*.[18] Above all there was 'mutual expectancy' and, in restricted languages at least, redundancy. But he does not seem to have extended his theory to comprehend the whole of the problems of lexical compatibility or to have seen that the kind of formal grammatical analysis which he recommended is dependent upon the recognition of mutually collocable classes of lexical items. Grammar should have been for him as much dependent upon collocation as phonology is upon grammar.

The notions of *colligation* and *exponent* derive directly from Firth's emphasis on theory. His categories were essentially abstractions.[19] Grammar is not, therefore, merely concerned with the arrangement of morphemes, if morphemes are seen in any sense as 'concrete' bits of language, but with the 'interrelation of the categories in colligation'.[20] But it is essential at some stage to return to actual language material or as Firth puts it, to provide 'renewal of connection' with the 'phonic data'.[21] This was the function of the exponents. But Firth insisted that it was not necessary that all the phonic data should be assigned once and once only to the abstract categories and units. There could be 'overlap of phonic reference' and non-assignment of some of the data. To do otherwise suggested a 'false realism' in phonetics.[22]

Structure and *system* suggested that linguistic analysis should be undertaken in terms of syntagmatic and paradigmatic relations. Firth's structures and systems were of course essentially abstractions. Even the order of the elements of structure was not 'merely a sequence',[23] i.e. it did not relate directly to the sequence of items in the language material. But Firth did not, I think, really see the problem in differentiating between sequence and order.[24] Firth took from de Saussure (while rejecting much of de Saussure's theory)[25] the notion of *value* (valeur). There was *commutation* of the terms in each system and the values of the terms were derivable from the system itself. Indeed, the following quotation might almost have come from the *Cours de linguistique générale*: 'A singular in a two-number system has different grammatical meaning from a singular in a three-number system or a four-number system such as Fijian which formally distinguishes singular, dual, "little" plural and "big" plural.'[26] But there was one big difference. Firth's linguistics was essentially *polysystemic*.[27] He rejected the view of language as a single system (the *monosystemic* view) and in particular Meillet's addition 'où tout se tient'.[28] Even within a single structure there could be several systems. The consonant system in word-initial position would be different from the system in word-final position. Firth saw no reason to identify initial and final phonological units in terms of the 'logic of distributional relations',[29] and the subsequent necessity to account for differences in terms of limited distribution or neutralization; he simply declined to make the identification. His polysystemic approach is, in my view, one of his most important contributions but it is perhaps the least recognized. Yet language *is* essentially polysystemic. Seldom are two systems (in Firth's sense) identical. Firth was prepared to accept this. Most linguists are not; they seek simple solutions, small neat inventories with, of necessity, subsequent restrictions and qualifications.

Restricted languages. Firth believed that the very great complexity of language forced the linguist to limit his field of interest and to focus his attention upon one part of language at a time. This belief underlay his view of the level of analysis (the spectrum of meaning) and of the polysystemic approach. In addition he argued that 'descriptive linguistics is at its best when it concentrates on what I call "restricted languages"'.[30]

As I have already suggested, even the most difficult aspect of language study—meaning in the usual sense—could, he thought, be handled in terms of context of situation provided we were dealing with restricted languages. Translation, too, lost some of its problems if the languages could be restricted. 'It is easier to build the bridges from the source language to the target language if the situational content is mutually assimilated by cultural convergence.'[31] The objection is, of course, that the linguist wants to do more than look at restricted languages. But Firth was a realist and held that it was quite impossible to do everything at once.

Prosodic analysis. The starting-point for the prosody was essentially the complete rejection by Firth of the phoneme as a satisfactory basis for phonological analysis. There are two major characteristics of the prosodic approach. First, its elements are not confined to the narrow segments of the phoneme but might extend beyond these segments to parts of the syllable, the syllable, the word, or even the 'longer piece'.[32] Secondly, it rejects the rigid division between morphology and phonology of American linguistics which was, Firth said, 'to all intents and purposes *phonemics* with an additive *morphemics* plus the supplementary amendments of *morphophonemics*'.[33] I cannot accept Robins' remark that Firth himself never espoused seriously the opinion 'that to anyone at all sympathetic to prosodic analysis the phoneme and all its works were dead and probably damned as well'.[34] Firth did not of course deny the right of others to do their linguistic analysis as they pleased, but he was quite firm in his utter rejection of 'theories of distribution' which are basic to phonemics which he himself, he said, had once held but had later abandoned.[35] There is indeed a famous story which I do not think is apocryphal that once Firth said to Bernard Bloch, 'The phoneme is dead', and Bloch replied, 'It's got a pretty lively ghost'. Nor can I accept Robins' omission of the morphophonological aspect of prosodic analysis. This is illustrated by numerous articles including, e.g. my own 'The "broken plurals" of Tigrinya',[36] and is the subject of an entire section of 'A synopsis of linguistic theory 1930–55'. It can be argued that this aspect of Firth's approach stemmed essentially from his views on the interdependence of levels but it was in the phonology, i.e. in the prosodic analysis, that this interdependence (between grammar and phonology) was most clearly illustrated in practice by Firth and his colleagues.

Today Firth's name is linked with M. A. K. Halliday's 'neo-Firthian' 'scale and category grammar' which Halliday explicitly states in his

'Categories of a theory of grammar' to have derived from Firth.[37] But Halliday's essentially monosystemic categorization seems to me to have little in common with Firth's approach which, as Firth so constantly stressed, was essentially polysystemic and in which the levels were no more than 'a heirarchy of techniques for the statement of meanings'. Most significantly of all, Halliday's theory retains the phoneme, a linguistic unit that so typifies the kind of segmentation and classification that Firth rejected. Of course the terminology is largely Firth's, but Firth was particularly aware of the danger of equating terms in what were essentially different theories.[38]

At the time Firth was writing, linguistics was largely dominated by the American phoneme-morpheme school and it was against this that Firth directed most of his attacks. Not surprisingly then some of his viewpoints seem similar to those of the transformational-generative school, but in a negative sense, in his rejection of some of the basic tenets of post-Bloomfieldian linguistics—discovery procedures, the rigid separation of levels, the phoneme. But it is not surprising to see that whereas the first edition of *Studies in linguistic analysis* which was published in 1957 (and contained 'A synopsis of linguistic theory' plus a number of articles by Firth's disciples) was almost utterly damned in an uncomprehending review by R. P. Stockwell[39] (before his conversion to transformation-generative grammar), yet the second edition was sympathetically and thoughtfully discussed in 1964 by a scholar from M.I.T., D. T. Langendoen.[40] Firth, like Chomsky, considered that linguistics was concerned with abstract rather than with concrete elements.[41] There is a reference in one article, a favourable reference, to rules,[42] whose meaning, however, is not entirely clear, and I do not think Firth ever doubted the need for handling transformations within linguistic description. But he placed transformation where I believe it belongs, in the exponents (Chomsky's 'interpretive component'[43])— 'The exponent of interrogation in English may be intonational, but when we employ inversion or front shifting, the twenty-four operators are the finites affected by the inversion'.[44] But Firth was not himself impressed by *Syntactic structures* and he would have had no place at all for the mentalism with which transformational grammar has now been associated.

For all his emphasis on theory, Firth never forgot that the task of linguists was to talk about language and languages; he rejected utterly 'linguistics without language'. At the same time he wished to avoid 'dehumanizing' language. For him, undoubtedly, part of the meaning of his texts was that they were uttered (or written) by human beings.

Notes

1. **'Structural linguistics', 44.
2. The quotation is not an invention; it was made to me by an American colleague discussing the lack of any impact of Firth's theories in America.
3. London: O.U.P., 1957.
4. 'General linguistics in Great Britain 1930–60', *Trends in modern linguistics*, edd. C. Mohrmann, F. Norman and A. Sommerfelt, Antwerp: Spectrum, 1963; obituary article 'John Rupert Firth', *Language* 37.2.199–200 (1961); 'Aspects of prosodic analysis', *Proceedings of the University of Durham Philosophical Society*, Volume I, Series B, No. 1, 1–12, 1957.
5. **'Structural linguistics', 43.
6. cf. N. Chomsky's *Syntactic structures*, The Hague: Mouton, 1957, 51 ff.; but contrast R. E. Longacre, *Grammar discovery procedures*, The Hague: Mouton, 1964.
7. *'Personality and language in society', 183.
8. **'Linguistics and translation', 90.
9. **'Synopsis of linguistic theory 1930–55', 200.
10. **'Synopsis of linguistic theory 1930–55', 192–4.
11. *Word* 3.3.15–72 (1947).
12. **'The languages of linguistics', 30.
13. cf. P. M. Postal's review of R. W. M. Dixon's *Linguistic science and logic*, in *Language* 42.1.84–93 (1966); and N. Chomsky's review of B. F. Skinner's *Verbal behavior*, in *Language* 35.1.26–58 (1959).
14. B. Malinowski, *Coral gardens and their magic*, London, 1935, II, 59.
15. cf. J. J. Katz and P. M. Postal, *An integrated theory of linguistic descriptions*, Cambridge, Mass.: M.I.T. Press (1964).
16. *'Personality and language in society', 182.
17. **'Linguistics and translation', 87.
18. **'Synopsis of linguistic theory 1930–55', 179–80.
19. cf. e.g. **'Linguistic analysis as a study of meaning', 24.
20. **'Synopsis of linguistic theory 1930–55', 181.
21. cf. e.g. **'Descriptive linguistics and the study of English', 99.
22. **'Synopsis of linguistic theory 1930–55', 184–5.
23. **'Synopsis of linguistic theory 1930–55', 186.
24. See my '"Sequence" and "order"', *Monograph series on language and linguistics* 17, ed. C. I. J. M. Stuart, Georgetown University, 1964.
25. cf. *'Personality and language in society', 179–80.
26. **'Synopsis of linguistic theory 1930–55', 191.
27. cf. e.g. **'Linguistic analysis as a study of meaning', 24.
28. **'Structural linguistics', 41.
29. **'Synopsis of linguistic theory 1930–55', 187.
30. **'Linguistics and translation', 87. For examples of restricted languages see e.g. **'The languages of linguistics', 29.
31. **'Descriptive linguistics and the study of English', 109–10.
32. Robins (rightly) divides this into two aspects: 'Generally speaking two reasons may be seen for the allotment of given features in a language to a prosody: (1) The phonetic extension of the feature over the whole of, or a

part of, a stretch of utterance correlatable with a definable structure, and (2) the syntagmatic function ascribable to the feature, even though itself of segmental extent, as demarcative of a given structure or a structural division.' ('General linguistics in Great Britain 1930–1960', 29).

33. **'Structural linguistics', 40.
34. 'John Rupert Firth' (obituary article), *Language* 37.2.196 (1961).
35. **'Synopsis of linguistic theory 1930–55', 187.
36. *BSOAS* 17.3.528–66 (1955).
37. 'Categories of a theory of grammar', *Word* 17.3.241–92 (1961).
38. **'The languages of linguistics', 28.
39. *IJAL* 25.4.254–9 (1959).
40. *Language* 40.2.305–21 (1964).
41. N. Chomsky, *Current issues in linguistic theory*, The Hague: Mouton, 1964, 9. Firth, **'A synopsis of linguistic theory 1930–55', 199: 'An isolate is always an abstraction from the language complex.' Cf. his reference to 'Schematic constructs' in *'Personality and language in society', 181.
42. **'Structural linguistics', 43.
43. *Current issues in linguistic theory*, 9.
44. **'Descriptive linguistics and the study of English', 104.

One

Linguistic analysis as a study of meaning†

The present article arises from the Nice Colloquium on semantics sponsored by the Société Linguistique de Paris, organized and presided over by Professor Benveniste and supported by the Rockefeller Foundation.

The study of meaning was examined and exemplified from at least as many angles as there were members of the group, and all the principal theories of semantics considered in one connection or another. The most valuable results of such meetings are intangible and the effects will probably not be recognizable in the subsequent work of the participants even by themselves.

For the present writer this article provides a very welcome opportunity of making explicit some of the more fundamental issues as they now appear to him after the colloquium.

All systematic thought must start from presuppositions and in dealing with meaning some scholars have supposed single words listed in a dictionary and single sentences each bounded by full stops could be safely examined as to their meaning in complete abstraction from specific environment.[1] Similarly a sentence as such has been regarded as a logical proposition expressed in words, which must have a subject, that which is not the subject being the predicate, the whole sentence affirming or denying the predicate. Logicians continue to treat words and sentences as if they somehow could have meanings in and by themselves. Some linguists follow this centuries-old method of linguistic analysis merely because of the weight of philosophical and logico-grammatical tradition. Both these pre-suppositions are misleading in

---

† Apparently prepared for publication in 1952 or 1953, but never published.

linguistics and wholly inadequate for the handling of speech events which is the main object of the discipline.

The meaning of any particular instance[2] of everyday speech is intimately interlocked not only with an environment of particular sights and sounds, but deeply embedded in the living processes of persons maintaining themselves in society. 'Spoken language is immersed in the immediacy of social intercourse',[3] and 'voice-produced sound is a natural symbol for the deep experiences of organic existence.'[4] The sounds of speech are *ex intimis*. They are not merely molecular disturbances of the air. It is not the acoustic disturbances which matter, but the disturbances in the bodies of speakers and listeners. The dominating interest of the immediate situation, the urge to diffuse or communicate human experience, the intimate sounds, these are the origins of speech.

Since science deals with large average effects and these within certain modes of observation,[5] it is necessary to generalize typical 'texts' or pieces of speech in generalized contexts of situation. The basic presuppositions or postulates are from this point of view in three groups:

1. The human being is a field of experience in which the life process is being maintained in the social process. The human being in society is endowed[6] with an urge to 'diffuse' and 'communicate' his experience by voice and gesture.

2. All language text in modern languages has therefore:

(a) the implication of utterance, and must be referred to
(b) participants in
(c) some generalized context of situation.[7]

These categories must also cover 'talking to oneself'.

3. The participants in such contexts are social persons in terms of the speech community of which they are members. The key notion is one of personality, the essentials of which are:

(a) Continuity and the maintenance of the life process, the social process. In this connection the concepts of context of culture and context of experience[8] are necessary abstractions in stating the continuity as well as the change of meanings.
(b) The creative effort and effect of speech, including talking to oneself. The preservation of the essentials of life in society from the point of view of the participants in the situation forms a large part of the meaning of language as creative activity.
(c) Personal responsibility for one's words.

(d) The organization of personality and of social life depends on the built-in potentialities of language in the nature of the human beings and on what is learned in nurture.

In the most general terms, the basic principle is the unity, identity and continuity of the human personality, bearing constantly in mind that 'we are in the world and the world in us'.[9] As far as possible the linguist should remain in one world, resisting all theories which demand the acrobatics of balancing on two worlds, oscillating between two worlds or seeking a machine with an escape velocity by means of cybernetics.

It is of course true that all language presupposes 'other' events linguistic and non-linguistic issuing from each other. But this does not necessarily lead to a dualist theory of the sign, still less to the setting up of a naïve binary opposition based on the two much abused general words *phonetic* and *semantic*.

The contextual theory of meaning[10] employs abstractions which enable us to handle language in the interrelated processes of personal and social life in the flux of events. As I emphasized in my little book,[11] published over twenty years ago, 'In common conversation about people and things present to the senses, the most important "modifiers" and "qualifiers" of the speech sounds made and heard, are not words at all, but the perceived context of situation. In other words, "meaning" is a property of the mutually relevant people, things, events in the situation. Some of the events are the noises made by the speakers.'[12]

The abstractions the linguist makes must always presuppose communicativeness or tendency to diffusion of experience as a human predisposition, but he must never forget converse with oneself which starts with babbling in infancy, as one of the origins of all speech.[13] It is on this basis that in further converse two or more articulated memories become, so to speak, one.

There are many difficulties in dealing with written language, which may itself be considered as 'an abstraction from insistent surroundings'. But a great deal can be done with writing which 'is immersed in the immediacy of social intercourse', and any remoter text which can be apprehended in use can be regarded as having such temporary meaning as is given to it by the reader.

At this point two contemporary journalistic discussions of the meaning of 'words' will point what I venture to think is the inevitability of the contextual approach to meaning.

The *Sunday Times* correspondent in Korea reports as follows on 7th October 1951:

> One vital necessity is for the already largely standardised Anglo-American military vocabulary to be extended to cover tactical situations as well as equipment, signal procedures and headquarters nomenclature. A powerful contributory reason for the heavy losses suffered by 29th Brigade in April was the tactical misunderstandings which arose between the staffs of the brigade and the U.S. 3rd Division—misunderstandings equally inspired by British understatement and American over-statement.
>
> It is true that American staff officers are quicker to use such expressions are 'surrounded' and 'cut off', and that those expressions do not always apply to situations as Commonwealth staff officers see them. But the British are no less guilty of misrepresentation in a mixed command when they describe imminent disaster as a 'shaky do'; or assure anxious Americans that 'everything is under control' when, as the Americans themselves would declare, 'all hell is breaking loose'.

As an illustration of the contextual theory of analysis, I would point out that the main categories could be applied to the events referred to in the above report: the nature as well as the nurture of the participants, the *texts* or verbal actions, the non-verbal behaviour of the participants, the relevant objects and the effects of the verbal actions.

Much more interesting is the recent correspondence[14] in the *Observer* on what Mr Philip Toynbee called the 'wanton privacy' of Edith Sitwell whom he accused of cheating in using a phrase he quotes as *Emily-coloured hands*. His complaint of wanton privacy is based on the fact that such writers publish material 'which is *by its nature* inaccessible to all readers except their personal friends. It is almost equally unjust when Joyce demands of his readers a detailed acquaintanceship with the geography of Dublin.' This again reminds him of Mr Ivor Brown's previous article on the *Laziness of readers*, which refers failures of communication to the shortcomings of the reader and the social situations of our times. A writer should certainly be conscious of his readers. But of what readers? 'You cannot broadcast to people who are without receiving sets.' Such discussions show how far such professional writers are from the naïve approach to the meanings of words, characteristic of nineteenth-century semantics, which regarded them as if they were immanent essences or detachable ideas which we could traffic in.

However, it turned out that it was Dr Edith Sitwell who had been wronged. She graciously accepted an apology and pointed out that 'taking a line out of its context helps to obscure the meaning,[15] in many cases', and supplied the three relevant lines:

> For spring is here, the auriculas
> And the Emily-coloured primulas
> Bob in their pinafores on the grass.

She pointed out that the intention was to call to mind 'the pink cheeks of young country girls'. Such 'intention', however, is not the concern of the linguist. The intention of a particular person in a particular *instance* of speech is never the concern of linguistic science. We study the flux of experience and suppress most of the environmental co-ordination of what we examine, regarding the essentials as *instances* of the general categories of the schematic constructs set up. We see structure and system as well as uniqueness in the instance, and its essential relationship to instances other than itself.

But before Dr Sitwell's explanation had appeared another correspondent had written to say that she knew quite well what 'Emily-coloured hands' were like. They had the tang as well as the colour of 'white' pepper. She had not been cheated. And Dr Sitwell charmingly accepts this approach adding '*the phrase gave a sensory impression*, that is all that matters'.

In a recent study of meaning[16] I have avoided any attempt to approach individual 'reified' words as isolates of conceptual meaning. In examining Swinburne's poetic diction, for example, the language 'pieces' are chiefly verses, stanzas and poems, and in the study of prose whole sentences and paragraphs form the quoted material, not just 'words'. They were examined by applying a set of modes excluding historical details such as those given in telling the story of *Emily-coloured*.

In the prosodic mode the compound *Emily-coloured* certainly suits the verses in which it comes. At the level of collocation something might be learned from other contexts of *coloured* and generally of such *-ed* forms in compounds. Similarly studies of collocations in which personal names and such flower names as *primulas* occur might prove interesting. Before briefly exemplifying this approach, all conceptualist and associationist psychology must be laid aside together with the traditional figures of rhetoric.

We have the verbal text, and Edith Sitwell's poems, her personality, language and diction are possible subjects of study. Linguistic analysis must first state the *structures* it finds both in the text and in the context. Statements in structural terms then contribute to the statements of meaning in various modes.

I have already mentioned the structure of the verses in which *Emily-coloured* has its place in the design. This is a statement of meaning in the prosodic mode. The grammatical mode of meaning will be better understood if in addition to a statement of *syntagmatic structure* (i.e. of the nominal phrases including *Emily-coloured primulas*) we set up *systems of constituents* each one of which is a *term* having *function* or 'meaning' by interior relations with the other terms of the system.

I have not made a study of Dr Sitwell's English, and can only offer open systems of collocations in which *coloured* is commonly preceded by (1) closely related nominals, and (2) closely related adverbs. Most of us are familiar with (1a) *rose*-coloured, *coffee*-coloured, *chocolate*-coloured, *plum*-coloured, perhaps *flame*-coloured, *honey*-coloured and *canary*-coloured; (1b) *dark*- or *light*-coloured, and *darkish*- and *lightish*-coloured, *funny*-coloured; (1c) phoneticians refer to *h*-coloured or *r*-coloured vowels; and (1d) *multi*-coloured, *parti*-coloured. And with adverbs, (2) *brightly*-coloured, *gaily*-coloured and *highly*-coloured.[17] In terms of the above very tentative system, the constituent *Emily* is first of all not a sectional term in (2), nor in (1b, c, d), but has its value as a sectional term in (1a), which itself has the functional value of *not* being (1b, c or d), or (2), which as a section is a function of a group of given sections or sub-sections.

It will now be clear that whatever the 'intention' of the poet, whatever imagined concepts are invented for *Emily-coloured*, such things are not relevant. In all systematic thought there is a putting aside of notions, and of suggestions, with the prim excuse that of course we are not thinking about such things.

We have, however, seen *Emily-coloured* as part of a syntagmatic structure, a structure of categories. We have also very tentatively set up paradigmatic systems of which it is a term. And such functions as are there given by way of example can be stated as meanings at various levels of analysis. Having made a series of abstractions at various levels, it is necessary to establish *renewal of connection*.[18] If the context is about not very aristocratic flowers in English country gardens, the odds against *Emily-coloured* seem to be decidedly less than twenty to one. The odds in favour can perhaps be guessed when the collocational improbabilities of some of the phrases in (1a) with the word *primulas* are borne

2

in mind. According to my analysis part of the meaning of *Emily-coloured primulas* is collocation with *Bob in their pinafores on the grass*. This level I have termed meaning by collocation, which may be personal and idio-syncratic, or normal.

Proceeding from the three lines of text to fuller contextualization makes it clear that no independent conceptual 'meaning' can be given to *Emily-coloured*. If poetry can be defined as any piece of prose for which another piece of prose cannot be adequately substituted,[19] then '... Emily-coloured primulas Bob in their pinafores on the grass'.

And though my employment of these controversial lines has been entirely linguistic, I am happy to say that thanks to the poet I *have* seen them bobbing in their pinafores on the grass, the Emilys *and* the primulas.

There is, however, a possibility that a statement of meaning in the phonaesthetic mode[20] might be made, if the association of personal and social attitudes with certain proper names be considered relevant. There is the trinity of Tom, Dick and Harry, and Mary Ann, Mary Jane, Polly, Martha, Rosie, even Emily. And what would English low comedy do without Wigan?

The important points for the present purpose are (1) the inadequacy of the traditional categories of semantics, (2) the impossibility of the conceptualist word-idea approach in descriptive linguistics, and (3) the indication that the time has come to try other abstractions using the larger contexts in which words are embedded, necessitating new types of ordered series of words and pieces, and new systems of stylistics. The conceptualist or psychological approach to words as units in the linguistic analysis of meaning is already in its grave, but not yet buried. The 'one morpheme one meaning' approach in the United States will probably follow it.

Words must not be treated as if they had isolate meaning and occurred and could be used in free distribution. A multiplicity of *systems*[21] derived from carefully contextualized *structures* would seem to be indicated.

The *structures* attributed to 'texts' are not to be given ontological status. They are schematic. Only within such limited systems can commutation provide the basis of a functional or meaning value, and substitution not amounting to commutation, the absence of such value.

Two or three further examples may be useful. The final assibilation of words in English is homophonous for the plural and the genitive of nouns, and the third person singular of the present indicative of verbs. I have employed the traditional terms since here at any rate they can be formally established in English. Take three texts, which can be fully contextualized:

(a) He got the orders for cement.
(b) He orders cement once a month.
(c) Have you forgotten the Ancient Order's name?

First the structure of appropriate contexts of situation must be stated. Then the syntactical structure of the texts. The criteria of distribution and collocation should then be applied. Three formal scatters can be established:

(a) order, order-s;
(b) order, order-s, order-ed, order-ing;
(c) order, order-'s, order-s, order-s'.

We may consider the categories of noun substantive and verb established, since grammatical collocation and distribution provide differentiating criteria. The categories of singular and plural both in the noun substantive and the verb present indicative are similarly guaranteed.

The simple form of the noun and the genitive form are also determined by distribution and collocation. There is clearly a functional meaning for the noun substantive and the present indicative verbal forms in a system of formally established grammatical categories. Text, context, distribution in collocation, guarantee the binary opposition of singular and plural, and also of the zero form and genitive forms of the noun substantive. At the levels of the situation, syntax, and distribution in collocation, abstractions can be made from the structures, and systems of word-classes and morpheme-classes set up. Within these systems each term or member functions and has a clearly determined meaning.

The linguist must be clearly aware of the levels at which he is making his abstractions and statements and must finally prove his theory by *renewal of connection* with the processes and patterns of life. Without this constant reapplication to the flux of experience, abstract linguistics has no justification.

The lexicographer has to face the difficult problem of definitions and the forms of entry. One of the most valuable results of the Nice Colloquium was the frank recognition that truly descriptive dictionaries did not exist, that we are still a long way from real historical dictionaries, that most of the citations we meet were far from satisfactory, and that great opportunities awaited the lexicographers of the future.

During the Nice discussions the suggestion was made that a lexicographical definition of the English verb *get* might be possible, and I made some sort of statement which turned out to be highly complex, but at any rate not just nebulous and vague. I shall not repeat it, but suggest a schematic summary compiled independently of the N.E.D., giving some of the structures in which distribution in collocation may be stated.

My purpose is to suggest what was in my mind during the discussion, namely, that the various formal structures and collocations of which *get* is a constituent or 'word' can be regarded as criteria for setting up a system of distributed variants, in which each variant is a function of the others and of the whole system. Each sectional definition in shifted terms is *not* a statement of a concept or of the 'essential' meaning of the word *get* itself, but a descriptive indication of the relation of the collocations to generalized contexts of situation.

1. To have and to hold in secure possession. To be given something for certain, perhaps forcibly, or by creative effort.

get, gets, got, getting.
(a) He has got plenty of money.
     He's got the blues.
     She's got the measles.
     I've got him.
(b) He has succeeded in getting a house at last.
(c) This music just gets me.
     He got ten years.
     I don't get it.
     You'll get it.
     He won't get the sack.
     He's got what was coming to him.

2. Securing or obtaining possession.
get, gets, got, getting.
(a) Get me one too.
(b) It's difficult to get.
(c) He got a pass.
(d) Get yourself a wife.
(e) That won't get you anywhere.

3. In binomial verbs—making the effort to possess, or putting in possession, movement towards possession.

(a) Go and get it yourself.
Come and get it to make sure.
Run and get it before it is too late.
(b) I'll try and get one for you.

4. Growing, becoming, moving towards having something, arriving successfully at some destination, securing progress towards some end.

(a) He gets better every day.
You'll get dirty.
(b) You'll never get there at this rate.
(c) How do you get to work?
(d) You'll get lost.
You'll get caught if you are not careful.
You'll get mixed up in intrigue.
He got married.

5. Obligation, forcing, forced, making effort towards some end.

(a) Get it done (—made, —written, —finished).
(b) When I get going, you'll see.
He's got moving at last.
(c) You've got to go through with it.
(d) Get rid of it.

6. In phrasal verbs or with particles one at a time. Various combinations of the creative effects suggested above in situations involving becoming, conation, successful effort.

(a) He can't get in.
He can't get out.
He can't get through.
(b) He knows just enough to get by.
(c) I got up at six.
(d) When am I going to be able to get down?
(e) You do get about.
(f) Where do we get out?
(g) He must be getting on.

7. With following nominals.

(a) This gets me down.
(b) We got her off.

(c) I can't get it in.
   I can't get it out.
   I can't get it through. (Cf. I can't get through it.)
(d) They got the fire under. (Cf. They got under the fire.)
(e) We'll get it over. (Cf. We'll get over it.)

8. With more than one particle.

(a) I've at last got down to it.
(b) I can't get on with him.
(c) There's no getting away from it.
(d) They'll never get away with it.

9. With particle and nominal.

(a) What are you getting at?
(b) She gets on my nerves.
(c) I can't get through it.
(d) He's got under your skin.
(e) I got up a play.
(f) She got in a rejoinder.
(g) He got out a prospectus.
(h) You'll get to it in the end.
(i) You'll get to like it in time.

10. With more than one particle.[22]

(a) You can't get out of it now.
(b) I shall perhaps get over to that tomorrow.

It must be remembered that the above rough scheme is in no sense intended as a criticism of any lexicographical method. It is merely a tentative system of collocations for *get, gets, got, getting*, bearing in mind the types of situation in which the collocations as wholes may be used. The classification is admittedly imperfect and the generalized descriptions of situational usages are not mutually exclusive. But there are over *thirty* formal types of collocation in ten sections to provide not only an internal set of determinants for forms of the verb *to get*, with general conditions of use indicated in general terms, but also a basis for the highly complex statement necessary to define the forms of *get* in a dictionary. There is no doubt about its unique position nor about the inadequacy of any so-called synonymous substitutions. However, summary indications may be given in the following list of words.

(a) have, hold, possess, grasp, grip, catch;
(b) secure, obtain, procure, acquire;
(c) earn, profit, gain;
(d) am, is, etc., grow, become;
(e) progress, advance, arrive, reach;
(f) obliged, force, forced;
(g) succeed, surmount, subdue, defeat, overcome, overpower;
(h) contrive, extricate, insert, apply, escape, avoid;
(j) learn, understand, express.

Some of these words may be substituted for *get* in collocations the distribution of which may be marked by formal structure, but by no means all. The possibility of substitutions not amounting to commutation is an indication of similarity of value or function. There are a sufficient number of such non-commutative cases to suggest that parallel distribution of this kind justifies the use of the above nine lists of words to summarize the general situational conditions of the use of *get*.

Get is formally involved and widely distributed in a large number of collocations functioning in creative, possessive and highly conative situations. It is easy to understand why taboos grew up about this word of power, especially among puritans and schoolmasters.

The study of the collocations in which a word is normally used is to be completed by a statement of the interrelations of the syntactical categories within the collocation. The distribution of the collocations in larger texts, and the distribution of the word under examination in collocations will probably provide a basis for functional values or meanings for words of all types. The homophones *by* (two values), *bye* (two values), *buy* in English can be dealt with by applying these categories, and definitions are possible for all of them if other words or phrases are used to describe the generalized situations, as with *get*.

Again the notion of substitution in collocation and context of situation not amounting to commutation may prove adequate. Such substitutions are not to be regarded as synonyms, nor need all the *bai* homophones be regarded as homonyms. *by*, *bye* and *buy* are easily distinguished formally. We can even have *by byes* (cricket), *by buying*, *byes by chance*, *buying by the State*. The distinction between prepositional and adverbial *by* is clearly established by distribution in collocation, by substitutions not amounting to commutation, supported by syntactical relations.

For example: (a) They go by night.
(b) They go by night after night.

The substitution of *past* in (b) does not amount to commutation with reference to the situation, but is impossible in (a). Intonational and other differences in utterance can perhaps be shown by oscillograms.

Finally, I submit the barest summary of some of the terms I have used with technical intention, the distribution of which in collocation and context should be adequate definitions for the present study.

Processes and *patterns* of life in the environment can be generalized in *contexts of situation*, in which the *text* is the main concern of the linguist. *Order* and *structures* are seen in these, and after examining *distribution* in *collocations*, '*pieces*', *words* and *morphemes* may be arranged in ordered series, resulting in *systems* and *sets of systems*, the *terms* of which are functions of one another and of the systems. On a previous study I have outlined linguistic analysis as a study of meaning in the following terms:

> I propose to split up meaning or function into a series of component functions. Each function will be defined as the use of some language form or element in relation to some context. Meaning, that is to say, is to be regarded as a complex of contextual relations, and phonetics, grammar, lexicography and semantics each handles its own components of the complex in its appropriate context.[23]

The *abstractions* or *schematic constructs* set up are made at a series of distinct mutually complementary *levels*. *Renewal of connection* with the *processes and patterns of life* in the *instances* of experience is the final justification of abstract linguistics. Linguistic analysis must be polysystemic. For any given language there is no coherent system (*où tout se tient*) which can handle and state all the facts.

I venture to think, even to hope, that this approach to linguistic analysis as a study of meaning may be found to offer opportunities of a synthesis of contemporary theories. Science is not proved wrong, it develops. It is more probable that we are all in that sense right, than that we are all wrong, and only dogmatic interpretations of de Saussure are right. 'The span of life for modern scientific schemes is about thirty years.'[24]

Notes

1. cf. A. N. Whitehead, *Modes of thought*, Cambridge, 1938, 90; and Gordon Holmes, M.D., F.R.S., *Introduction to clinical neurology*, Edinburgh, 1947, 138: 'Single words are meaningless unless related to other words.'
2. 'Instance' is brought forward as a technical term.

3. Whitehead, op. cit., 55.
4. Whitehead, op. cit., 45.
5. Whitehead, op. cit., 123.
6. cf. Norbert Wiener, *The human use of human beings*, London, 1950, 84, 85, 93, 94, 103, 104, 108. Though this work will interest linguists, it does not show much understanding of their work or recent developments. Three principal notions, however, are in harmony with the presuppositions put forward in this article: (1) Man's 'preoccupation with language . . . is built into him'; (2) Personality and therefore language has to do with 'continuity of pattern' and 'continuity of process'; (3) 'Individual and social process centers around the process of learning.' To apply these three valuable concepts to human beings and the products of engineering alike seems to me nothing more than metaphor. And I am inclined to think the whole cybernetic theory of communication applicable only to engineering, and can only refer to human beings in the manner of telephone exchange metaphors and analogies. Or possibly to a physiologist's decerebrate preparation. The essential elements of living personality in society cannot be 'built' into machines even with all the resources of cybernetics. The development of such machines, however, will undoubtedly affect the categories linguists employ at certain levels of analysis.
7. See *'Personality and language in society'.
8. See *'The use and distribution of certain English sounds'.
9. Whitehead, op. cit., 227.
10. See *'The use and distribution of certain English sounds', *'Technique of semantics'; *'Personality and language in society'; *'Modes of meaning'; *Speech; Tongues of men* especially Chapter 10; Malinowski in C. W. Ogden and I. A. Richards, *The meaning of meaning*, London; B. Malinowski, *Coral gardens and their magic*, London, 1935; A. L. Gardiner, *Theory of speech and language*, Oxford, 1932.
11. *Speech*, Chapter 5.
12. cf. Gordon Holmes, op. cit., 65. 'It is on the multiple nature of the impressions we receive that knowledge of what is happening in our bodies and of our relations to the external world depends. Though one or other sensation excited by a stimulus be dominant, it is the total sum of the impressions received that determines our reactions, not exclusively those of one nature or from one source only.'
13. The phrase 'converse with oneself' is not intended as an equivalent of *innere Sprachform* or 'internal speech' as used by neurologists. But the basic importance of babbling in infancy and of converse with oneself is heavily underlined by the experience of clinical neurologists. 'External speech depends on internal speech.' 'Gesture and pantomime or dumb show suffer when internal speech is disturbed.' 'Internal speech may remain intact in motor aphasia.' See Gordon Holmes, op. cit., 136, 193, 141.
14. 30th September, 7th October and 14th October, 1951.
15. i.e. The 'piece' under examination is really *Emily-coloured*.
16. See *'Modes of meaning'.
17. cf. N.E.D. Vol. II. A comparison of these entries with even the tentative and incomplete notes offered above may be taken as a first indication of how far short the best dictionaries often are of being either truly historical or adequately descriptive.
18. Whitehead, op. cit., 2.
19. Attributed to Paul Valéry.
20. See *'Modes of meaning', 195; and *Speech*, 183–8.

21. See *'Sounds and prosodies', 121–2.
22. [This section heading is identical with that of 8; this may have been an oversight, but it seems to me more likely that Firth thought that this was, in collocational and situational terms, a different section. F.R.P.]
23. See *'Technique of semantics', 19.
24. Whitehead.

Two

The Languages of Linguistics†

In the social sciences and in modern linguistics some of the epistemological conditions of scholarship are the vehicles in which it is carried,
the general national language. The Scandinavian languages, French,
Russian and English for example all determine certain aspects of linguistics. Even in what is called English, scholarship takes very different
forms in America in English from those we are developing on this side
of the Atlantic in European including British English. *Phonemics*,
phonemicize, *phonemicization*, *phonemicist* are American words and
are rarely used in England. *Phonetics* and *phonetician* are not nearly
so frequently used in America as in England, and the modern use of the
word *phonology* and its derivatives also is not widely current in America.
There are many other discrepancies in the technical language which
stand in the way of mutual interchange and quite obviously reduce
mutual quotations and references to negligible proportions.

Some of this discrepancy is due to the different technical employment
of such ordinary words as *environment, frame, juncture, context, contextual, situation, sound, segment,* by Americans, partly on account of
basic differences of usage and styles in American English.

In British English there are similar developments, for some of which
I am in part responsible—the student reading both languages tends to
equate American supra-segmental phonemes for example with the

---

† As stated on p. 3 this paper was in a completely unfinished state. It was
typed but with considerable handwritten emendations and additions. I have
omitted some of the typewritten and the handwritten material, but in general
have followed the text as emended with such additions as were clearly intended
to be part of the text. Internal evidence (see note 4) suggests it was written in
1953.

British use of the word *prosodies*, or indeed the American phoneme and what I may call the 'Joneme'. This sort of thing does not help the student very much. His teachers must see to it that personal scholarship is understood and that full cognizance should be taken of the part played by the national idioms.

Though I believe that the English face the Latin south rather than the Gothonic north and have developed a facility for Romance borrowing, we often upset the French by specializing our borrowings from them, in an English way. In 1923, Meillet asked me what we had done with the *phonème*, and noted our different uses for *implosion* and *implosive*, and asked what the French should do about it. I couldn't advise him. I did however work up quite a list of difficulties between us, e.g. in:

> phonétique : phonetics
> phonologie : phonology
> philologie   : philology

and pointed out that we had no equivalent to de Saussure's trinity: *le langage, la langue, la parole*, not including *les parlers*—in English. *Root, stem, radical, inflexion, flexion, base, endings, time, tense* and a whole lot more cannot safely be equated with what might seem at first sight fairly near equivalents in French.

In Norwegian and indeed all three Scandinavian languages, I imagine calque and translation borrowings are most easily made from German. Whole ranges of equivalents seem at first sight automatically possible. Is this really so? What are the difficulties if any? In English we do not readily borrow by calque or translation from German. We borrow much more readily from French.

Then to come to personal matters. My own technical use of the words *substitution, commutation* and *function* does not square with Professor Hjelmslev's employment of the analogues in Danish. A little book of mine entitled *Speech*, first published in 1930, has recently been translated into Chinese by a competent scholar who has had to devise expressions and adapt current words in new collocations to lead Chinese readers to take up certain attitudes and entertain new theories about speech. It is no longer my book. I suspect that Whitfield's American English translation of Professor Hjelmslev's Danish work is in fact also a new book. I therefore avoid the common belief in the internationality and universality of such subjects as linguistics in the sense that they can be possessed or shared by all as common united knowledge in a variety of languages. In epistemological terms each scholar makes his own selection and grouping of facts determined by his attitudes and theories and by the nature of his experience of reality of which he himself is part, and any statements he makes to like-minded fellow workers in the specific form of language employed must in the present state of affairs be referred to personal and social conditions and situations.

Nevertheless there is always a possibility that wider fellowship and co-operation is promoted when scholars agree that a certain set of attitudes and theories embraces a number of parallel and competitive attitudes and theories—or when it is agreed that a number of alternative theories can be regarded as special cases of the comprehensive theory provisionally adopted. We are far from this happy state in linguistics. A very useful approximation to some sort of general framework for descriptive grammar, agreed by a group of linguists, has been successfully promoted under the auspices of Unesco by Professor Sommerfelt. A tentative directive was issued in French and English. The English version has been included in an article of mine in the *Transactions of the Philological Society of Great Britain.*[1] I can say it has been welcomed and indeed applied by some of my colleagues. They have remarked on the value of its being endorsed without dogmatism by a small authoritative international commission. Such grouped influences in a subject like linguistics might well be developed, but only if the group embraces all the principal authorities.

To turn now to the language under study. The first essential is to circumscribe the field and to decide on the selection and grouping of material to be placed on the agenda and on what levels and by what techniques it is to be handled with a view to the final statement of the facts. Quite often the materials, the subject or topics of study, are isolated by circumstances or by conditions. Let us call the subject of study by the simplest possible expression—i.e. the language. I will give five examples of what I will call languages.

1. Air-war Japanese.[2]
2. A unique thirteenth-century Chinese text—The Secret History of the Mongols.[3]
3. Lear limericks.
4. Swinburnese lyrics.
5. Modern Arabic headlines.

These languages are then to be analysed at a number of levels with varying emphasis according to the subject, all levels with the first, fourth and fifth, grammatical and lexical levels with the second, very little at the phonological level.

In languages of the first type, the main field is easily delimited, already fenced off so to speak, for the linguist. It is more difficult when the linguist also has to make his own abstractions from what amounts to a whole linguistic universe—let us say from what is loosely called English or Norwegian.

What the linguist may decide to select and group in attention may be determined by his equipment, by the instruments of his calling. Very few linguists will wish to work only at the impressionistic phonetic level —but many have dealt with their languages at the phonetic and phonological levels. Even then they like to think the boundaries determining their circumscribed interests are reinforced at all levels. Pike for instance wrote on the grammatical prerequisites of phonemic analysis. In recent talks with him, I think I have convinced him that the use of the word *prerequisites* implies priorities and hierarchies and perhaps it is wise to believe that all levels are mutually requisite and should be congruent. This means that with a high degree of specialization in various branches or levels of linguistic analysis it is obviously desirable to promote team work, as for example is the case in the biological sciences. The need for concerted action I have mentioned before, coupled with the name of Professor Sommerfelt. May I add a comment in the negative. I do not believe very much in conferences on the standardization of terminology. Concerted action, i.e. freely organized international collaboration for specific purposes, implies that some sort of convergence in technical languages is bound to accompany it. I have previously referred to the selection and grouping of linguistic materials, to the agenda, and eventually to the statement of the facts. May I remark in passing that there are no scientific facts until they are stated. And statement is the final stage at several removes from the first experience of the material. The common view of facts as brute and basic ultimates for everybody is misleading. As Mr Angus Sinclair says: 'One must indeed at times in ordinary life say facts are facts, liars are liars and that's that.' But things are rather different in scientific statement.

It will be agreed that scientific priority cannot be given to spoken language as against written language, and I believe Bertrand Russell has somewhere said that we cannot even be sure in the dawn of humanity about the precedence of written marks and spoken signs. Written language materials, it is true, are however considered as having the 'implication of utterance'. This phrase, 'the implication of utterance', is in some sense a technical phrase since I believe that this even applies to formulaic expression in all subjects. It is, I think, a good practical guide in linguistic statement to regard all forms of writing as having the implication of utterance. All forms of speech have also the implication of writing for linguistic statement, even in literate societies. I well remember an African informant whose language had recently been reduced to writing, as the phrase goes, refusing to record certain spoken sentences, as he felt it would not be proper. How right he was in the general sociological sense. This is a point in connection with the use of informants. Our own practice is for the investigator himself to do the writing in such cases, not the informants, who very often can't, and sometimes won't.

The actual forms and systems of writing or spelling are a near concern of the linguist in dealing with his material. I think it is important that the three world systems of writing other than Roman, should be studied as such. I refer to Arabic, the Indian alphabets and Chinese. A Chinese friend of mine referred to us in the West as ABC merchants, and it is true that Western linguists tend to transliterate in those fields. And by that I do not mean to include phonetic or phonological notations. A great deal is lost in transliteration unless the structure, theory and practice of the Asian writing system is stated. The Arabic script in all its forms, and especially when fully pointed, offers what, in my terminology, I should describe as a prosodic analysis of the word and piece. In this system of writing, the unity of the word and piece is formally expressed. The initial, medial and final forms of what I will provisionally call the letters emphasize one of the features of prosodic analysis, which draws attention to the characteristics of the whole piece, including the word; that is to say, it notes syllabic structure and marks the beginning, middle and end, internal *junction* of syllables, interword *juncture*, such prosodies as length, stress, prominence, pitch, tensity and laxness, and what I term Y, W and central prosodies. The Chinese system of writing has often been described as ideographic, even pictographic. Perhaps this suited the attitudes and theories of the nineteenth century, but such descriptions are entirely misleading. The Chinese system of writing is a word script and the characters can in Chinese writing even be used for phonetic references.

I do not think myself that with either of these systems of writing as a basis of analysis, an Arabic or Chinese scholar could have produced a phoneme theory of the Western type. The Indian systems of writing, best illustrated by the Devanagari script, are syllabaries, also exhibiting what I would call the prosodic approach which represents the unity of the piece or word. The so-called inherent vowel of the Indian syllabary is from their point of view no vowel unit. A vowel sign may be actually written before the consonant though in reading aloud it is heard after it; that is to say, our notions of alphabetic place do not in this script apply. Like the Arabic Sukuun which is a prosodic sign, the Indian use of hələnta or Virama, and of conjunct characters are also related to syllabic structure and again it is what I should call a more prosodic system of writing than our Roman transliterations. Those of us in the London group who have specialized in the South-east Asian languages and in Chinese are inclined to the view that the phoneme theory, whether of the Jones, Prague or American type, is not the best approach either in principle or in notation for the phonological analysis of these languages. Indeed three competent young linguists, including two Egyptians, have turned down these phonemic theories, often regarded as universally applicable, in their expositions of the structure of the Arabic word and piece.

It is of course necessary to undertake the study of spoken language in pre-literate communities, and indeed in our own societies, where there are great differences of matter, form and style between the spoken and written languages. There are those who specialize in research in pre-literate communities with a view to bestowing on the speakers the benefits of the Roman alphabet. I must say, I find it difficult to suppress a smile when I hear in this connection the phrase 'reducing a language to writing'. In so many cases it is reduction indeed. However, notations must be established in the preliminary research, and in the statements of the results and presentation of the texts.

In the study of spoken language, I stress the study of specific persons. Perhaps some would prefer to say representative persons. I have very little belief in the collection of haphazard and colloquial oddments here and there, from a variety of speakers at random. I feel it is important to show that the texts are referred to the representative person or persons, in typical contexts of situation, with due attention to the form of discourse, to the style, tempo of utterance and other relevant characteristics. In support of any linguistic analysis formally presented, there should always be texts. It is perhaps never possible or desirable to present the whole of the materials collected during the observation period, but some sort of 'corpus inscriptionum' seems to me essential in almost all studies. I have previously referred to our custom of transliteration, in works on linguistics. There is also the question of translations. In the last number of the *BSOAS*,[4] there is an article on 'Particle-noun complexes in a Berber dialect (Zuara)', by one of my colleagues, Mr T. F. Mitchell, in which no translations are given. Mr Mitchell and I discussed this matter, and as an experiment, I advised him to omit what we in London are accustomed to refer to as *translation meaning*, both of words and sentences. In most texts such translation meanings are not really equivalents, but are merely convenient identification or reference labels. Nevertheless, they should be most carefully chosen, if used at all. One of the languages of linguistics consists of the words, phrases or sentences, to give what we in the London group refer to as the translation meaning of the materials studied. I will not, at this point, go into the question of the translation of texts presented in linguistic work. According to the principles and methods of analysis I have proposed, total meaning is dispersed to be dealt with at various levels, and this involves a recognition of what I have called in a recent article, *'Modes of meaning' phonetic, phonological, syntactical, collocational, to mention only the lower end of the spectrum. If this is so, it follows that there are also modes of translation. Most of these modes would be considered impossible of translation from one language into another. I therefore feel that in the matter of textual translation, the freer they are the better.

I have already referred to the differences between the usage, idiom and style of the English used in linguistic works in America and on this side of the Atlantic. These differences are in what one might describe as the general vehicle. One cannot escape the implication of the general vehicle, in which technical phrases and technical terms are embedded. But even in America there are notable discrepancies in the use and application of what must be regarded as technical terms and phrases. There is no consistency, for example, in the use of the term 'zero'. And the symbol of crossed parallel lines, rather like a sharp in music, is not used with a single intention. More examples of the same kind can be found in American linguistics. Technical terms and phrases cannot always be defined in the dictionary manner. Indeed, the attempt to express in other words, as the saying goes, the power of the technical term, contributes little to the result. It has been my own practice to employ the words *prosodies* and *prosodic* in such a way that they are contextually specialized in the articles in which the words have appeared. And they are, so to speak, defined operatively, that is to say, instead of being equated with other words, they find part of their meaning in collocation in the text. In operational terms, they mean what they do.

Though it is difficult to give isolate meaning to any technical word or phrase, linguists should be the first to control, direct and specialize almost every word they write in linguistic analysis. I am convinced that there are very few really invented words, though there may be new words arising always from some known language background.

The main purpose of this paper is to point out the need for all linguists to be language conscious at all levels and at every point to emphasize that the more we take humanism out of linguistics the more we must take distance from our languages and techniques of statement and examine them to see if they form a fit and proper set of languages for a science of language. How can we build such a science without the scientist's regard for the terms in which we state our results not only for one another, but for all who may need them?

Notes

1. [*'General linguistics and descriptive grammar', F.R.P.]
2. [A handwritten comment of interest—'Redundancy and expectancy'. F.R.P.]
3. [M. A. K. Halliday, *The language of the Chinese 'Secret history of the Mongols'*, Oxford 1959, Publication of the Philological Society 17. F.R.P.]
4. [*BSOAS* 15.2.(1953). F.R.P.]

Three

Structural Linguistics†

The organizers of the First International Congress of Linguists, which met at The Hague in April 1928, indicated that one of the fundamental problems of linguistics, and one of growing insistence, was the necessity of developing a satisfactory method for the complete analysis of a given language. They realized that a systematic analysis of any language can be achieved only on a strictly synchronic basis, perhaps with the aid of analytical comparison of different types, without specific regard to their historical relations.

In 1936 Professor Mathesius of Prague underlined the insight then shown, and pointed to the increasing attention being paid to what even at that time he called *linguistic analysis*[1] based on such principles, i.e. regarding a language as a structure of interdependences between co-existing facts of the same language—that is to say a structural theory of language as a system of signs. The first instalment of this grand conception was the establishment of structural phonology—largely the work of Trubetzkoy, with some indebtedness to phonetics and indeed, as I know from personal contact with him, to British phoneticians.

In an article included in Kroeber's *Anthropology today*,[2] André Martinet says 'It is a difficult task' to define structural linguistics and to show how it differs as a whole from pre- or non-structural linguistics. There are the proclaimed structuralists, and those who may be said to be basing their work on 'applied' and what Martinet described as 'understood' structuralism, and yet other silent scholars, who just get on with their work, along lines not differing too much from those widely 'publicized by their more vocal fellow scholars'.

---

† *TPS* 1955, 83–103.

Expressions such as grammatical structure and phonetic structure have quite a long history. For instance, in Volume v of *Conférences de l'Institut de Linguistique de l'Université de Paris*, 1937, there are two papers, the first entitled 'La structure de la langue hongroise', by Professor A. Sauvageot, and a second entitled 'Structure de la langue basque', by G. Lacombe, neither of which could be classed as contributions to structural linguistics. Indeed, Sauvageot refers to the structure of Hungarian today as composite, as a mixture, and with archaisms of structure. We get nearer to structural concepts if we turn to our own country at a much earlier date, even as far back as Sweet. Everyone interested in structural as distinct from *structuralist* linguistics should study his 'Words, logic and grammar'.[3] A large and important section of the article appears under the sub-title 'Structure of English', and opens with the following words:

> I now propose to say something about the structure of English, and the proper method of treating its grammar. I may state at once that I consider the conventional treatment of English to be both unscientific and unpractical, starting as it does with the assumption that English is an inflexional language like Latin or Greek.

Further he adds:

> Every language has the right to be regarded as an actual, existing organism, not merely as the representative of earlier stages.

And even more pointedly:

> The only rational principle is to look at the language as it is now, and ask ourselves, How does this language express the relations of its words to one another?

He points out 'the many-sidedness of its structure' and 'the peculiar complexity of English grammar and the difficulty of attaining a just and adequate view of its characteristic features'. His concluding remarks are a penetrating analysis of the parallel study of *forms* and *meanings*. He even says that 'the whole of syntax is nothing else but an investigation of the meanings of grammatical forms'. He clearly recognizes meaning at the grammatical level of analysis, and declares that 'an essential part of English grammar is *intonation*'. The final paragraph must be quoted in full:

> If English grammar were treated in this way, it would give the student just notions not only of the structure of his own language,

but also of language generally, and a solid foundation would be laid for historical and comparative philology. The ordinary grammars, which ignore many of the most characteristic features entirely, and subordinate others to purely exceptional ones, not only give the student an entirely erroneous idea of the structure of English, but also train him to habits of erroneous and superficial observation, the evil results of which are seen every day both in scientific philology and in the practical acquisition of foreign languages.

In his paper on 'Russian pronunciation'[4] he refers to the 'exceptionally difficult *sound-system*'. He refers to what he terms 'the elementary vowels' of Welsh, mentions the need to study the *tonology* of Danish dialects (1873), and in the same year, over eighty years ago, he employed the notion of distribution:

> The question whether these close and open vowels are distributed according to any fixed principles, has, as far as I know, been answered by Danish phoneticians in the negative: they say that no rules can be given. I have taken the trouble to draw up exhaustive lists, and the result is that the character of the vowel is determined by the following consonant, although there is considerable irregularity.[5]

Then follow two pages of tentative rules of distribution based on exhaustive lists of words and phrases. The whole of his work in phonetics, perhaps especially his systematic presentation of a number of notations, including both Visible Speech and Broad Romic, prepared the way for the phoneme theory and functional and structural phonology. In the first volume of his *New English grammar*[6] there are well over two hundred pages which all those interested in the beginnings of general linguistics in England should read with respect.

In the United States, Sapir laid down the first American outlines much later. An interesting article appeared in *Language* in December 1929, entitled 'The status of linguistics as a science', from which the following passages[7] deserve quotation in the present connection:

> Linguistics would seem to have a very peculiar value for configurative studies because the patterning of language is to a very appreciable extent self-contained and not significantly at the mercy of intercrossing patterns of a non-linguistic type ...

> One can only hope that linguists will become increasingly aware of the significance of their subject in the general field of science. ...

Of linguistics:

> Its data and methods show better than those of any other discipline dealing with socialized behaviour, the possibility of a truly scientific study of society.

> Linguists should, on the other hand, become aware of what their science may mean for the interpretation of human conduct in general.

Turning to our own time, there are successors to Sweet: there is an article in the *Transactions* of the Society,[8] by Daniel Jones, entitled 'The phonetic structure of the Sechuana language', in which Jones states that Sechuana appears to contain twenty-eight phonemes, i.e. twenty-eight sounds or small families of sounds which are capable of distinguishing one word from another. He finds five main tones, modifiable for grammatical purposes, at points in the sentence determined mainly by grammatical considerations. There are seven tonal conjugations. In Memorandum VI of the International Institute of African Languages and Cultures, Jones dealt with 'The tones of Sechuana nouns', in which the tonal analysis is associated with grammatical distinctions or with syntactical relationships. Incidentally, Jones was one of the first to use the expression 'environment' in referring to the phoneme. In an article on chronemes and tonemes in *Acta linguistica*, Volume IV, he describes phoneme variants as being 'used in particular phonetic environments'.

The expression 'Phonetic structure' also appears as the heading for Chapter 8 of Bloomfield's *Language*, 1933, in which he points out that 'even a perfected knowledge of acoustics will not by itself give us the phonetic structure of a language'. He is emphasizing the importance of what he calls 'distinctive features' and the parts phonemes play in the structure of our language. He adds that the grammatical structure of a language implies groupings of the phonemes, and points out that the structural pattern differs greatly in different languages. In his chapter on form-classes and lexicon, he states that on the one side the lexical form in the abstract 'exhibits a meaningful grammatical *structure*' and on the other in any actual utterance it appears in some 'grammatical *function*'.[9] He used the expression 'structural order' in a different sense, but nowhere finds any technical use for the word *system*. The index enters *phoneme* and *phonemic*, but not *phonemics* or *phonemicize* and, we may be thankful, not *re-phonemicize*. Strange as it may seem, there are only three entries for the word *structure*.

I doubt very much whether Jones' articles would be considered as completely structural by many contemporary linguists. They are only the beginnings of systems of analysis, which provide very practical means of stating in terms of articulatory and acoustic phonetics certain phonetic features which are said to mark grammatical structure. In 1935 Professor Paul Menzerath, of Bonn, published in *Acta psychologica* (The Hague), an article entitled 'Die phonetische Struktur—eine grundsätzliche Betrachtung'. The summary in English[10] states:

> This paper presents fundamental views, won by both theory and experiment, on various forms of phonetic structure with special regard to articulatory structure. The conception of a word as a series of sounds resembling a 'chain' of phonetic elements independent of one another could be proved erroneous. As a matter of fact, there can no longer be any question of single speech-elements in a word; the sounds of a word run together, the word itself being intended as a unit.

The expression 'phonetic structure' has no place in my own theory, since elements of structure are mutually inter-related abstract categories set up by the linguist, and are timeless and 'ineffable'. Even Aristotle stated quite explicitly in his remarks on quantity that syllables could not be regarded as co-terminous.[11]

Aristotle lists seven items to which the term quantity properly applies, and these are divided first into discrete and continuous quantities, and secondly into quantities the parts of which are positionally interrelated and quantities without positionally related parts, and in the last mentioned sub-group (without positionally interrelated parts) are *time*, *number* and *speech*, of which time is a special case, but number and speech are both discrete and without positionally interrelated parts. Syllables are discrete and may be long or short, but they do not have common boundaries. In actual speech he recognizes that speech, like time and number, may be said to have relative order in sequence. My colleague Mr R. H. Robins tells me that the commentators ancient and modern have nothing useful to offer which might relate this chapter to some of the problems of structural linguistics. It is just possible that a tentative parallel may be drawn with my own approach which recognizes that the stream of speech flows in time[12] and that temporal sequence can be recognized in the *phonic* material as such, but that is all. All other interrelations of parts within larger wholes subsist, not in the phonic material, but in the *structures* and *systems* set up by the linguist at the phonological and grammatical levels.

Menzerath's emphasis on *the word as a unit* is a useful corrective for linguistics suffering from over-segmentation and fragmentation, and is to that extent in harmony with the prosodic approach which, however, extends to the piece and to the sentence as the main items on the linguist's agenda.

The prosodic point of view is further supported by the following statement, but it does this at the level of phonetics in dealing with the phonic material:

> Two more concepts must be added: Original or Sound-Steering, and Superposing Steering. Both factors influence speech movements at the same time. The articulation of a vowel is steered (determined) by the following consonant and vice versa (up, pu, upu). The nature of the articulatory movements in a word also depends on the idea underlying the sentence. Thus the idea involved steers the sound (in a word) differentiating it with regard to duration, loudness, accent, melody and colour.[13]

No proclaimed structuralist would accept either the idea or the term 'articulatory structure'. It is not easy to formulate a framework of categories and terms in which to state the phonetic structure as distinct from the phonological categories. The general terminology and alphabet of the I.P.A. as used for an impressionist description of the pronunciation of words and sentences, would not, I imagine, be regarded as structuralist. Moreover, it is manifestly inadequate for contemporary phonology which demands more and more phonetic categories to keep pace with the rapid development of linguistic analysis at all levels.

And yet, as we shall see, it is largely the later development of the phoneme theory which has provided most of the subject matter of structural linguistics, especially in America, where linguistics is, to all intents and purposes, *phonemics*, with an additive *morphemics*, plus the supplementary amendments of *morphophonemics*.[14]

Nevertheless, a great deal of attention is being paid in America to acoustics and to analysis by spectrograms. For instance, Roman Jakobson's *Preliminaries to speech analysis*, dealing with distinctive features and their correlates, is very much concerned with the phonic data, consequently with phonetics, concentrating on acoustics and not on articulation. The phonetic findings, however, are treated as correlates of linguistic values in the Saussurean sense. He gives a special paragraph on p. 11 to this one sentence—'In short, for the study of speech sounds on any level whatsoever their linguistic function is decisive'. In correspondence with me he has been emphatically in agreement with my suggestions repeatedly made since 1935, that meaning in a *strictly linguistic sense* is our concern at all levels of linguistic analysis—I repeat the qualification, *meaning* to be interpreted strictly within an autonomous linguistic discipline.

These preliminary remarks lead me to what I believe is the best introduction to the subject under discussion.

Three very common words in the new language about language are *system, structure* and *phoneme,* with all their derivatives. There is, however, no real agreement on their use, and neither the Americans nor the Scandinavians have controlled and distinguished the use of *system* and *structure*[15] as we have in the linguistics group at the School of Oriental and African Studies.

The beginnings of structuralist linguistics of the phonemic type are with Baudouin de Courtenay and his Slav group, and also of course with the real founder of it all, de Saussure, followed by Meillet whose famous sentence still reverberates: 'Chaque langue forme un système, où tout se tient . . .'

Trubetzkoy's work with the Prague Circle provided firm foundations for a *structural* phonology which might combine the achievements of Russian and Polish linguists with the general linguistic theories of de Saussure. Although the basis of a great deal of the linguistic analysis of this group is one type of phoneme theory, it differs in almost every essential from structuralist phonemics as practised in the United States. The following comments are taken from 'Notes autobiographiques de N. S. Trubetzkoy, communiquées par Roman Jakobson' to Cantineau's translation of the *Grundzüge*[16] 'de Saussure, tout en enseignant que "la langue est un système" n'a pas osé tirer les conséquences logiques de sa propre thèse'. If he had, there would have been contradictions of much traditional historical linguistics. Meillet, who added to 'système', the emphatic clause 'où tout se tient', even found it possible to say 'le progrès de la civilisation détruit le duel'. Trubetzkoy rightly believed all such speculations were 'out of order' from the point of view of the newer structural approach:

Cependant une étude attentive des langues orientée vers la logique interne de leur évolution nous apprend qu'une telle logique existe et qu'on peur établir toute une série de lois purement linguistiques indépendantes des facteurs extra-linguistiques, tels que la 'civilisation', etc.[17]

Trubetzkoy, Jakobson and the others who sympathized with them were greatly encouraged by the First International Congress of Linguists at The Hague in 1928.[18] This is another indication that, although de Saussure's *Cours de linguistique générale* dates from 1916–17, contemporary structural linguistics really begins to develop the outline of its foundations about 1930, or just about ten years after the publication of Jespersen's *Language*, the first sentence of which is: 'The distinctive feature of the science of language as conceived nowadays is its historical character.'[19]

Trubetzkoy turned to the general theories of phonological and morphological structure. 'La langue étant un système il doit y avoir un lien étroit entre la structure grammaticale et la structure phonologique de la langue.' While fully recognizing the contributions of Baudouin and Ščerba and of de Saussure, he and Jakobson advanced and won new positions. Trubetzkoy did, however, recognize brilliant earlier work of men ahead of their time, such as the Swiss J. Winteler, and goes out of his way to mention that

> le célèbre phonéticien anglais Sweet a exprimé à plusieurs reprises la même idée et l'a transmise à ses élèves, dont le plus remarquable, Otto Jespersen, a mis tout particulièrement l'accent sur cet aspect des vues de son maître. Malgré cela, Sweet aussi bien que ses disciples ont toujours traité de la même façon toutes les oppositions phoniques, que ces oppositions servissent ou non à différencier des sens, et la méthode employée était celle qu'on utilise dans les sciences naturelles pour l'observation.[20]

At the Congresses in Rome (1933) and in Copenhagen (1936), Trubetzkoy was clear that structural linguistics, especially in phonology, had really made a successful beginning and said in one of his letters 'nous sommes suivis par les jeunes qui ont été formés par nos écrits et qui peuvent travailler d'une façon indépendante'.[21]

Every British empiricist must warm to Jakobson's further comment on Trubetzkoy:

> Il rejette catégoriquement 'toute tendance à philosophailler en dehors du travail concret sur les faits', bref toute tendance à maltraiter les détails en faveur de l'ensemble, mais d'autre part il blâme sévèrement la négligence de l'ensemble en faveur des détails,

ou de la théorie au nom de la pratique: 'Le mathématicien peut se passer de l'ingénieur, mas l'ingénieur ne peut se passer du mathématicien'.[21]

Since in my own view, languages are to be described from a poly-systemic point of view, I am naturally pleased to quote Trubetzkoy's view that a language may be considered as 'un ensemble de plusieurs systèmes partiels'.[22]

It is greatly to be regretted that Trubetzkoy never brought out a new edition of the 'Anleitung zu phonologischen Beschreibungen' covering both 'sounds and prosodies', and adding to his eleven rules. His rules quite appropriately do not attempt to axiomatize phonology. They are rules for description, and though they would not now be acceptable as they stand, the notion of rules for structural description is valuable. A linguist drawing up such rules would no doubt direct them towards linguistic description at a series of levels, morphological, syntactical, stylistic, lexical, even situational. Though I should not develop my approach in those directions I see no objection to the replacement of axioms by rules.

There are then, several approaches in linguistic analysis: the axiomatic approach, the procedural approach, the theoretical approach, and a combination of the theoretical and the empirical approaches. Professor Zellig Harris claims in his Preface[23] that his 'procedures of analysis are the product and outgrowth of the work of linguists throughout the world, to whose investigations the meager references cited here are an inadequate guide'. This is a wholesale over-simplification of the subject. In an immediately following sentence he does, however, say that he owes most to Sapir and Bloomfield.

Bloomfield was quite clearly convinced of the value of the method of postulates and axioms, and believed he was moving into a more scientific methodology akin to mathematics. The postulational method involves the strict definition of terms. He has been faithfully followed by Professor Bernard Bloch in his 'A set of postulates for phonemic analysis': 'Any procedure for which no tenable assumption can be found is for that very reason open to the gravest suspicion.'[24] It is unfortunate that Professor Bernard Bloch appears to distinguish between what he calls the facts of a language and facts that can be put into words. For me, a *fact* must be technically stated and find a place in a system of related statements, all of them arising from a theory and found applicable in renewal of connection in experience. It is probably true that even in mathematics the possibilities of complete axiomatization have been over-estimated.

The procedural approach does not necessarily imply axiomatization. As practised by Professor Kenneth Pike it is a kind of linguistic assembly-line technique for the production of 'linguisticians'. Professor Zellig Harris describes his work as a system of methods and procedures for research or teaching

> for those who are primarily interested in the logic of distributional relations, which constitutes the basic method of structural linguistics, a minimum of knowledge about language and linguistics has been assumed.[25]

The first sentence of his Introduction goes further, and baldly states that the methods are those used

> in descriptive, or, more exactly, structural, linguistics. It is thus a discussion of the operations which the linguist may carry out in the course of his investigations, rather than a theory of the structural analyses which result from these investigations. The research methods are arranged here in the form of the successive procedures of analysis imposed by the working linguist upon his data.[26]

It would, I think, be safer to say that such methods and procedures are used in structuralist linguistics which proceeds by segmentation of utterance, and endeavours to link unit-length and phoneme-length.[27]

Structuralist descriptions are limited to collections of utterances which can be phonemicized by segmentation. Such descriptions may be valuable, but they form only one part of one branch of what might properly be called *structural* linguistics. A coherent structural analysis in terms of descriptive linguistics has recently been made of a medieval Chinese text, without any attempt to reconstruct a complete phonological analysis.[28]

Professor Louis Hjelmslev's 'Prolegomena to a theory of language'[29] is, in effect, linguistic philosophy. Though he proceeds by the partition of texts it is not segmentation in the American sense:

> The analysis thus consists in registering certain dependences between certain terminals, which we may call, in accordance with established usage, the parts of the text, and which have existence precisely by virtue of these dependences and only by virtue of them.[30]

A summary statement of Hjelmslev's general approach is to be found in his 'Structural analysis of language',[31] from which the following key quotations are taken:

> On the contrary, the real units of language are not sounds, or written characters, or meanings; the real units of language are the relata which these sounds, characters and meanings represent. The main thing is not the sounds, characters and meanings as such, but their mutual relations within the chain of speech and within the paradigms of grammar. These relations make up the system of a language, and it is this interior system which is characteristic of one language as opposed to other languages, whereas the representation by sounds, characters and meanings is irrelevant to the system and may be changed without affecting the system.

> This is why the structural approach to language, in the real sense of the word, conceived as a purely relational approach to the language pattern independently of the manifestation in the linguistic usage, has not been taken up by philologists before the present day.

> If talking of one's own efforts would not be considered too pretentious. I should like to state, modestly but emphatically, that such a structural approach to language, considered merely as a pattern of mutual relations, has been and still will be my chief concern in all my endeavours within this field of study. In contradistinction to conventional philology, I have proposed the name *glossematics* (derived from Gk. γλῶσσα 'language') to denote this purely structural kind of linguistic research.

> It is obvious that the description of a language must begin by stating relations between relevant units, and these statements cannot involve a statement about the inherent nature, essence or substance of these units themselves.

> We can wind up this discussion by stating that linguistics describes the relational pattern of language without knowing what the relata are, and that phonetics and semantics do tell what those relata are but only by means of describing the relations between their parts and parts of their parts. This would mean, in logistic terms, that linguistics is a metalanguage of the first degree, whereas phonetics and semantics are metalanguages of the second degree.

Professor Hjelmslev gives five fundamental features which he considers are involved in the basic structure of any language in the conventional sense, namely the following:

1. A language consists of a content and an expression.
2. A language consists of a succession, or a text, and a system.
3. Content and expression are bound up with each other through commutation.
4. There are certain definite relations within the succession and within the system.
5. There is not a one-to-one correspondence between content and expression, but the signs are decomposable in minor components. Such sign components are, e.g. the so-called phonemes, which I[32] should prefer to call taxemes of expression, and which in themselves have no content, but which can build up units provided with a content, e.g. words.[33]

Hjelmslev concludes his 'Prolegomena' with a list of one hundred and six technical words with brief definitions and references to the text. He also uses 'segments' and 'procedure' with an entirely different purport from the commonly accepted application of these words in American linguistics, or indeed in the rest of this article. Two key words that need to be followed up throughout the list and text are *function* and *functive*.

At this point it is convenient to discuss the attempts that are made to axiomatize linguistics and to develop general theorems of universal application. Applying my own technique, I would suggest that the meaning of the one hundred and six listed terms in Hjelmslev's 'Prolegomena' is to be found by collecting and classifying the collocations, first in English and then perhaps in Danish, proceeding thence to frame a summary grammar of the structures regularly employed in the text. Any linguist proposing to apply the theory would then have a rigid framework in which to test this special language for linguistic analysis in English and Danish. But even this short review will show the limitations of the approach by axioms and postulates and general theorems of a philosophico-mathematical character.

The empirical data of such sciences as linguistics are usually stated in technical restricted languages which must, nevertheless, involve indeterminacy, since technical terms are collocated with words of common usage in general language. Linguistics which does not fully recognize this element of indeterminacy cannot very well be applied to the study of language in society. There is need to recognize indeterminacy, not only in the restricted technical language of description, but also in the language under description, in describing, let us say, familiar colloquial English as used in professional circles in southern England; but the point is that the restricted language of linguistics used for statements of fact, must use other related forms of the language, shared with common colloquial, hence this double character of indeterminacy.

It would be absurd to say that there is no room for mathematical thinking in linguistics. I would rather suggest that language presents an open field for applied mathematics of the right kind. Moreover, linguists are developing various forms of notation and symbolization for such of their systems of relations as lend themselves to formulaic statement. The group of linguists at the London School of Oriental and African Studies have made a number of experiments in these directions, the results of which have been published either in the *Transactions* of the Society[34] or in the *Bulletin* of the School.[35]

In a recent number of *Word*,[36] appearing under the misleading title 'Linguistics to-day', the first editorial article, by André Martinet, is in general terms unfortunate in its emphasis, but there are four sentences at any rate which deserve notice:

Instead of brushing away as irrelevant, or disregarding as subordinate, semantics, phonetics or both, they will have to look for information wherever information is to be found, taking of course great care to evaluate the reliability of every piece of it. The description of a language is not achieved through taking apart all the elements of its delicate machinery any more than a watch would be usefully and exhaustively described through the linear display on a green cloth of all its springs and cogwheels. It is necessary to show how all the elements of both the language and the watch co-operate when at work. . . . So far we have had, in descriptive linguistics, a little too much anatomy and not enough physiology, and the rigor after which some of us are striving too often resembles rigor mortis.[37]

The quotations raise two questions relevant to the present state of structural linguistics: firstly, the emphasis on segmentation and phonemics with the so-called exclusion of 'meaning', and secondly, the attempt to frame a sort of linguistic mathematics or a completely axiomatized science. In my opinion, any fully axiomatized mathematical linguistics will not be found workable in a truly empirical science, and will, as Martinet says, become a dead technical language perhaps only applicable to dead languages, and perhaps not even then with any effective result.

Reverting to the first point, I believe we have all been *au régime* and fed too exclusively on a diet of phonemics, and indeed on segmentation and fragmentation phonology of all sorts. As Professor Kenneth Pike once said, phonemics involves cookery, but it is a very limited cuisine and the time has now come for an improvement in our standards of living and a more international outlook. Phonological analysis and the notations arising therefrom will always provide the basic data for most descriptive work dealing with spoken languages. Moreover, specialist phonological studies, even accepting a continuing proliferation of phonemic analyses, will not exhaust fundamental research which might be of some use to linguistics at other levels, not excluding historical and comparative linguistics.

In my view, there can be no unity of linguistics, if that is considered desirable, and certainly no synthesis of all the approaches here reviewed, unless we all turn to what Roman Jakobson has described as the 'second front',[38] or the application of our discipline and techniques to statements of meaning at all levels. In his 'A set of postulates for phonemic analysis', Bloch provides one of the characteristics of the 'excluded meaning approach' in the following sentence:

> The basic assumptions that underlie phonemics, we believe, can be stated without any mention of mind and meaning; but meaning, at least, is so obviously useful as a short cut in the investigation of phonemic structure—one might almost say, so inescapable—that any linguist who refused to employ it would be very largely wasting his time.[39]

And in a footnote he is pleased to quote Daniel Jones who said:

> The fact that certain sounds are used in a language for distinguishing the meanings of words doesn't enter into the definition of a phoneme.[40]

The truth is, of course, that phonemicists holding to these views merely wish to circumscribe the field of investigation and define the level of their analysis. The work done happens to be called structuralist linguistics by some, but it is in fact only a branch and should be specifically named phonemics or structuralist phonemics, although the latter phrase would perhaps be a tautology. Bloch himself says that it is only in the wording that semantic criteria are avoided. There is no implication that meaning is necessarily ruled out of what are called practical devices in the actual work of making a phonemic analysis. All phonological analyses, however, contribute one band of abstractions from the meaningful complex, and it is an inescapable duty for linguists to add other bands of abstractions at other levels, all congruent, in order to provide any description which can comprehensively be called linguistic.

The treatment of meaning by Zellig Harris would appear to be less carefully considered; to begin with, in his *Methods in structural linguistics* he uses translation meanings throughout, sometimes almost casually; for example in dealing with a set of grouped Swahili examples, the following occur: 'in the corner', 'cat', 'it soars', 'rubber', 'beach'. Whether the Swahili words form any kind of system of comparables is doubtful. The translation meanings themselves raise doubts. Other translation meanings grouped together are 'carry ye', 'they called us'.[41] Another curious group of translation meanings runs as follows: 'leap!' 'interpreter', 'in-law', 'ship'.[42] Bit for bit translations of rather a different kind are also used in the analysis of certain Arabic isolates, for example '*kataba*', '*kaðaba*', etc., which seem to require such translations as 'write', 'he', 'perfective', 'intensive', 'reciprocal'.[43] There are other less satisfactory translation meanings, for example in *victrix bona* 'good victor (f.)', also . . . *ix* . . . *a* meaning 'female'.[44] There are many such bit for bit translations throughout. This unsystematic use of translation is of so loose a character that it cannot be taken as a constituent of the analysis proper—but it is there expressly included in the author's text.

It may clarify the issue if we assume that in stating his facts the linguist must carefully consider (1) the restricted language under description, (2) the language of description,[45] including technical terms, collocations, notations and formulae, and (3) the language of translation,[46] including (a) translation meanings or *systematic* identification names, (b) bit for bit translations where considered absolutely necessary and always referred to one level at a time, (c) a running translation, (d) free translation. My submission is that in a great deal of present-day *structuralist* linguistics insufficient attention is paid to all these methods of stating linguistic facts. Much of the prevalent philosophizing on metalanguages and the like does not face the essential problems of statement. Dispensing with translation meanings, and the increasing use of typographical specialization appropriate to levels of analysis and formulaic expressions, might possibly be wrongly interpreted by some

4

as excluding certain elements of 'meaning'. They are in fact attempts at statements of meaning in more precise linguistic terms.

From my point of view, *structural* linguistics aims at employing all our technical resources systematically for multiple statements of meaning in the appropriate linguistic terms. Structural linguistics, therefore, deals with meaning throughout the whole range of the discipline, but it only does so within its own circumscribed fields and exclusively in its own terms. The question, therefore, is not how much meaning can be *excluded*, but how much meaning can legitimately be included. It might even be said that meaning *must* be included as a fundamental assumption.

The coming together of anthropologists and linguists in recent conferences may have the highly desirable effect of demonstrating to linguists that they are concerned with the statement of meaning in linguistic terms and that 'linguistics limited to the signal factor' was a 'necessary but fragmentary stage'.[47] Professor Lotz remarked that linguists should not feel so pessimistic about statements of meaning in linguistics. They should certainly avoid mis-statements of meaning in linguistics, especially the casual use of undefined translation.

In conclusion, I should like to draw attention to the remarks of Professor Roman Jakobson summing up his impression of the American Conference of anthropologists and linguists mentioned above. He declared that:

> One of the most symptomatic features of this Conference was that we lengthily and passionately discussed the questions of meaning . . .[48] Thus, meaning remains a No Man's Land. This game of Give-away must end. For years and decades we have fought for the annexation of speech-sounds to linguistics, and thereby established phonemics. Now we face a second front—the task of incorporating linguistic meaning into the science of language.[49]

In England we have been on the second front since the days of Sweet, and in London we have been interested in the theory and practice of linguistic statements of meaning at all the main levels of structural analysis since the early thirties.

Notes

1. Malinowski used the expression *linguistic analysis* in referring to his own work as early as 1921 in his *Argonauts of the Western Pacific*, 428, and frequently in later work—e.g. Supplement 1 to Ogden and Richards *Meaning of meaning*, 1927, 302, 305, 308–9, 312.

2. University of Chicago Press, 1953.

3. *TPS* 1875–6, 470–503. Reprinted in his *Collected papers*, Oxford: Clarendon Press, 1913. The same paper also appeared, with some modifications, in the *Journal of the Anthropological Institute*, May 1877, under the title 'Language and thought'.

4. *TPS* 1877–9, 543–60. *Collected papers*, 448–64.

5. *Collected papers*, 352–3.

6. Oxford: Clarendon Press, 1892.

7. 212.

8. *TPS* 1917–20.

9. 264–5.

10. 262.

11. Aristotle, *Organon*, Chapter 6. Compare this with Bloch's notice of the difference between his definition of segment and Pike's in his *Phonetics*, Ann Arbor, 1943, 107, which runs 'A *segment* is a sound (or lack of sound) having indefinite borders with a center that is produced by a crest or trough of stricture during the even motion or pressure of an initiator . . .'. It is interesting that Bloch nowhere defines the term *syllable*, but wisely remarks in his 'A set of postulates for phonemic analysis', *Language* 24.1.41, that it is 'often useful as the name of a structural unit determined by phonemic analysis; and we have included no postulates on which a definition might be based'. I think I would have regarded the term *syllable* as applicable to an element of word structure which cannot be determined by phonemic analysis. I would add that I think Aristotle has something to say to us in this connection.

12. See my *'The semantics of linguistic science', from which the following is quoted: 'An utterance happens in time. The stream of speech with all its items integrated unrolls itself so to speak on the *time track* of occurrences. But the systemic abstractions which we isolate in language systems are not limited by the time track dimensions of the utterances from which they are taken.'

13. Menzerath, 'Die phonetische Struktur—eine grundsätzliche Betrachtung', 1935.

14. See Zellig Harris' *Methods in structural linguistics*, University of Chicago Press, 1951, 219, 224–5.

15. See my **'A synopsis of linguistic theory, 1930–55'. See also R. H. Robins' 'Formal divisions in Sudanese', *TPS* 1953, 109.

16. See Trubetzkoy's *Principes de phonologie*, Paris, 1949, xv–xxix.

17. xxv.

18. See above, p. 35.

19. Preface to Jespersen's *Language*, London: Allen and Unwin, 1922.

20. Trubetzkoy's *Principes de phonologie*, 4. I hope I may be allowed to appreciate in the highest terms the full and generous recognition Trubetzkoy always gave to any work, however small and from whatever country it came, if he found it of value in developing his own arguments. May I be allowed to mention the liberal references in the Grundzüge to quite a number of English phoneticians in addition to Daniel Jones, all of whom are in one way or another 'pupils' of Sweet.

21. 'Notes autobiographiques', *Principes de phonologie*, xxix.

22. ibid., 3.

23. Preface to *Methods in structural linguistics*.

24. 43.

25. Preface to *Methods in structural linguistics*.

26. Introduction to *Methods in structural linguistics*, 1.
27. See op. cit., 44.
28. By Dr M. A. K. Halliday in his thesis for the Ph.D., Cambridge, 1955. [See p. 34, n. 3. F.R.P.]
29. Supplement to *IJAL* 19.1 (1953).
30. op. cit., 17.
31. *Studia linguistica* (1948).
32. i.e. Professor Hjelmslev.
33. See also my **'General linguistics and descriptive grammar'.
34. J. Carnochan, 'Glottalization in Hausa,' *TPS* 1952.
35. See note 46.
36. 10.2–3 (1954). Though the volume runs to 279 pages the subjects treated cannot be said to be representative, and for some reason no mention is made of any contribution from Great Britain either in historical, descriptive or general linguistics. As I have shown in this short article, a good deal of work that can be described as structural has been characteristic of English work since the days of Sweet and before; but then I distinguished *structural* from structuralist.
37. op. cit., 125.
38. Supplement to *IJAL* 19.2 (1953). Report of the American conference of anthropologists and linguists.
39. 'A set of postulates for phonemic analysis', 5.
40. ibid., 6.
41. 99.
42. 100.
43. 165.
44. 166.
45. The contribution of Malinowski in the development of the study of meaning from the ethnographic as well as from the linguistic point of view, is fully dealt with in an essay to appear in a forthcoming volume on the significance of his work in anthropology and linguistics.
46. Some linguists of the London group have experimented with notational and formulaic statements excluding translation meanings. See T. F. Mitchell's 'Particle-noun complexes in a Berber dialect', *BSOAS* 15.2 (1953). See also R. K. Sprigg's 'Verbal phrases in Lhasa Tibetan', *BSOAS* 16.1, 2 and 3 (1954), and his 'Tonal system of Tibetan (Lhasa dialect) and the nominal phrase', *BSOAS* 17.1 (1955).
47. Supplement to *IJAL* 19.2 (1953).
48. op. cit., 19.
49. op. cit., 21.

Four

Philology in the
Philological Society[†]

If I am to give a title to this Address—may I take it from a heading in
the second Address by A. J. Ellis in 1873, 'Philology in the Philological Society'.

He had given the first Annual Address at the Anniversary Meeting on
Friday, 17th May 1872. He opened with the following words:

> Gentlemen, it was, as you are aware, the intention of our late
> lamented President, Professor Goldstücker, to make our Anniversary
> conform to those of other learned Societies, by delivering an Annual
> Address. We have been hitherto accustomed to make our anniver-
> saries in no respect differ from ordinary meetings, except in the
> passing of accounts and election of officers. In other Societies, the
> retiring President usually delivers an address, thus giving the
> proceedings on that occasion a distinctive character.

I cannot say that I have anything very distinctive to offer you in the
matter of my Address except possibly to put before you interesting facts
and views from earlier Presidential Addresses and to follow them to
some extent in reviewing in the customary words of my predecessors,
the 'progress of philology' in this country since the War.

The last Presidential Address was delivered by Professor Wrenn on
the 10th May 1946. In his opening words, Professor Wrenn said: 'It
happens also that this Anniversary Meeting is the first occasion that
wartime conditions permit us to commemorate, besides Sweet's
centenary, that of the foundation in 1842 of our Society itself.' As

---

† *TPS* 1956. Presidential Address delivered to the Society on Friday, 4th
May, 1956.

Professor Wrenn also reminded us, Henry Sweet was one of our greatest pioneer leaders and also perhaps the greatest philologist that our country has so far produced. A study of the early years of the Society's Proceedings, especially between 1869 and 1885 shows Henry Sweet as a dominant factor in the work of the Society.

Sweet delivered the sixth and seventh Presidential Addresses in May 1877 and May 1878 respectively. Remembering Sweet's place in English philology and in the history of our Society, it is a matter of high significance to record his emphasis in 1877–8 on the catholic interests of the Society. Reviewing the papers delivered during 1876–7, which beside English and French included Serbian, Persian, Common Tamil, the non-Aryan languages of India and Akkadian phonology, he said:

> These papers represent a very wide range of subjects. It is enough, I think, to acquit our Society of any accusation of one-sidedness to consider how large a proportion of our papers are on Oriental languages—this, too, in spite of the formidable rivalry of a 'Royal Asiatic Society', endowed by Government.

Subjects in which England took a decided lead in those days were phonetics, phonology and lexicography. Of phonology as the science of linguistic observation, he said:

> The truth is, that phonology is not only the indispensable foundation of all philology, but also that no department, from the highest to the lowest, can be investigated fully without it, whether it be accidence, syntax, or prosody, or even that fundamental problem— the origin of language.

This leads him to mention the concentration of our energies mainly on what may be called 'living philology'. He referred to his own work the *Handbook of phonetics*, now rare and still valuable, pointing out that it aimed at being

> a guide to the study of sounds generally whether as a preparation for the practical study of languages or for scientific philology. The distinctive feature of the work is that it summarizes and—as far as possible—harmonizes the often widely-divergent results of English and Continental phonetic investigation.

Finally, referring once more to his own work in 1877, he pointed out that almost the only paper that dealt with any of the fundamental problems of language was his own on 'Words, logic and grammar', in which he tried to upset some of the conventional dogmas of philology, logic and grammar, partly by means of a consistent phonetic analysis, and to explain the real meaning of the parts of speech; and again in 1878, he said that the only papers dealing with general questions were two of his own—'Gender' and 'Practical study of languages'. He added a comment which is a good deal less true today, namely that 'the inability to grasp general principles is, indeed, one of the most marked characteristics of English philologists'. The evils he denounced were, he said, 'not due to any defect in the English character, but simply to want of systematic training'. Philology in the Philological Society in these days includes substantial contributions to the fundamental problems of language, and there is no lack of systematic training. The wide range of the Society's interests is also reflected in the earlier Presidential Addresses. I have already quoted from Ellis' first Address in 1872, attributing the holding of an Address to the suggestion of a well-known Sanskritist of those days, Professor Goldstücker, Professor of Sanskrit at University College London. All the early Presidential Addresses reviewed the work of the Society but also included reports from leading authorities on many branches of the subject, this custom being broken by the Rev. Professor Sayce in 1888. He apologized for the omission and, referring to Sweet's 'living philology', also apologized for the 'antiquarian philology' which he said he represented. If he had had to present an account of the work of the Society, he would have referred to papers on the language of the Cayapas Indians of Ecuador, on the languages of Mexico, on Russian as well as Celtic.

A. J. Ellis gave five Addresses. The first, I have already mentioned. In reviewing the work of the Society, under the heading of 'Philology in the Philological Society' in the second Presidential Address in 1873, he noticed three papers on Sanskrit, on both lexicography and grammar, and further papers on Basque, Hungarian, Pennsylvania German, the Mosquito Dialect[1] and a paper by Ellis himself on the relation of thought to sound which he had announced as the pivot of philological research in his first Address. He, too, was interested in general subjects such as the philosophy of the origin of language, reduplication, as well as in his own specialization in phonetics and transcription. In those years too, there were papers on Etruscan and Semitic, five papers on Latin and Greek including pronunciation, on Celtic and one on the English Dialect Society.

When Ellis delivered the tenth Address in 1881, he found it necessary to go out of his way to address the lady members, expressing regret that more women did not enter the Society. He had, of course, by that time the routine report on the Society's Dictionary based on material supplied by Murray, on spelling reform, on Graham Bell and Visible Speech. In the eleventh Address in 1882, the wide variety of the Society's interests was again headlined in the report on the Yaagan language of Tierra del Fuego, on the South Andaman language, on research in Mongolian, on cuneiform and on important contributions to phonetics, especially by the Bells and Sweet who provided reviews of work in phonetics and general philology as well as on Germanic and English philology. Skeat submitted material on the English Dialect Society and on a German linguistic atlas.

My purpose has been to show that at any rate down to 1888, the Society so established its traditions that Wharton, who was Secretary of the Society from 1915 to 1930, was able to record in 1920 and 1921, a considerable amount of what is referred to as 'non-English work'. 'We must', he writes, 'tread a very wide field if we are to follow our own traditions.'

The greatest achievement of the Society is undoubtedly the Dictionary, and during the most active period there was a tendency to regard English philology and etymology as a main interest. It was not until Murray became President in 1880, that a Dictionary report became an annual feature. In giving the ninth Address, Murray expressed the opinion that the President might give his Address either on election or retirement, and, in speaking of the Dictionary, made two interesting remarks. I should put first the obvious connection between lexicography and linguistic theory. In referring to the historical character of the Dictionary, he notices the question of what is a word and what is merely a form. A good Dictionary entry, I should say myself, makes statements of meaning at a number of different levels and touches general linguistic theory at all of them. Secondly, in passing, he almost exclaims:

> It is marvellous, and to the inexperienced incredible, how Dictionaries and Encyclopaedias simply copy each other, without an attempt either to verify quotations or facts . . . so entries, which are mere blunders, are ignorantly handed down from Dictionary to Dictionary, each writer entering them as boldly and authoritatively as if he really knew of their existence.

In 1884, Murray delivered the thirteenth Address, telling the Society that he was unable to say when he expected the Dictionary to be finished. 'All depends upon the amount of time which I can be enabled personally to give to the work, and the number of competent assistants whom I have to help me.'

On 1st June 1928, there was a report by Dr Onions on the completion of the first part of the Dictionary. This almost coincided with the seventieth anniversary of the proposal adopted by the Society under the inspiration of Trench to prepare a *New English Dictionary* of the English language.

At this point, I should like to mention an observation by Dr Onions that may account to some extent for the current title for the Dictionary, which is usually the *Oxford Dictionary*. 'By the way,' remarked Dr Onions,

> let those whom it may concern observe that here we have the origin of the title *A New English Dictionary on Historical Principles* which has nothing to do with the use of 'New English' as a representative of German *neuenglisch*, meaning English of the modern period. It is clear how the work became known as the *New English Dictionary*, with the legitimate abbreviation N.E.D., which is still the official use with the Oxford University Press itself. Not that there is any quarrel with those who prefer O.E.D., the symbol of the *Oxford English Dictionary*, a style adopted now for many years on the covers and wrappers of our sections and parts, and on the binding cases of the quarter-persian edition, but not incorporated in the title page.

Dr Onions also announced the continuation of the work for a Supplement which, as he pointed out, could not be a full Supplement of addenda and corrigenda to the whole work. The intention was merely to fill up gaps unavoidable in a Dictionary compiled on historical principles, the preparation and publication of which had extended over the best part of half a century.

The Dictionary reports continued to be given from time to time, eventually by Sir William Craigie, who submitted three paragraphs of four lines each in September 1933, one paragraph each on the *Dictionary of the Older Scottish Tongue* and on the *Historical Dictionary of American English* and four brief and momentous lines announcing that the editorial work on the Supplement to the *New English Dictionary* was finished by the end of August. The work of seventy-five years was thus completed, for it was on the 18th January 1858 that the Society resolved to begin its new Dictionary. The year 1933 I do not myself forget since it was in that year I joined the Society.

In order to emphasize once more the wide scope usually associated with the expression 'philology in the Philological Society', I would mention the fourth and fifth Addresses delivered by the Rev. Richard Morris in 1875 and 1876. In 1875, he again gave the warning that we are apt to take too narrow a view of comparative philology and this in spite of the fact that the report on the work of the Society included references to Chinese, Semitic, Sanskrit, Pali and Sinhalese, a memorandum on the vernacular languages of India as well as the normal studies in English. In 1876, there was even a report on North American Indian languages.[2]

There would appear to have been a narrowing or reduction of the scope of the Society between 1889 and the end of the century. In this decade, there seems to have been more concentration on English and Celtic subjects and a good deal less notice of the wider interests which had early become established traditions of the Society. In consulting the publications list at the end of *Transactions* 1955, recently revised by our Publications Secretary, Professor Allen, you will find no publications of the Philological Society properly so-called before 1913. There were, however, eighteen independent volumes and other works distributed by the Society between 1862 and 1952. With the exception of a collection of 'Medieval Greek texts', these were either Presidential Addresses or works on English, Germanic and Celtic, including dialect studies.[3] There would appear to have been no works distributed between 1887 and 1903. During this period, and more especially between 1889 and 1901, subscriptions dropped steadily.[4]

I have already mentioned Wharton's note in *Transactions* 1920–1, in which he said he was proud to report on the considerable amount of what he described as non-English work, followed by the sentence I have already quoted 'we must tread a very wide field if we are to follow our own traditions'. In 1920–1, Wharton again reported that we had entered on a new era and challenged the 'unfortunate impression' to use his own words, 'that the Society cared nothing for general philological study and cared nothing for the wonderful achievements of the Society's past'. He expressed his pride in the special position of the Society in that it had nominated delegates officially to the International Oriental Congress. Later in 1924, the Society showed its interest in tone languages and more notice is given to the study of African languages. In 1930, membership stood at 120 and subscriptions amounted to £70.

I shall now turn to the second part of my Address which is to deal with philology in the Philological Society since the War and, to begin with, I

would link my previous figure of 120 members in 1930 with membership
of 200 in 1945. In that year, nineteen ordinary members and five
libraries joined the Society. It is, I think, of some importance that we
should first review the progress of the Society in terms of membership
and finance. Membership has risen steadily year by year as the following
annual figures will show for a period of ten years between 1946 and
April 1956, as follows: 227 in 1946, 260, 284, 307, 312, 349, 372, 383,
398, 405 and the Honorary Treasurer the other day supplied me with
the latest figure of 408 on 15th April of the present year, which is a
record.

Our subscription rate was doubled in 1947, which accounts for a jump
in the subscriptions from £263 in 1947 to £554 in 1948. It stood in
1954 at £748, not including recovery of income tax under covenant
arrangements. Our Honorary Treasurer, Sir Ralph Turner, has served
us in that capacity and as a member of Council since 1931, in which
year the effective membership, he reports, was round about eighty.
Unfortunately, he could not attend this Anniversary Meeting since he
has been chosen as one of the representatives of Her Majesty the Queen
at the Coronation of the King of Nepal.

This year the membership has reached the record total of 408.
During the past five years alone, there has been a net increase of just
under 100. The Society's balance in 1931 when Sir Ralph Turner first
took office was about £174; today, it is nearly £7,000. In the twenty
years previous to 1931, only four volumes of *Transactions* were published. Since 1931, *Transactions* have been issued year by year and in
addition a number of separate volumes have been published by the
Society, and it is confidently anticipated that with the funds at our disposal more will be published.

I think we may safely say that the remarkable growth of the Society
during the past twenty-five years gives ample proof of the wise conduct
of its affairs by its Council, and of the good work of its officers.

In reviewing these post-War years, mention must be made of Sir
William Craigie's Presidential Address in 1944 on 'The outlook in
philology'. Looking back on the achievements of the Society since its
foundation, he thought that even the highest expectations any of the
earlier Presidents might have entertained would have fallen far short of
what was accomplished even before the Society had reached its Jubilee.
He was thinking mainly of our achievements in English and Germanic
studies, especially in lexicography and, indeed, his own work and the pro-
posals he put forward arising out of it make up a good deal of the story.

The Middle-English Dictionary is now in Ann Arbor, Michigan, and there are achievements to report in American and Scottish work. He also referred to the comprehensive *Dictionary of Modern Norwegian*, with which our distinguished Honorary Member, Professor Alf Sommerfelt, is closely associated. He foresaw there would be a considerable development of linguistic studies in other fields than English and Germanic. He remarked that the Indo-European languages had had a long run and it seemed to him doubtful whether indefinite continuation of the traditional lines of these studies was likely to lead to anything new.

Sir William foresaw there would be a return to a wide variety of languages and methods of approach and welcomed the carry-over of any ideas gained in such studies into general works on the nature of language. At this point, it is sufficient to mention the circumstances which gave rise to the Scarbrough Committee and the developments which have arisen from it, backed by public funds.

It will be remembered that the Scarbrough Committee was concerned with Oriental, African, Slavonic and East European studies. It is perhaps particularly in Oriental and African studies, including language and what may be generally described as philology, that most has been accomplished, and this is paralleled in the wide variety of subjects upon which papers have been read to the Society and published in *Transactions*.[5]

The two branches of linguistics in which British scholars have excelled are phonetics and lexicography and this has been reflected in the work of the Society since its foundation. It is a healthy sign that six papers have been published on phonetics and phonology since the War and nine on lexicographical topics. However, remembering Sweet's emphasis in 1878 on the importance of general principles, our published work on general theory in the years since the War, roughly fifteen papers, is barely adequate, in view of the vigorous development of linguistics since 1930 and the widespread interest in the study of language by other disciplines and, perhaps especially by philosophers, acousticians and those interested in cybernetics.

Dialect studies have always been one of the specialized interests of the Society and, for a number of years, beginning with the second Address by Ellis in 1873, reports on the work of the English Dialect Society were read at meetings. In 1946, the project of a Linguistic Atlas of Great Britain was discussed. It was decided to set up a Committee called the Dialect Survey Sub-committee, to report from time to time on steps that could be taken to encourage scholars to develop this work. The Planning Committee was appointed and recommended to Council that the Society should proceed to initiate a preliminary survey of the English dialects of Great Britain in a limited number of areas with a limited questionnaire. Professor Wrenn, together with Professor Orr and Professor Orton, were named as Directors of the Survey in 1947, and, as the result of progress made both in England and Scotland, the names of Professor Angus McIntosh, and Professor Dieth of Zürich, were added to the list of Directors. In June 1952, the Dialect Survey Planning Committee received a report of the Directors of the Survey, under the Chairmanship of Professor Wrenn, and it was at this point that some specialization of treatment was recognized in England and Scotland. Professors Dieth and Orton had completed their questionnaire published and financed by the Leeds Philosophical and Literary Society. The distribution of the Scottish questionnaire submitted by Professor McIntosh was organized with the co-operation of the Educational Institute of Scotland and the Association of Directors of Education, and financed from funds derived from the University Grants Committee and by a grant from the Carnegie Trust. It was a project of the University of Edinburgh controlled by an inter-departmental Committee of the University.

In 1953, in recognition of the progress made independently in Scotland and England, the Council considered the connection of the Society with the Survey to have come to an end with the receipt of the Final Report of the Planning Committee and it hoped for the successful continuation of the work which it had helped to initiate.

Professor Orton, Professor McIntosh and Professor Kenneth Jackson have been good enough to let me have details of the work done in their respective spheres of activity. Professor Orton heads his notes 'The linguistic atlas of England' and associates with this his agreed collaboration with Professor Dieth as early as 1946. The Leeds questionnaire was first drafted in 1947 and the second draft was completed by the Long Vacation of 1948. Recording in the field was begun in earnest in November 1950, dealing with twenty-five places in Yorkshire. Up to the present, over 160 localities have been visited by field workers and records completed. These localities are distributed over the six Northern counties and also in Lincolnshire, Derbyshire, Cheshire, Worcestershire, Herefordshire, Monmouthshire and Oxfordshire. Further recording is in progress in Leicestershire, Cambridgeshire, Gloucestershire and Somerset. Edited excerpts from tape recordings in some of these districts are re-recorded on discs by the Phonetics Department of Leeds University under the direction of Mr MacCarthy. Over 130 of such disc records provided a check on the phonetic transcriptions made by the various field workers. Material for seventy-three localities is now being prepared in Leeds for publication in list-form and maps based on this material may be issued from Zürich. The Survey continues to enjoy the most generous backing of the University of Leeds in staff, apparatus and money.

Turning now to the Scottish side of the Linguistic Survey, the main principles on which it is operating have been set forth in Professor McIntosh's book *An introduction to a survey of Scottish dialects*, published early in 1953. In addition, Mr J. S. Woolley has compiled a *Bibliography for Scottish linguistic studies*, published in 1954. They have used postal questionnaires designed to elicit detailed distributional information about over 400 lexical items. Information about their occurrence has been obtained from about 2,500 places and recorded on about half a million slips. An analysis so far indicates the importance attached to the study of word distribution, and steps are now being taken to publish the more significant parts of the information assembled. The inadequacy of the postal method is fully recognized and after trying out a number of preliminary questionnaires for field workers, a more or less definite questionnaire of about 900 items now in regular use has been prepared by Mr J. C. Catford. Mr Woolley has applied it throughout South-west Scotland as well as in a number of other experimental places scattered all over the country. The questionnaire is of a predominantly phonological nature and Professor McIntosh is of the opinion that the systemic orientation of the questionnaire has already justified itself. He tells me also that the Survey is envisaged as having several different phases, including collaboration with sociologists. In Scotland, too, there is the closest collaboration with the Department of Phonetics directed by Mr David Abercrombie, who has interest in special phonetic investigations in progress. The University of Edinburgh has given its fullest support throughout the planning stage and we look forward to the fruits of these investigations in the years ahead.

On the Celtic side, we had the pleasure of hearing Professor Kenneth Jackson's paper in 1954 on the Gaelic work of the Linguistic Survey of Scotland. He has kindly provided me with supplementary information. Field work on the mainland is pretty well completed, leaving only the Hebrides. The collections are on similar lines to the Leeds Survey, employing a questionnaire of 1,200 items using phonetic transcription. The chief points of morphology are noted from both the descriptive and the historical point of view. Tape recorded conversations and stories have been collected and will provide illustrations for syntactical and lexical studies. All this work will benefit greatly from the collections of Gaelic folk tales and folk songs by the School of Scottish Studies. I understand that the University of Wales is planning a similar survey of Welsh dialects.

I do not wish to exaggerate the part the Society has played in the actual work of the Dialect Surveys of England and Scotland, but rather to emphasize our active interest which has the backing of a well-established tradition of the Society, so well expressed in recent years by Professor Wrenn.

I am indebted to Professors Orton and McIntosh for their reports to me on the English side of the Survey and to Professor Kenneth Jackson for the Gaelic.

Everyone knows that the Society was an important centre in the development of phonetics in this country in the nineteenth century and, in that connection, we remember first of all Sweet, but also Ellis and their association with the Bells. I should like to mention the great work of Professor Daniel Jones and to remind you that he continues to revise his works and that he has maintained his interest in the Society since he first joined in 1913.

In reviewing linguistic developments in this country since the War, it is an indication of the growing strength of a subject in which we have excelled, that two Phonetics Departments were established in 1948, one in the University of Edinburgh when Mr D. Abercrombie was appointed in that year, and one in Leeds when Mr P. MacCarthy succeeded him there. In 1948, the Department in Edinburgh had neither staff nor premises. It now has a well-equipped laboratory with a technician, a library, a growing collection of recordings and a teaching staff of five. Mr Abercrombie has been kind enough to send me a report in which he states that the Department remains firmly a Department of Linguistic Phonetics, though they have elaborated their instrumental means of observation and have devised new techniques. Research interests are very varied and the syllabuses of the University require a good deal of teaching of phonetics. They have naturally collaborated with the Linguistic Survey of Scotland since its foundation.

I would like to thank Mr MacCarthy for allowing me to use his report on the Department at Leeds which at present has a staff of three and a technician. Their teaching covers general phonetics and student courses in the phonetics of English, French, German, Italian and Spanish, and they do a great deal of recording.

In London, the Department of Phonetics at University College continues its work and much research has been done under the direction of Dr Fry in the perception of speech, including work for the deaf and further developments in acoustic analysis and synthetic speech. May I also, in this connection, refer to the work of the Department of Phonetics and Linguistics at the School of Oriental and African Studies, on the staff of which there are two Readers in Phonetics and six Lecturers in that subject, and, of the total, seven are members of the Society, having contributed five papers. If it would not be considered too presumptuous, I would like to mention the establishment in 1944 by the University of London of the Chair of General Linguistics, to which I was appointed and which I shall vacate at the end of the present session. I shall refrain from inflicting on you an apologetic account of what has been achieved during my tenure. Mr Robins now holds an established Readership in General Linguistics and there are two Lecturers in Linguistics; all three are members of the Society and all have publications to their credit.

At a recent meeting of the Language Commission of Unesco, of which I have been a member since 1950, the eight members, representing European and American linguistics, observed that linguists 'are now prepared to return, in the entirely different intellectual climate of today, to language problems recognized long ago'. Since 1930, the new approaches in linguistic studies at all levels have been shaped into a discipline with its ancillary techniques, which is satisfactorily described in English as 'General Linguistics'. In addition to the Chair in London, the subject is recognized in the Chair held by Professor McIntosh in Edinburgh, by the Chair in Birmingham, a newly established Lectureship in General Linguistics in Manchester and also in Glasgow.

At the School of Oriental and African Studies, we have regarded phonetics and phonology as levels of linguistic analysis congruent with other levels so that linguistics and phonetics become really one. This unity of purpose includes the laboratory which is used for inquiries in linguistics, that is to say we take linguistics into the laboratory and in no sense can we be said at the School to be interested in experimental phonetics as such, though this work is being developed in other centres in this country, especially in University College London.

The work of British linguists in London and elsewhere has been published in our *Transactions*, in the *Bulletin of the School of Oriental and African Studies* and also with the aid of subventions granted by the Publications Committee of the School.[6]

The challenge of translation in our modern Babel is ever with us and

British linguists have undertaken a number of useful projects in this direction ranging from obscure Nepalese and Tibetan texts to texts in African languages requiring translation and commentary. The Language Commission of Unesco, to which I have previously referred, has recently recommended the publication of two descriptive analyses, one of Igbo by Mr Carnochan and a second of Fijian by Mr Milner, both members of our Society.

These two monographs were suggested by the Commission and were reviewed at a meeting[7] which issued a second draft report in continuation of an earlier directive published in 1950.[8]

The following extracts will give some indication of the results of the discussions:

> In the study of patterns of linguistic structure account must be taken of social systems and social conditions of use, and therefore it is becoming increasingly apparent that we can and must learn to build bridges between any two languages whatever their cultural matrix.
>
> This involves a new approach in the setting up of grammatical and lexical categories. Although we must draw upon a common stock of grammatical terms, that does not imply the recognition of grammatical universals. On the contrary, the grammatical forms of a language are never in a strict sense precisely paralleled in another language. A first essential is not to assume a common grammatical base in all tongues, but to state such correspondences and differences as there may be between the structures.
>
> The statement of lexical facts involves much the same principles. There are no one-to-one correspondences between the vocabularies of two languages, but the statement of such correspondences and differences as there may be in the lexical patterns of the two languages is a further way of bridging the gap between them. In all probability such studies would help overcome the problem of discrepancies in translation. This is an essential part of the total bridge of translation, particularly between languages of widely different cultures. No translation is itself enough, we must also provide the basis upon which it is constructed.
>
> Although the three monographs are devoted in large part to the grammatical aspects of the languages described, the authors have, in a number of instances, stated precisely certain correlations between grammatical and lexical categories on the one hand, and

situational context and social conditions of use on the other. The relatively brief time allowed for the studies did not permit the authors fully to develop these correlations, nor to systematize and organize them. What has been done, however, is sufficient to indicate that further and more detailed research along the same lines will lead to greater accuracy in the language of description and the language of translation.

To achieve a bridge between a language and the other social and cultural systems with which it is associated, it is necessary to achieve a thoroughly integrated analysis of both the language and the cultural matrix in which it is embedded.

... the historically long and fruitful association between linguistics and social anthropology in particular leads us to emphasize this especial collaboration.

I have elsewhere[9] laid a good deal of emphasis on the challenge of translation to linguistic theory. If we recognize phonological, phonaesthetic, grammatical, stylistic and other modes of meaning in the linguistic analysis of the source language and of the target language, it becomes possible to consider modes of translation not perhaps in parallel with the modes of meaning in each language, but in close relations with them, even if the relations cross. The modes of translation would of course be different in each direction of translation. There would appear to be great opportunities in linguistics for the construction of such inter-lingual bridges. The main question is—how are we to bring the technical linguistic description into relation with the translation of texts? If we can answer this in technical linguistic terms we shall begin to understand what we translate and how we translate and be on the way to the formulation of a new and comprehensive general theory of language and firmer foundations in philosophy.

Though the scope of this Address could not possibly extend to a review of 'Linguistics today', my subject, which is 'Philology in the Philological Society' permits me to notice our publications and the work of our members. Professor André Martinet, one of our distinguished members whose work we have published, edited a recent number of *Word*, published in 1954, which did, as I think, inappropriately bear the title of 'Linguistics today'. I do not think you will find in it any connection with any item which I have been able to include in this present Address. Professor Martinet in the first editorial article of the volume offers valuable criticism of some aspects of present-day structuralism, to which I have referred in my sketch of structural linguistics published recently in *Transactions*.

It would be a colossal task for any scholar to examine thoroughly the origins and present forms of linguistics. The discussion of the principles and methods of contemporary linguistics in America, the Soviet Union, Western Europe and elsewhere would involve different and complex social contexts, differing intellectual climates, quite apart from the personalities of linguists themselves.

It will be readily agreed that linguistic analysis owes a great deal to the pioneer work of Slav scholars, beginning with Baudouin de Courtenay and his group and, coming down in our own day, to Trubetzkoy, Jakobson, Mathesius and other members of the Prague Circle. To give a satisfactory account of the relationship of linguistics to the intellectual climate of the relevant periods for, let us say, Russia, would be a considerable undertaking. For the Soviet period alone it would involve the study of the relationship of Soviet linguistics to Marxism of various kinds and the work of such eminent names as Marr, Meshchaninov, Vinogradoff and Stalin himself. Those names provide hints of four periods—I have nothing to suggest for the post-Stalin period!

In America the background and impetus for the vigorous and continuous development of linguistics are to be found in the inescapable compulsion to take a lively cultural interest in the American Indian. Anthropologists and linguists had their field work awaiting them on the doorstep, or at least just over the garden fence. Moreover, the need to record and establish texts in American Indian languages demanded reliable methods of reducing these languages to writing by alphabetic means. This is as good a reason as any for the disproportionate attention given to the principles and methods of spelling by employing the minimum number of letters consistent with the avoidance of alphabetic ambiguities. It is no accident that phonemics is an American rather than a Chinese, Indian or Arabic science. In the great American missionary endeavours the necessity of producing orthographies for unwritten languages is only the first step to the translation of the Gospels.

In addition to these basic conditions, it is relevant to note the development of assembly-line production methods, the high development of machine tools and of characteristic American philosophies such as 'behaviourism' and important new schools of logic and related subjects. On the other hand it must be noted that the pioneer work in machine translation by electronic computers was done by Dr Andrew Booth of Birkbeck College, who continues to direct research in this field, and, in

Cambridge, a group of scholars are also at work on similar problems which involve, in addition to the physical sciences, both mathematical and linguistic analysis as well as logic and other branches of philosophy. I have had some association with both these groups and am convinced that the theory and practice of translation is one of the most interesting subjects for linguists in the future. As I have pointed out elsewhere, the problems of translation are a challenge for linguistic theory and for philosophy.

The notion of machine translation shocks many people and some may even scoff at the idea. Swift may be aptly quoted here:

> Every one knew how laborious the usual Method is of attaining to Arts and Sciences; whereas by his Contrivance, the most ignorant Person at a reasonable Charge, and with a little bodily Labour, may write Books in Philosophy, Poetry, Politicks, Law, Mathematicks and Theology, without the least Assistance from Genius or Study.

He describes the machine as twenty feet square, placed in the middle of the room, the parts linked together by slender wires. On paper stuck on bits of wood were written

> all the Words of their Language in their several Moods, Tenses and Declensions, but without any Order. The Professor then desired me to observe, for he was going to set his Engine at work. The Pupils at his Command took each of them hold of an Iron Handle, whereof there were Forty fixed round the Edges of the Frame; and giving them a sudden Turn, the whole Disposition of the Words was entirely changed. He then commanded Six and Thirty of the Lads to read the several Lines softly as they appeared upon the Frame; and where they found three or four Words together that might make Part of a Sentence, they dictated to the four remaining Boys who were Scribes. This Work was repeated three or four Times, and at every Turn the Engine was so contrived, that the Words shifted into new Places, as the square Bits of Wood moved upside down.

The Professor had made 'the strictest Computation of the general Proportion there is in Books between the Numbers of Particles, Nouns and Verbs, and other Parts of Speech'. The concluding sentence of my extract from Swift is even more topical:

> I told him, although it were the Custom of our Learned in *Europe* to steal Inventions from each other, who had thereby at least this

Advantage, that it became a Controversy which was the right Owner; yet I would take such Caution, that he should have the Honour entire without a Rival.[10]

My reaction to this quotation is entirely favourable since I believe that the study of grammatical structure of the longer pieces and also of the mutual expectancy of words in clichés and high-frequency collocations is one possible approach to machine translation. I have no doubt that some of the results of our present-day machines would be quite like Swift's description in which he says three or four words together might make part of a sentence. The broken sentences when pieced together would no doubt appear rather like extreme forms of modernistic verse pouring out of a confused unconscious mind, but then, I hold the view that some of the stylistic peculiarities of Joyce are symptomatic of cultural disintegration in a chaotic world.

Problems of meaning and of translation have especially interested British scholars. The well-known work *The meaning of meaning* connects the interest of linguists with what is after all a characteristically English tradition in philosophy. The empiricist tradition in particular stands in the direct line of descent from Locke and Hume. The logical positivism of the Vienna Circle is not without inspiration from this country.

The study of the problems of meaning in all its aspects can be well illustrated from English sources. The development of lexicography and phonetics as well as other branches of linguistic analysis is, perhaps, to be considered a contribution to the study of meaning. If I may be permitted again to refer to my own work, I should like to mention 'The technique of semantics' which appeared in *Transactions* in 1935 and on which a useful commentary appeared in Mr W. Haas' article 'On defining linguistic units' nearly twenty years later.[11] He made an especially interesting contribution in pointing out that the kind of situational analysis I suggested in my article assumes no *parallelism* between utterance and situation, nor do interior relations in structures and systems 'correspond' to situational analysis. It is, however, a fundamental assumption that the text is itself a constituent of the context of situation. No statement of use can be made without taking into consideration the relations between the text and the other constituents of the situation. Further reference was made to this approach in my *'General linguistics and descriptive grammar'.

In the same volume[12] there appeared Sir Alan Gardiner's contribution

'A Grammarian's thoughts on a recent philosophical work'. The recent philosophical work referred to was entitled *Essays on logic and language* and these were concerned with the linguistic movement in philosophy. Judging from a recent similar work, *The revolution in philosophy* (with an Introduction by Professor Gilbert Ryle, comprising eight broadcast talks), the philosophers are still unaware of the developments in linguistics during the last thirty years. Mr Warnock, for example, after noticing problems which linguists have been dealing with during this period, actually says:

> Comparatively little such study of language has in fact been attempted, and it is hard to see good reason for adopting a defeatist posture in advance. On the contrary, I would not mind at this point venturing the prediction that this little-trodden path will be trodden to some purpose before very long.

In the opening words of the following paragraph he reminds us of the fairly common contention that systematic research in the functioning of language is not philosophy. My rejoinder is that the kind of language analysis so frequently indulged in by philosophers is not linguistics, so perhaps both sides can be happy—though, with Sir Alan Gardiner, I pray that the philosophers be led to pay a little more attention to linguistics. This is all the more important since the development of linguistics in this country coincides in time with one of those periods of rapid development which, as Mr Pears reminds us in the same work, historians of ideas call revolutions. 'The centre of the new movement was England, and, more particularly, Cambridge, and its leaders were Moore, Russell and Wittgenstein.' Once more then, we may say with Gardiner:

> There can be no doubt that such opening of the doors of the philosophic sanctuary will be greatly welcomed by the more enlightened students of linguistics. For they, too, have become increasingly aware that but little progress can be made in their terminology and their definitions without the building up of a general linguistic theory.

There has been a good deal of this building up in England during the last twenty-five years, both in linguistics and philosophy. Considering linguistics as concerned with problems of meaning, and this has been on the whole, as I have said, characteristic of British scholars, I had better speak from experience. In the 1930s, I enjoyed the privilege of long discussions with Sir Alan Gardiner and the late Professor Malinowski, both of whom contributed to the progress of linguistic theory. I think that *linguistics*, as represented by Sir Alan himself, by Malinowski and, may I say, by myself, and *philosophy*, as represented by Professor Ryle, Professor Ayer and others, meet in the controversy suggested by the following quotation from Gardiner's paper:

> Take any seriously intended statement or assertion you like—is it true to say that this, considered by itself, apart from any extraneous circumstances, signifies or means some definite so-and-so? Professor Ryle appears to think that it does, since he takes no account of the speaker and the listener and the situation which play so large a part in my own linguistic theorizing.

I would like to take this a little further to give yet one more example of the spread of linguistic analysis. Sir Alan Gardiner takes as his first example from Professor Ryle, the statement 'unpunctuality is reprehensible'. This involves ethics which has also become a linguistic subject, and I quote a work by Professor Charles Stevenson *Ethics and language*, published in 1944, and frequently reprinted. In the chapter on 'Working models', Professor Stevenson says:

> The object of the present study is not to devise, in arbitrary fashion, a sense for ethical terms that suits them to a limited, technical purpose; it is rather to free the language of everyday life from confusion. It is essential, for this purpose, to realize that everyday life presents us not with 'a' usage of terms but with many different usages.

The first few lines of the following chapter on 'Some pragmatic aspects of meaning' run as follows:

> If we are to reach a more detailed understanding of ethics, guarding its issues from confusion, and opening them to economical types of inquiry, we must pay constant attention to ethical language . . .

Professor Ryle has stated that research into the nature of philosophical inquiry has for some thirty years inevitably been a pre-occupation of English-speaking philosophers. The story of twentieth-century philosophy is very largely the story of this notion of sense or meaning. The word 'meanings' is a trouble-making plural noun, as Professor Ryle says, and there is also a good deal of plurality about the meaning of meaning—so much so that I would take the liberty of quoting another sentence of Professor Ryle's, with an addition—'and yet, meanings are just what in different ways, philosophy and logic *and linguistics* are ex-officio about '. I have added 'linguistics' to philosophy and logic.

There may have been a revolution in philosophy but there has been no revolution in linguistics. I have already noticed the importance of Sweet's paper 'Words, logic and grammar' and the obvious connection of lexicography and linguistic theory. In my view, even phonetics and phonology must be linked with studies of meaning. The Society has even glanced with Professor Brough at 'Theories of general linguistics in the Sanskrit grammarians' and 'Some Indian theories of meaning'. Once more, I would quote the unanimous opinion of the Language Commission of Unesco that linguists are returning to language problems they have long been concerned with but they do this in the intellectual climate of the present age, and that these new approaches, especially since 1930, have been shaped into a discipline with its ancillary techniques and I submit that in English the name of all this is 'General Linguistics'.

On one of the preliminary pages of every volume of *Transactions*, you will find that the Society was established to investigate and promote the study and knowledge of the structure, the affinities and the history of languages. That is indeed a wide commission and would include all the contemporary developments in structural and statistical approaches in linguistics. It is in that broadest sense that our members at our meetings and through their publications have promoted philology in the Philological Society.

Notes

1. Mosquito Coast and Reserve, a division of the republic of Nicaragua bordering the Caribbean Sea. Called after its principal inhabitants, the Misskito Indians.

2. Reference to the importance of these studies has recently been made in Council. One of our members, Mr Robins, has done considerable reasearch on Yurok, an Indian language of California. His work is now in the press to be published by the University of California. A younger member under his supervision is at the moment in Peru doing similar work in association with one of our American colleagues, Professor Kenneth Pike.

3. In the list of the twelve official publications of the Society between 1913 and 1936, these studies still predominate: no. 6 was a Russian historical epic and no. 10 was on a Romance subject. Since the War, however, publication has been more varied and more representative of the wide interests of the Society; e.g. Professor Palmer's 'Grammar of the post-Ptolemaic papyri', Professor Thomas' 'Nam', Professor Martinet's 'Phonology as functional phonetics' and in 1954, Dr Gershevitch's 'Grammar of Manichean Sogdian'. At the moment, there is a Special Volume in the press, *Studies in linguistic analysis*.

4. In 1889, the Treasurer reported subscriptions amounting to £101 17s. In 1892, they stood at £93 9s., in 1895 at £70, in 1900, £50 and in 1901, £48 6s. Some slight improvement followed but Council found it necessary in 1911 to issue a notice to members and an appeal for general support to philologists. Sir William Craigie indited a forceful letter. Even in 1920, subscriptions had only risen to £65.

5. They include five in Sanskrit and related studies, nine in Oriental languages, three on African languages and half a dozen in Slavonic and East European studies. If we restrict statistics to articles published in *Transactions*, and if we bear in mind the work and interests of the distinguished philologists who are members of our Society, it will be seen that the distribution of the subjects is significant having regard to the personalities of our leading scholars and also with reference to those broad traditions of our Society which I have already emphasized. The total of papers read since the War can be broken down as follows: Indo-European Comparative Philology 19; Indo-Iranian 13; Germanic 6; Greek 7; Latin 5; Celtic 5; Tokharian 3; Hittite 4; Romance 3; languages of South-east Asia 2; and, among all these, 20 are on English subjects, including 4 on dialect studies.

6. Such work includes 'Phonetics in ancient India' by Professor Allen, as Vol. 1 of the London Oriental Series, which also includes Dr Segal's 'The diacritical point and the accents in Syriac', and Dr Boyce's 'The Manichaean hymn cycles in Parthian' inspired by the work of Professor Henning; Professor Lambton's 'Persian grammar', Mr Robins' outline study of 'Ancient and mediaeval grammatical theory in Europe', very useful practical handbooks on 'Writing Arabic' and on the various forms of the Devanagari scripts, useful studies and practical works in African languages, the late Professor Stewart's 'Manual of colloquial Burmese' and, in the press, a 'Dictionary of Sea Dayak' by Mr N. C. Scott, our Honorary Secretary. We have under consideration a 'Dictionary of spoken Mon' by Mr H. L. Shorto, a member of our Society since 1953. There have been interesting reports published in *Transactions*. In 1947, Professor Palmer reviewed five years of Classical Philology. There are also his 'Grammar of the post-Ptolemaic papyri' and his paper on 'Mycenaean Greek texts from Pylos', following Mr Chadwick's contribution based upon his collaboration with Mr M. Ventris who deciphered the Mycenaean Linear B. Syllabary. Professor Bailey reviewed recent work in Tokharian in 1947, and we acknowledge his regular contributions to Indo-Iranian studies and also the contributions of Professor Henning.

7. Held at the School of Oriental and African Studies, University of London, 21st–25th November 1955, under the Chairmanship of Professor Alf Sommerfelt. There were present: Professors J. R. Firth, R. Firth, L. Hjelmslev, H. Hoijer and H. Vogt. Professors Benveniste and Lévi-Strauss were unable to attend on account of illness.

8. See my *'General linguistics and descriptive grammar', 221–4.

9. **'Linguistic analysis and translation'.

10. See *Selected prose works of Jonathan Swift*. Ed. by J. Hayward. London: the Cresset Press, 1949, 277–9.

11. *TPS* 1954.

12. *TPS* 1951.

Five

Linguistic Analysis and Translation†

In view of the extraordinarily rapid development of linguistics during the last thirty years, few people would venture the remark that, whereas historical and comparative linguistics is esoteric and technically difficult, linguistic description is comparatively straightforward. De Saussure over forty years ago rightly stated the difficult problems of linguistic science when he said: 'D'une façon générale il est beaucoup plus difficile de faire de la linguistique statique que de l'histoire.'[1] He no doubt had in mind the whole range of synchronic linguistics, and not merely phonology and phonetics. Great advances have been made in phonology since his day by Trubetzkoy and the Prague Circle, and by American and British linguists. Phonemics, morphemics and the morphophonemic bridge have been so far elaborated in the United States, that we may almost assume that in these directions ingenuity is exhausted. Recent publications can even be taken as marking the ending of one phase of descriptive linguistics, and, taken in conjunction with recent discussions between linguists, anthropologists, psychologists and even engineers, may point to the opening of a new phase, which Professor Roman Jakobson has referred to in general terms as the 'second front'.

We are now prepared to return to language problems recognized long ago, and while recognizing the richness of our traditional heritage we are setting up newly designed frameworks, taking the fullest advantage of the aggregate of our experience, in order to deal with any language under description, and by more securely based languages of translation.[2] All this, in the entirely different intellectual climate of today. How

---

† *For Roman Jakobson*, The Hague: Mouton 1956.

different, will be apparent if we turn to Whitney's ninth lecture in which
he attempts a characterization of 'the Polynesian languages':[3]

> Their roots, if we may call them so, or the most primitive elements
> which our imperfect historical analysis enables us to trace, are
> more often dissyllabic, but of indeterminate value as parts of speech:
> they may be employed, without change, as verb, substantive,
> adjective, or even preposition. All inflection is wanting: gender,
> case, number, tense, mode, person, have no formal distinctions;
> pronouns, indicative particles, prepositions, and the like, constitute
> the whole grammar, making parts of speech and pointing out their
> relations. Moreover, anything which can properly be styled a verb
> is possessed by none of these languages; their so-called verbs are
> really only nouns taken predicatively. Thus, to express 'he has a
> white jacket on', the Dayak says literally: 'he with-jacket with-
> white', or 'he jackety whitey'.[4]

As I have so frequently stated in other places, it is the business of
linguistics to make statements of meaning at all levels of analysis in
accordance with the intellectual climate of today. Anything bearing the
slightest resemblance to Whitney's approach, summarily illustrated
above, is to be avoided. Roots are not to be sought out by an imperfect
historical analysis, and although we must continue to draw upon a
common stock of grammatical terms, we must not thereby imply any
recognition of grammatical universals. A first essential is not to assume
any such common grammatical measure, and it is nowadays contraven-
ing every canon of description to say 'gender, case, number, tense,
mode, person, have no formal distinctions', or to state that a language
has no verbs. The statement of meaning by interlinear word for word
or literal translation *as an aid to analysis* is equally inadmissible though
often still met with.

In this paper I wish particularly to draw the attention of linguists to
the use and abuse of the statement of meaning by translation as part of
linguistic analysis. To begin with, one must beware of building bridges
between two different languages by means of 'naked ideas'. It may be
that even engineers are programming machines for linguistic use on the
'naked idea' principle, and if results are achieved they must necessarily
be crude. Again, we have primitive examples of this kind of thinking in
Whitney:

> The Chinese words, for example, are still to no small extent roots,
> representing ideas in crude and indefined form, and equally

convertible by use into noun, verb or adverb. Thus, *ta* contains the radical idea of 'being great', and may, as a substantive, mean 'greatness'; as an adjective, 'great'; as a verb, either 'to be great', or 'to make great, to magnify'; as an adverb, 'greatly'.[5]

All linguists must, of course, make constant use of common human experience and even all the highly abstract concepts of the common human situation, in order to bridge the gulf separating one language from another. But they must always bear in mind that the English word 'kindness', for example, does not represent a 'naked idea' of any value to linguistics, and in that sense no other language in the world has a word for 'kindness'. It is equally unprofitable to make statements such as, this language has no word for 'the' or 'lamb', or that it has no verb 'to be'.

In the history of English linguistics Malinowski was the first scholar to deal with the systematic use of translation in the statement of meaning of ethnographic texts.[6] It was to this sort of translation scheme that he applied the term 'linguistic analysis'. It is one of the great merits of Malinowski's methods that he nowhere even implies that 'naked ideas' form any sort of possible bridge between Kiriwina and English.

In Whitney's ninth lecture there is an example of double translation of Chinese into English taken from Schleicher:

> How different is the state of monosyllabism which precedes inflection from that which follows it in consequence of the wearing off of inflective elements, may be in some measure seen by comparing a Chinese sentence with its English equivalent. The Chinese runs, as nearly as we can represent it, thus: 'King speak: Sage! not far thousand mile and come; also will have use gain me realm, hey?' which means, 'the King spoke: O sage! since thou dost not count a thousand miles far to come (that is, hast taken the pains to come hither from a great distance), wilt thou not, too, have brought some thing for the weal of my realm?'[7]

Such shots in the dark, however lucky, are invariably the result of inadequate analysis at the grammatical, lexical, collocational and situational levels. The basis for any total translation (and by total I do not imply final or complete) must be found in linguistic analysis at these other levels. But the reverse process of using a translation as a basis for linguistic analysis at any level is usually the foundation of error. There are many examples in recent linguistic literature.

Translation methods are often employed in American Indian linguistics, and here again Whitney provides early examples of the type still with us:

> The Mexican name for 'goat', *kwa-kwauh tentsone*, literally 'head-tree (horn)-lip-hair (beard)', or 'the horned and bearded one' . . . on the other hand, and what is of yet more importance, an unwieldy aggregation, verbal or *quasi*-verbal, is substituted for the phrase or sentence, with its distinct and balanced members. Thus, the Mexican says 'I-flesh-eat', as a single word, compounded of three elements; or if, for emphasis, the object is left to stand separate, it is at least first represented by a pronoun in the verbal compound: as 'I-it-eat, the flesh'; or 'I-it-him-give, the bread, my son', for 'I give my son the bread' . . . An extreme instance of excessive synthesis is afforded in the Cherokee word-phrase *wi-ni-taw-ti-ge-gi-na-li-skaw-lung-ta-naw-ne-li-ti-se-sti*, 'they will by that time have nearly finished granting [favours] from a distance to thee and me'.[8]

For all I know the 'Mexicans' referred to may have many words for the animals generally described as 'goats', 'he-goats', 'billy-goats', 'she-goats', 'nanny-goats', 'mountain goats', 'wild goats', not to mention 'giddy goats' in English, and may have none for 'sheep'. In French, for example, the word 'mouton' has certainly not the same linguistic value as the English 'sheep'. It will be noticed that two attempts are made at literal translation, including bracketed words. In the Cherokee word phrase there are seventeen separated syllables, there are also seventeen English words in the translation—this is probably an accident.

There is no point in denying the concept of translation. The fact is, translation is a necessity on economic and on general human grounds. Moreover, the fact of translation is a main challenge both to linguistic theory and to philosophy. I am not here referring to translation as an end in itself or as an art, nor am I discussing the relation between outer and inner language form and similar problems of German 'Sprachphilosophie'. I am concerned with the necessity of building a bridge with many strands, and even levels, between one language and another, and the construction of this bridge with the materials and techniques of linguistics. It may be true that wherever and whenever we enter into the speech of someone else, or our own past speech, we are really translating.[9] It is necessary then, for the linguist, while regarding translation in the widest and most general terms, including for example 'translation' within the 'same' language, constantly to maintain a critical, analytical attitude towards all the methods and levels of translation employed in the statements of meaning in linguistics.

The absurdities and futilities of interlinear word for word translations without foundations in linguistic analysis are well illustrated in the Appendix to Richards' *Mencius on the mind*,[10] which gives 'Passages of psychology from Mencius'. For example: 'With not-bear-others-of-mind, carrying-out not-bear-others-of-government, rule the world can (be) turned around its palm-on.'[11] I find no profit in the effort to state the total meaning of a word, nor is my phrase 'total translation' to be taken as anything more than a comprehensive application of all known techniques in the statement of meaning in linguistic terms. The method of multiple definition illustrated in that work is a different road from the one linguists normally take, and I think does not fall within the discipline of linguistics. Richards does, however, state his problem briefly as follows:

> Can we in attempting to understand and translate a work which belongs to a very different tradition from our own do more than read our own conceptions into it? Can we make it more than a mirror of our minds, or are we inevitably in this undertaking trying to be on both sides of the looking-glass at once? To understand Mencius, for example, must we efface our whole tradition of thinking and learn another; and when we have done this, if it be possible, will we be any nearer being able to translate the one set of mental operations into the other? Is such translation, at best, only an ingenious deformation, in the style of the clever trick by which the children's entertainer makes with his fingers and thumbs a shadow really like a rabbit?
>
> It is not to be supposed that most Orientalists, Egyptologists, classicists, mediaevalists, field-anthropologists ... have not had their wakeful nights over the problem. To put it more precisely, can we maintain two systems of thinking in our minds without reciprocal infection and yet in some way mediate between them? And does not such mediation require yet a third system of thought general enough and comprehensive enough to include them both? And how are we to prevent this third system from being only our own familiar, established, tradition of thinking rigged out in some fresh terminology or other disguise? There is nothing new about the problem, that is obvious.[12]

It appears to me likely that the answers to these questions would lead again into that nebulous region or heaven of 'naked ideas'.

In repeating the statement that no translation is either complete or final, I wish to make the reservation that every additional translation of a well-known text raises some interesting problems in linguistics. The *Gita*, for example, has been translated many times into many languages, but quite recently there has been a new translation by Adeltaa Siitaa Devii entitled *Giitaa, A Samskrit-English bridge with the barriers removed*.[13] In the Preface[14] the new plan is explained. The text is printed in the Devanagari script with a Roman transliteration and an interlinear translation in the Sanskrit order. The reader is expected to turn to the original for the writing, sound and linguistic pattern, even if this means a neglect of English syntax. The translator, in giving an account of her method, again stresses the rhythm of the Sanskrit order and the importance of realizing the grammatical correspondences and differences between English and Sanskrit. Parentheses and square brackets are used somewhat unsystematically, it is true, to deal with these matters. No effort is made to seek word for word equivalents and a whole phrase is needed to translate the one word *tapas*. She points out that:

> A negative is always translated as NOT its positive rather than as its positive's opposite. Good and Non-Good are definitely not Good and Evil and Samskrit has a word for Evil as well as for Non-Good. Similarly with Success and Non-Success, Victory and Non-Victory, etc. The unsuccessful may not be a failure. The unvictorious may not be a defeat.[15]

She adds the remark that:

> We can make compounds in English almost as easily as we do in Samskrit and we have our possessive with the apostrophe which obviates the need for the use of the preposition 'of'. We can say 'the God-intoxicated man', 'the Gold-desirer', just as it is said in the direct Samskrit, and we need not descend to such phrases as 'the man who is God-intoxicated', or 'the man who desires gold'. An example is to be found in XI-17: 'Diademmed with mace, discus, too, splendrous mass everywhere flaming, I see Thee, dazzling to be seen from everywhere, a flaming Fire-Sun-Glory immeasurable.'[16]

The following is an example of the result in English:

Material contacts, verily, . . .—of cold, heat, pleasure, sorrow, the givers, Coming near and vanishing, inconstant—these endure patiently, O Thou of Bharata's Race. Whom, indeed, (these)* do not distress, (that) man, O Man-Bull, The same in woe and weal determined, he for immortality's nectar is fit [formed]. Never for the non-existent is there being; never non-being is there for the existent. Of the two also (has been) seen the ultimate, verily, of these by the Reality Seers. As imperishable, verily that know by which all this [world] is spread out [as on a loom]. The ruin (of this)* undiminishable, never (is) anyone to accomplish able. 'As having an end' (are called)* these bodies belonging to the constant embodied one, Indestructible, immeasurable. Therefore, fight, O son of Bharata Race! [17]

More barriers would have been removed if the linguistic analysis at the grammatical, collocational and lexical levels could have been systematic in both languages and keyed to the translation.

Linguistic analysis coupled with translation offers a vast field of work for linguists and social anthropologists. The building of the bridge between the language under description and the language of translation will call for highly trained workers in both these disciplines with all their techniques. Quite soon we may expect scientific workers from the less developed communities, working on their own languages using English as the language of description and of translation. In a recent work on the *Funeral dirges of the Akan people*,[18] by a young West African scholar, a good deal of modern linguistic analysis is stated as a basis for the translations given. In referring to the scope of his study the author says:

The requirements of social life often impose forms of linguistic behaviour on individuals or groups of individuals in given situations, to which are attached values that appear to govern their continued practice. The study of verbal expressions in such situations is important not only for a clearer understanding of problems of meaning in a language, but also for a deeper understanding of a people's life from which their meaning is ultimately derived.[19] . . . a synthetic approach has been our guiding principle. Its context of situation and its meaning in social life, its performance, its themes, language, structure, style, scope for creativeness and its links with other texts of Akan oral literature form the framework within which it is examined and discussed.[20]

The author devotes a section to the language of the dirge under four headings: 'Prosodic features', 'Vocabulary', 'Collocations' and 'Sentence structure', and an interesting statement of the musical features corresponding to the verbal linear units. In his conclusions the author again indicates the linguistic approach to his translation as follows:

> In order to express these themes, the dirge makes use of a number of verbal conventions containing a dispersal of meaning at the prosodic, word and syntactical levels. Great use is made of repetitions ranging from repetitions of single phonological terms to the terms in complete utterances. In building up dirges, some words such as personal names, kinship terms, place names and words for indicating origin and identity are pivotal and have the greatest collocability. The use of constructions with front placed nominals in linked or free position is a marked feature of the language of the dirge.[21]

The problems of stating meaning in linguistic terms are more manageable if we distinguish between two of many possible methods of approach. First, the approach of the 'linguistic engineer' who hopes to arrive at the mechanism of rendering material in one language, the source language, into a second language, the target language. It may well happen that recourse to some theory of 'naked ideas' will at first prove attractive. Where are the materials for the bridge to be found? Presumably in some sort of analytical segmentalized dictionary based on units of meaning, whatever those might be. It is faintly possible that we translate that way, but do we really know how we translate? Do we even know what we translate? The second method of approach is by linguistic analysis. This proceeds on the assumption that language is polysystemic, and that multiple statements of meaning in linguistic terms can be made at a series of congruent levels. The language under description, which must be a restricted language, is subject to analysis in terms of the categories of linguistics at all levels, and the resulting statements, which I submit are statements of meaning, are made in the language of description. In the language of description various methods of translation may be used, such as identification names or translation meanings, and finally, some or all of the texts in the *corpus inscriptionum* may be rendered in an *ad hoc* language of translation based on the findings stated in the language of description. This approach ensures that statements of meaning in the language of

6

description, at the grammatical and lexical levels, are keyed to the language of translation. In this way the linguist should be able to render the texts of the *corpus inscriptionum* in an *ad hoc* language of translation. This second approach does not require a bridge of hypothetical 'naked ideas'. It is difficult to see how 'naked ideas' may constitute any sort of serviceable inter-lingua.

The bridge of linguistic analysis has to be constructed by various techniques, of materials shaped by phonetics, phonology, of branches of grammar, lexicography, discourse analysis and perhaps even stylistics. From this point of view, it is clear that phonemic materials do not provide the main elements of structure. A comprehensive description of a given language is perhaps itself the bridge enabling the linguist to frame what I have described as a total translation. This total translation cannot be in any theoretical sense a complete translation.

Since the 1930s I have firmly held to the view that descriptive linguistics fulfils its function best if it regards language behaviour as meaningful over the whole range of its relations with life in society, and, in order to deal with such a vast subject, proceeds by the dispersal of the total complex at a series of levels of analysis, probably constantly increasing in number and specialization. Some indication of this approach was sketched in 1935, and a further example is shown in my *'Modes of meaning'. There I have recognized phonological, phonaesthetic, grammatical and other modes of meaning from the point of view of linguistic analysis, and it is possible to link such analysed modes of meaning with modes of translation, these various modes being examined in connection with the inter-lingual bridges.

The main question I wish to put here is, how are we to bring the technical linguistic description into relation with the translation of texts? If we can answer this in technical linguistic terms we shall begin to understand what we translate and how we translate.

Let us recognize at the outset that all linguists rely on common human experience as part of their own experience. From this common human experience we may make abstractions for our guidance and, I would submit, set up common human situations of an abstract nature to form one of the bridges between the source language and the target language. This abstract inter-situation may be considered to have common elements in everything but language text.

If we wish to assume that there are general or universal elements of verbalization in the common situation, it could not be in terms of universal grammar. There is no such thing. But between any two languages, especially if cognate or mutually assimilated, the grammatical bridge might bear some relations in general terms to the common situation. In such cases it might be possible to state that in the common situation the verbalization could be described as nominal or verbal, even though the noun and verb categories in the source language did not bear a one-to-one relation with those of the target language.

Traduttore, traditore, is only too often true of linguists who constantly make use of translation in linguistic analysis, generally without systematic statement of the nature and function of the translation methods used. There have been long discussions on meta-languages and clashes of opinion on the technical languages of linguistics, but the place of translation in linguistics has not been adequately studied. The achievement of translation is a main challenge to linguistic theory and philosophy. Do we know how we translate? Do we even know what we translate? If we could answer these questions in technical terms we should be on the way to the formulation of a new and comprehensive general theory of language and firmer foundations in philosophy.

Notes

1. See *Cours de linguistique générale*, 3rd edition, Paris, 1931, 141.
2. Dr M. A K. Halliday of the University of Cambridge has successfully applied a linguistic analysis of this type to a thirteenth-century Chinese text, *The secret history of the Mongols*. [See p. 34, n. 3. F.R.P.]
3. *Language and the study of language*, London, 1870.
4. Ibid., 338.
5. Ibid., 330.
6. This is fully dealt with in **'Ethnographic analysis and language with reference to Malinowski's views'.
7. Whitney, 331.
8. Ibid, 348–9.
9. See *The spirit of language in civilisation*, by Karl Vossler, London, 1932.
10. London, 1932.
11. Appendix, 12–13.
12. Chapter 4, 86–7.
13. Madras, 1955.
14. By Dr C. Kunhan Raja.
15. Ibid., 8.
16. Ibid., 9.
17. Ibid., 54–5.
18. By J. H. Nketia, published at Achimota, 1955.
19. Ibid., 1.
20. Ibid., 4.
21. Ibid., 132.

Six

Linguistics and Translation†

The two words in the title of my lecture are common enough but I suppose that most people feel they know more about translation than about linguistics. Perhaps they do. You may not have 'done' linguistics, as they say, but most of you will have 'done' translation. Do you really know what you translate or how you translate? We know a good deal more about why we translate than about the 'what' or the 'how', just as we all speak and write English but do not know very much about the processes. We can learn the use of our own language without knowing very much about the language itself. We learn foreign languages in rather a more orderly manner. And so, we may become quite wonderful translation machines—I wish we knew more about how it is done.

Let me turn first to the question of what we translate, from a source language to a target language. Most people would say in the most general terms that we translate the meaning; but we cannot just stop there, taking it for granted that we all know the meaning of meaning. Even if you read the well-known book bearing that title, you will be no nearer the solution of your problem. In any case, that book is a contribution to the theory of knowledge, or an enquiry into how we know and how we state our knowledge. Most people in the West since Descartes would refer all problems of meaning to an analysis of thought, so that the problems of philosophy have been logical, psychological and, nowadays, even linguistic. Corresponding, I suppose, to the two-sided relation of mind and body, we have also the two-sided relation of thought and its expression. Recently in this country, philosophy— perhaps more especially in Oxford as the result of the influence of Cambridge—has become principally a study of meaning by what is

---

† Read to an audience at Birkbeck College in the University of London, June 1956.

called analysis, and a good deal of this analysis is concerned with the expression or language. This is not, however, linguistic analysis properly so-called as practised by present-day linguists.

I hope it will be already clear to you that I cannot discuss the bearing of linguistics on translation without considering meaning, but the whole problem of meaning is bedevilled by linguistic difficulties caused by the use of the word 'meaning' and all its derivatives. Just think of them. The word 'meaning' itself, the book title referrred to, the plural of the word which as Professor Gilbert Ryle says is 'a trouble-making plural noun', and we have such embarrassing usages as primary meaning, basic meaning, generic meaning, secondary meaning, transferred meaning and many others of the same sort, and all the apparatus of logic and rhetoric. Logic is concerned, I suppose, with the question of truth or falsity of propositions—and so is etymology if we pay any regard to views such as those held by Skeat, namely that the true meaning of a word is its original meaning. I am now lost in a welter of insuperable difficulties if I turn to translation without linguistics, to find out what becomes of all these meanings. I should probably manage something without bothering about theory perhaps, just going ahead and getting the main ideas, and with a lot of intuition and hunch, inspiration and even perhaps flashes of genius, creating in the target language something deriving from the source language. The bridge between the two would consist of ideas, ill-defined—perhaps just naked—without any form expressed or rather with two forms expressed, one in the source language and the other in the target language, the translator being the creator of the bridge, without any working drawings whatever.

So let us turn to linguistics to examine the difficulties and to provide some breaking-down of the problem in the hope that we may construct a framework of interpretative theory with its technical language. This process should lead to useful criticism and throw light on the problem of meaning by making statements about it in purely linguistic terms.

I have often said that the main concern of descriptive linguistics is to make statements of meaning in its own terms. This implies first that the main attention of the linguist is concentrated on the text, that is to say the material, the 'what'. In America, linguists have attempted to exclude meaning from linguistic analysis and by that they mean the exclusion of all psychological—or, as Bloomfield called it, mentalistic, references. They have concentrated, and still do, on what they call the 'basic code' of the language, upon particular messages in it in which they happen to be interested, not forgetting all other possible messages. Those familiar with recent developments in what is called communication theory will realize that in the extreme cases, such linguists—but more especially communications engineers—are interested in what they call the information in the message as coded and decoded and not at all with the effective result or what is ordinarily considered its meaning. The telephone people are only concerned with the electrical transmission of the message, so that adequate information is accepted or put in at source and transmitted to the receiving end. What the people at each end are thinking, intending, doing or not doing is completely irrelevant. Communication theory is not concerned with meaning in any psychological or social sense. But, of course, they make the fullest use of this so-called meaning in all their research, that is to say, they are squinting at meaning all the time. Bernard Bloch, for instance, in his 'Postulates', which are concerned with the minimal units of the phonemic signalling system of a language, states that 'the basic assumptions that underlie phonemics, we believe, can be stated without any mention of mind and meaning; but meaning, at least, is so obviously useful as a short cut in the investigation of phonemic structure—one might almost say, so inescapable—that any linguist who refused to employ it would be very largely wasting his time.' And in a footnote, he is pleased to quote Daniel Jones who said 'the fact that certain sounds are used in a language for distinguishing the meanings of words doesn't enter into the definition of a phoneme'.

An approach to translation from the point of view of communication theory would involve the bringing together of two codes, of two sets of signs, which are to be brought into relation with one another—in the first instance by a human translator. The interrelations of the two codes and of any message framed in them can presumably then be handled mechanically either by the use of a systematic thumb-index of words and phrases—that is to say, a sort of grammar and dictionary—or by electronic devices. But, of course, the process of bringing these two languages together involves comprehension by someone. So, looking at translation from the point of view of linguistics, I should suggest there are four main types with only one of which I myself am professionally concerned.

First of all, there is the creative translation inspired by a foreign source but mainly intended as literature in the language of the translator. Perhaps one of the best living examples of this would be the poetry of Arthur Waley. The second type I should describe as official translation, exemplified in treaties, international agreements and other institutional-ized, controlled or restricted languages. From some points of view, perhaps all technical and scientific languages could be regarded as somewhat similar. The third type of translation is used by descriptive linguists and is met with in the identification names given to items of the foreign language material and in the translations of the illustrative texts. As I have said elsewhere, descriptive linguists are concerned with the language under description, preferably a restricted language, the language of description and also the language of translation, and the languages of translation must be especially closely related to the language of description and to the analysis which itself consists of statements of meaning in linguistic terms. Finally, there is mechanical translation, pioneered by Dr Andrew Booth who continues to develop his researches which are a challenge to so many branches of study, including linguistics.

Descriptive linguistics is at its best when it concentrates on what I call restricted languages. A restricted language serves a circumscribed field of experience or action and can be said to have its own grammar and dictionary. From this point of view, the English of Arthur Waley's poems derived from the Chinese—perhaps 'derived' is a better word than 'translated'—would be a very interesting restricted language to analyse. If we could compare this analysis with the restricted Chinese languages at source, we should soon appreciate the present enrichment provided by the poet-translator. Ezra Pound also translates from the Chinese and it is interesting to note that he believes it is possible to 'translate' the structure or linguistic form of the characters of Chinese into English expressions.

The restricted languages of official translation, in spite of careful control and attempts at valid equivalents deserve detailed study. They have often been the source of international friction caused by mis-understanding, the misunderstanding of course being explained by mistranslation. (Examples—controller, *contrôleur*.) Here, I would emphasize the restriction of research in translation to the circum-scribed fields of restricted languages. It is in the study of the restricted languages of science and politics, both national and international, that part of the translation problem is met, in the mutual assimilation of the languages in similar contexts of situation. My suggestion is, therefore, the study of the more or less mutually assimilated restricted languages, necessitated by present-day world conditions. But there is, of course, a danger which I have long realized. In the developments of my own work I always go back to *'The technique of semantics' in which I first pointed out the great importance of the study of focal or pivotal words. I have sometimes used the expression 'key-words'. In 1935, I suggested it was only just beginning, but that was an overstatement—it is only just beginning in 1956. The recently admitted German members of Unesco are proposing an international approach to these problems. A small group in Bonn have, as I discovered when recently in Germany, taken my suggestion seriously and Professor Schmidt-Hidding has pointed out that crucial problems appear if we try to translate our own key-words, leading words or watchwords into other languages. He has, however, made and defined two new German words based on English, *Leitwörter* and *Schlüsselwörter*, and under this heading he has associated with key-words and leading words words referring to organization, especially words referring to forms of organizing people such as 'annual international meeting' or 'the Council' and 'the Committee', etc.

The kind of translation I am dealing with at the moment leads me again to the consideration of translations in the study of history and literature. I hope students of English have read the Prefatory Note by Professor Bruce Dickins to Dr Garmonsway's translation of the *Anglo-Saxon chronicle* in the Everyman Library. He says that:

> For lack of these obvious preparations more than one academic historian of the last fifty years has followed grotesquely antiquated translations and given a fresh lease of life to extraordinary mis-renderings, particularly of the Peterborough Annal for 1137, which, like *Hamlet*, is full of quotations.

Professor Dickins cites the following examples:

> H. W. C. Davis in *England under the Normans and Angevins . . .* renders *þa diden hi alle wunder* as 'then did they wonder' (*recte* 'Then they committed every atrocity') and *hengen bryniges on her fet* as 'hung burning things (*recte* coats of mail) on their feet'.

> Sir Charles Oman in *On the writing of history* translated *War sæ me tilede. þe erthe bar nan corn. For þe land was al for don. mid suilce dædes*, as 'The Earth bears no corn: you might as well have tilled the sea: the land is all ruined by evil deeds' (*recte* 'Wherever there was tillage the earth bore no corn, for the land was ruined by such deeds').

It is well to remember that different disciplines have entirely different attitudes towards the use of translation. For example, the historian and the lawyer. A text for a lawyer must always be contextualized for its present meaning. The original meaning or intention is irrelevant. So, from the legal point of view, the seventeenth-century politicians and lawyers interpreted Magna Carta for themselves in their own time. The historian, I maintain, must serialize his contexts and must face the interpretation, let us say of the Charter, not only in its own day, but also at each stage through the thirteenth century and, again, when it was used by the Roundheads in the seventeenth century. May I point out in passing that literary criticism at the moment is in a dilemma. There are a few, however, who would agree with me that contextualization of literature should begin with present reading and regressively return to the context of the original composition.

Such contextualizations and comparisons would prevent gross errors of translation of which historians are fully aware. I need only mention the translation of Stubb's *Select Charters* last century by Smith, the Master of Balliol. He appears to have translated Medieval Latin as though it were Ciceronian prose to be rendered by a humanist in contemporary English. I believe the result was such an embarrassment that, after his death, attempts were made to buy up all surviving copies.

There would appear to me to be many opportunities for the study of the place of translation in the history of literature and perhaps particularly in the history of criticism. There is still room for clearer statements in linguistic terms of the relations between translations and selected works of Shakespeare, Milton, Shelley and Swinburne, to mention only four fairly obvious names in this country. On the German side, there is the very interesting fact that Shakespeare holds the popular theatre perhaps better than in England because all the great plays are presented in linguistic modern dress, that is to say, in the German of the early nineteenth century or later.

It occurs to me that an interesting comparative study might be made of the place of translations of the Bible in English and German. This should be done by a scholar acquainted with the original languages if the anticipated interesting results are to be stated in linguistic terms. The present-day use of English expressions which can be referred to Biblical sources and similar ones in German have, I imagine, all moved a long way from the source languages in their contexts. In any event, this is rather like the law that takes no account of the first historical context, but applies the text in its contemporary relevance.

I do not think I can deal with the third type of translation, which is that technically employed in linguistics, without introducing a brief survey of recent developments in linguistic analysis in this country.

Though I do not wish to lay too much stress on the derivative nature of written language, and fully subscribe to the view of Archbishop Trench in the early nineteenth century that a word exists as truly for the eye as for ear, I must nevertheless remind you that the sounds and prosodies of speech are deeply embedded in organic processes in the human body, most of them intimate and secret. As Whitehead once said, 'voice-produced sound is a natural symbol for the deep experience of organic existence'. The notion of pure thought in abstraction from its expression is not one of the most useful figments of the learned world. The disastrous separation of body and mind fixed on European thought by Descartes is responsible for much blindness in certain sciences and especially in linguistics. Again, Whitehead realized that to see order in the mush of general goings-on, it was necessary to state the finding of structure and system. To be human, he once said, requires the study of structure. Animals enjoy structure. What has this to do with translation? you may ask. Before I can answer that, I must explain my position.

From my own point of view, first stated in 1930, maintained and developed since, the whole of our linguistic behaviour is best understood if it is seen as a network of relations between people, things and events, showing structures and systems, just as we notice in all our experience. The body itself is a set of structures and systems and the world in which we maintain life is also structural and systematic. This network of structures and systems we must abstract from the mush of general goings-on which, at first sight, may appear to be a chaos of flux.

Such an approach requires no dichotomy of mind and body, thought and its expression, form and content. It does, however, recognize the distinction between the language texts which are the linguist's main concern and the matrix of experience in which they are set. Meaning is, therefore, a property of all systems and structures of language. At the highest level of abstraction, it may be possible to maintain that the meaning of language may be stated in two sets of relations, the interior relations within the language and the exterior relations between structures and systems in the language, and structures and systems in the situations in which language functions. This monistic view of meaning shows us why some pedants are able to maintain that complete translation is impossible.

As I have so often said, the most important modifiers of words are things and events and, if we are not to refer structures and systems of language to structures and systems of thought, we have the alternative of regarding language as embedded in the matrix of living experience and the human body as the primary field of human expression and as continuous with the situations of life. Indeed, if we are fussily exact, we cannot define where the body begins and where what we erroneously call external nature ends.

Whether we begin with situations or the language texts which are characteristic of them is immaterial as long as we realize that they are intimately wedded. If I start with the word *sunset*, by itself it can have meaning only at the level of spelling or at the level of pronunciation with its stress pattern. I can from common experience decide that this word *sunset* belongs to a certain situation involving tables of times including such abbreviations as a.m. and p.m., perhaps lighting-up time too. We can perhaps find linked situations in which the two words *sunset* and *sunrise* occurred together and, indeed, the phrase *from sunrise to sunset* can easily be found. Eventually, one can connect these with *the sun sets* and *the sun rises* and structure begins to be evident without reference to history and we can identify the word *sun* and the word *set*. In due time, there is *the setting sun* and *the rising sun, the setting of the sun* and *the rising of the sun*. I have not moved into those situations or contexts where compounds such as *sundown* and *sun-up* are to be met with, least of all *sundowner*. These belong to other restrictive languages altogether. At this stage, it would be impossible to deal with *the Rising Sun on the corner which one can see on the darkest night* and, as for *sunflower*, we are again in a set of situations which would take time to connect with what I have just stated.

I want to make it clear that the linguistic systems and structures are related to the systems and structures in the events, relevant objects and people and what they are doing. You have the option of connecting structures and systems of language with structures and systems of thought or with structures and systems in situations comprising the human participants, their non-verbal behaviour, the relevant objects and other events and of these two alternatives, I suggest—difficult though it may appear—that the situational matrix is the more manageable one and more easily related to problems of translation.

As you will now realize, a translator has frequently to introduce in the target language, specific references to the situation; indeed, he may have to describe some of it, though in the source language these references would not appear. Mrs Atia Husain in a recent broadcast on the problems of an Indian novelist writing in English, made constant reference to her Indian language Urdu with special reference to the pronominal system and to terms of personal address and reference for which no parallel equivalents are at her disposal in English.[1]

Some of you may already have some idea of what some of my students have called the spectrum of linguistic analysis whereby the problem of what I may call total meaning of a text in situation is broken down and dispersed at a series of levels such as the phonological, the grammatical and the situational levels. One can never expect the modes of meaning in a given language to be translatable into parallel or equivalent modes of meaning in a foreign language. This is clearly true at the phonetic or phonaesthetic level. How should we translate the meaning of alliteration or assonance in English into a language with no such consonant clusters as *sl, cl, cr, str*. These are prosodies of the sentence or piece or of the verse, but other prosodies, I dare say, may sometimes find equivalents such as quantity, number of syllables to the line and certain regular features of stress, accent or prominence. It is not, of course, possible on any considerable scale to carry grammatical structures across the bridge of translation. For example, the English constructions such as *your having done that will spoil your chances*: the non-finite *your having done that* would require a separate clause with a finite verb in most European languages, but it is an important contribution to the technique of translation to know that this must be done. (On the other hand—*that goes without saying, impress* and *express*.)

I have previously referred to translations from the Chinese and have mentioned Mr Arthur Waley and Mr Ezra Pound. Let us compare these two. Arthur Waley presents us with this sentence based on Chinese—*to learn and at due times repeat what one has learnt, is not that after all a pleasure?* Ezra Pound's version runs *study with the season's winging past, is not this pleasant?* In this case, situational and other non-linguistic elements have found their way into Waley's sentence which is not communicating the Chinese but giving us comprehension of the Chinese. Ezra Pound, however, especially in his translation of the Confucian Analects, endeavours to translate the structure of written Chinese characters by a constant search for metaphor in English—that is to say, finding a mode of meaning in Chinese writing, endeavouring to carry it across the bridge of translation into English metaphor: thus the Chinese character, the translation meaning of which is usually given as *proud* has the character *high* written with the radical *horse*—and so Ezra Pound uses *high-horsey*. The Chinese character *fearful* includes *two eyes*, so a man who is fearful when approaching an action becomes in Pound's

version *a man who keeps both eyes open when appoaching an action.* The
previous example quoted, *study with the season's winging past*, is based
upon the character usually given the translation meaning of *repeat.* This
character has the *wings* radical but it is no good thinking of flapping
wings here, nor is the mode of meaning of the character structure any
help towards an English version.

Finally, we come to a subject about which I know little—translation
by machines. It is, of course, true that a human translator can be thought
of as a machine—the trouble is that we do not know how it works. If we
did, we could tell the engineers what to do. Strangely enough, the
neurologists' hopes are in the opposite direction, that is to say, when we
have invented a machine which can really translate, we may at last
discover what we translate and how we translate. The two points of
view meet, it seems to me, in linguistics which has its own method of
approach in statements of meaning and, so far as my own views go and
those who feel able to follow me, the longer units we study, the better
statements we can make. I do not believe in the short cut suggested by
some American linguists that we must find minimal segments of the
code and translate on the basis of the smallest number of minimal units.
I try to meet this need by suggesting a translation of restricted languages;
the more restricted they are, the more completely the mechanism of
translation can be investigated. I believe that it would be much easier to
invent a writing machine than a translating machine and I have even
toyed with the idea of sketching a plan for the writing of mass-produced
fiction by machinery—thrillers or detective stories for instance. Some
of the highly-coloured paperbacks that are sold in the back streets
could easily be produced by machinery without detailed composition
by the author. Indeed, Edgar Wallace used to keep a roomful of secre-
taries busy dealing with a number of stories at the same time by dictation
methods almost automatically. There is nothing new in this idea and, as
a linguist, I should like to refer you to *Gulliver's Travels* (1726) in which
Swift describes the Professor in a very large room with forty pupils. I
quote:

> Every one knew how laborious the usual Method is of attaining to
> Arts and Sciences; whereas by his Contrivance, the most ignorant
> Person at a reasonable Charge, and with a little bodily Labour, may
> write both in Philosophy, Poetry, Politicks, Law, Mathematicks and
> Theology, without the least Assistance from Genius or Study.

He describes the machine as twenty feet square, placed in the middle of the room, the parts linked together by slender wires. On paper stuck on bits of wood were written

> all the Words of their Language in their several Moods, Tenses and Declensions, but without any Order. The Professor then desired me to observe, for he was going to set his Engine at work. The Pupils at his Command took each of them hold of an Iron Handle, whereof there were Forty fixed round the Edges of the Frame, and giving them a sudden Turn, the whole Disposition of the Words was entirely changed. He then commanded Six and Thirty of the Lads to read the several Lines softly as they appeared upon the Frame; and where they found three or four Words together that might make Part of a Sentence, they dictated to the four remaining Boys who were Scribes. This Work was repeated three or four times, and at every Turn the Engine was so contrived that the Words shifted into new Places, or the square Bits of Wood moved upside down.

The Professor had made

> the strictest computation of the general Proportion there is in Books between the Numbers of Particles, Nouns, and Verbs and other Parts of Speech.

The concluding sentence of my extract from Swift is even more topical:

> I told him, although it were the Custom of our Learned in *Europe* to steal Inventions from each other, who had thereby at least this Advantage, that it became a Controversy which was the right Owner, yet I would take such Caution, that he should have the Honour entire without a Rival.

My reaction to this quotation is entirely favourable since I believe that the study of grammatical structure of the longer pieces and also of the mutual expectancy of words in clichés and high-frequency collocations, is one possible approach to machine translation. I have no doubt that some of the results of our present-day machines would be quite like Swift's description in which he says three or four words together might make part of a sentence. The broken sentences when pieced together would no doubt appear rather like extreme forms of modernistic verse pouring out of a confused unconscious mind, but then, I hold the view that some of the stylistic peculiarities of Joyce are symptomatic of cultural disintegration in a chaotic world.

There never was a time when there was more need of translation.

The spread of world languages such as English, but not forgetting Russian, Chinese and Arabic, multiplies the need for translation from and into all these languages mutually and also into dozens of other languages which serve what has become more and more a common world civilization. Electronics has become a key subject, mathematics and physics have always ruled us. I suggest that on the human side, linguistics in future will of necessity become their opposite number and my hope is that the universities will encourage its study as one of the more austere disciplines fitted to be ancillary at least to the sciences which promise us miraculous machines.

Note

1. [Firth added here: '(examples—*tu, ap, ap-log,* etc. Refer to Japanese and Korean, Japanese taxi-driver; terms of address and reference between husbands, wives and children—*the missus, the wife, the car, hubby, Smith*—what about translating these?)'. F.R.P.]

Seven

Descriptive linguistics and the study of English†

The title of my lecture might suggest at first sight that it is concerned with two or more disciplines. Indeed, the second half of the title is so general that it vaguely covers both language and literature, but it would be absurd within an hour to attempt such a vast survey. It would also be profitless and exhausting. In fact, I am going to deal only with my own subject which in England is described as 'General Linguistics', a discipline with ancillary techniques, including phonetics.

The first chair of General Linguistics in Great Britain was established in London in 1944. I have held it since then at the School of Oriental and African Studies. This was a most suitable institution for the subject since Europe is now more fully incorporated in the rest of the world than perhaps we realize and, to deal with the theory of language, a Western scholar must de-Europeanize himself, and, in view of the almost universal use of English, an Englishman must de-Anglicize himself as well.

I suppose the phrase 'descriptive linguistics' should be regarded as one branch or aspect of the theory of language in application, since general linguistics is also concerned with the theory of comparative linguistics, which is undergoing a profound change, and also with the more general theories of meaning. Interest in the meaning of meaning we share with the philosophers, the sociologists and perhaps the more biologically inclined psychologists. There is a well-established empiricist tradition in England from the days of Locke to Hume, and, more recently, to the Cambridge group of philosophers, Moore, Russell and Wittgenstein.

---

† Read in Berlin, May 1956. It is clearly designed for a German audience.

My own approach in general linguistics and especially in the study of meaning in purely linguistic terms dates back to about 1930 when the linguistic movement in philosophy was also arousing interest. My main concern is to make statements of *meaning* in purely linguistic terms, that is to say, such statements are made in terms of *structures* and *systems* at a number of *levels of analysis*: for example, in phonology, grammar, stylistics, situation, attested and established texts. I do not attempt statements about a speaker's or a writer's thoughts and intentions, ideas and concepts—these are for other disciplines.

The beginnings of structural linguistics of the English type can be traced to Henry Sweet, perhaps our greatest name in this field in the nineteenth century. But in England we have a long history of interest in our language. The analytic study of English may be said to have begun with the writing of our language before the Conquest. There was even a formal contribution by Aelfric in one of the earliest grammars of Latin in any European national language. We have an unbroken tradition of its formal study since Elizabethan times, certainly in orthoëpy, grammar and rhetoric, and in the invention of shorthand. Sir Thomas Smith, secretary to Queen Elizabeth, addressed his *Alphabetum Anglicum, de recta et emendata linguae Anglicanae scriptione* (1568) to all who could read Latin, especially on the Continent.

In the seventeenth century work developed in grammar and dictionary-making and in phonetics. These subjects, together with interest in universal alphabets and universal languages, and in signs and nomenclature, mark the beginning of general linguistic theory in English. Advances were made in the eighteenth century. We have Dr Johnson, Sir William Jones, Lindley Murray.

The second part of my title, 'the study of English', is so vast that it must be further circumscribed to make it at all manageable. To begin with, English is an international language in the Commonwealth, the Colonies and in America. International in the sense that English serves the American way of life and might be called American, it serves the Indian way of life and has recently been declared an Indian language within the framework of the federal constitution. In another sense, it is international not only in Europe but in Asia and Africa, and serves various African ways of life and is increasingly the all-Asian language of politics. Secondly, and I say 'secondly' advisedly, English is the key to what is described in a common cliché as 'the British way of life'. The expression 'the study of English' is overwhelming since it is not possible to devise any course of study which would

7

give you the English universe in twelve or in a score of intensive volumes.

And so, I come to the notion of a *restricted language*. Descriptive linguistics of the structural kind is at its best when applied to a well-defined limited type or form of a major language, let us say of English. The specialist languages of the sciences are restricted languages; so too are those of sport, of narrative, of specific political propaganda, of personal reference and address, of the lyrics of a poet like Swinburne or even of a single text, say Magna Carta in Medieval Latin, or of the American Declaration of Independence.

We have narrowed down the scope of the subject of my lecture to the circumscribed field of a selected restricted language which might be of a single author or of a single work or of a particular style or tempo of speech, provided this latter were recorded in phonetic texts. Further application of this sort of linguistic theory requires the recognition of other things besides the restricted language under study, which I describe as the *language under description* or the l.u.d. In the statements to be made about the l.u.d., we have to employ another form of language which is the *language of description*. This language of description might be English or German. The language of description would include the spelling employed or transcription, and the technical terms, phrases or expressions. Thirdly, there is usually the *language of translation* when more than one language is involved. The language of translation might be German for English or English for German and I should like to extend the concept of translation to include the definition languages used in, say, unilingual grammars and dictionaries; that is to say, in the Oxford Dictionary, we have the language under description which is current English in an historical perspective and the language of translation which appears in the definitions. The other technical statements in the entries would be in the language of description. For descriptive linguistics, the basic material of the restricted language or the language under description must be recorded in texts of some sort, either in orthography or some form of transcription.

For the linguist, the text is central and is kept in the focus of attention. I use the term 'text' to refer to the *corpus inscriptionum*, of whatever size. Texts will be attested and established either in orthography or some other form of spelling or transcription. A transcription may be phonemic or, according to the convenience of the linguist, an impressionistic phonetic transcription or, indeed, any form of reading transcription related to utterance if that is relevant.

And now, we are in phonetics. Let us assume we have to deal with a restricted language of English, having the implication of utterance. It could be careful polite colloquial, concerned with the discussion of a play or plays running in the contemporary theatre. To handle this, we must assume that the linguist has all the ancillary techniques of the language of description, especially in phonetics. Here we must make three distinctions: first of all, there is the *phonic material* which we hear and observe in all its fullness. The phonic material is part of the raw material of experience; it is the language under description at the phonic level. To this language under description at the phonic level, we apply the technical, descriptive language of *phonetics* which is part of the language of description; and there is the notation based upon established phonetic categories which is employed in the phonetic text. Beyond this again, and I shall refer to this later, there is the *phonological level* of analysis, a different level of abstraction, having its own language of description, and it will be readily understood that phonological categories, features or units will have exponents describable in the phonetic language of description, this phonetic language of description referring to what I have called the phonic material.

So, we have three clear and separate adjectival terms, phonic, phonetic, and phonological, to serve clarity of statement.

It is clear that phonetics does not, indeed should not, attempt a complete description of the phonic material. In phonology and grammar we must be selective; we do not need a description of the total phonic data. Our descriptions and notations, however, should always assist us to re-examine the phonic data, to recognize the named features in the phonic material on renewal of connection with experience. At the phonological level of analysis, we count what we call the vowels and consonants; we claim to isolate these minimal units in a language as a whole but phonemicists do not agree in the number and nature of the phonemes of either British or American English. Professor Daniel Jones in his *Outline of English phonetics* requires or uses sixteen vowel phonemes; Ida Ward, twenty-one; Bernard Bloch and other Americans, ten. I am not a phonemicist and do not set up unit segments, each of which must be occupied by a phoneme. I do, however, set up vowel systems applicable to particular elements of structure. The terms of the vowel systems vary according to the element—for instance, in final unstressed position, the system has fewer terms than in a stressed position. My six vowels are *i, e, a, ɔ* open, *o* close, *u*. These vowel units or phonematic units commute with one another but, in dealing with any particular word, the prosodic elements must be coupled with them so that the phonological structure of the word as a whole recognizes phonematic and prosodic elements as interdependent. The so-called diphthongs are dealt with at the prosodic level, recognizing *y*-closing features in *feed*, *w*-closing features in *food*, coupled with length. The so-called centring-diphthongs are dealt with by setting up an *r*-prosody, the exponents of which vary; with final it is often *shwa*; intervocalically it is a kind of *r*-sound: e.g. *swear, swearing, sworn*. (In passing, compare *a dawn* and the verb *adorn*.)

Phonetic features which mark initials and finals or characteristic medials are to be considered prosodic in that they are features which must be referred to the structure taken as a whole. Studies of junction or juncture between divisions of a word or between words in a piece, if these should be considered convenient, would also be prosodies of the word or piece. For example: *is she going to be there?*, *space-ship, those shoes.*

Descriptive linguistics in recent years has turned much more decisively to the sentence and the longer stretches of speech as the object of study. This is certainly true of the London group at the School of Oriental and African Studies and also of those associated with Professor Louis Hjelmslev of Copenhagen. This concern with what I shall call roughly 'the sentence' has made such demands on phonetics that the categories and terminology we associate with the International Phonetic Association have already been proved inadequate. As you know, England has always been strong in phonetics and I can assure you that in London we feel a great need for the development of phonetics as applied to what I have called the prosodic analysis of the sentence and of discourse generally. Henry Sweet in his most interesting paper 'Words, logic and grammar' contributed to the *Transactions of the Philological Society*, 1876, and which appears in his *Collected papers* published by the Oxford University Press, stressed the importance of intonation in the study of the grammar of English. This would apply with equal force to German. It is precisely the study of the intonation of the piece, phrase, clause and sentence, the study of the distribution of stress and of the distinctive features of words, pieces and sentences as wholes that Sweet foresaw as a study of synthesis and which is referred to nowadays in English as the prosodic approach.

The first step in the prosodic approach is to make a statement of various structures in general terms, employing a formulaic notation, say for English. The syllabic structure of characteristic word forms is stated in terms of *C*, representing the consonant element, *V*, representing the vowel element or unit, and inverted *e* (ə) or *shwa*, which is to be regarded as a syllabic and not as a vowel unit. Other prosodic features are indicated by *y* for fronting or front-quality, *w* for back or rounding or both, *h* for spirance, other features such as the glottal stop in English and Germanic by the I.P.A. symbols and, as a most general indicator of a prosodic element, the Greek letter *π*.

No general definition of a syllable is suggested though for each language syllabic structures are to be set up in the terms I have just suggested. Syllabic structures are entirely abstract and it is not always possible to mark their precise divisions and, as Aristotle pointed out in the Sixth Chapter of the *Organon*, we may state the quantities of syllables without regarding them as co-terminous. The syllabic structure, therefore, is not to be based on phonetic characteristics such as sonority. Any type of sound may be structurally syllabic, even voiceless fricatives in such English words, as, for example, *s'pose*, and the *for* in such a phrase as *two f'him and two f'me*. This of course is in rapid familiar colloquial, both in tempo and style.

Prosodic analysis of this kind indicates prosodic grouping which is useful grammatically as well as more practically in the teaching of pronunciation. For example, compare the following:

> '*concert* – *concert orchestra; concert engagements*
> *con*'*cert* – *concerted item*
>
> *con*'*tent* – *contentment*
> '*content*
>
> '*contest*
> *con*'*test* – *contested, contesting, contestable, incontestable*

In this last word, *incontestable*, there are only two vowel elements in the syllabics of primary and secondary stress. The rest are syllabics involving no possibility of stress or of vowel unit.

> '*transport* – *transportation*
> *trans*'*port*

Other interesting examples are such words as '*comfort, uncomfortable;* in the word *uncomfortable*, only two vowel elements of structures are seen, the rest being syllabics. Compare '*necessary, necessarily* with *ne*'*cessity* and *necessitous*.

To deal with plural forms of nouns and third person forms of verbs in the simple present, in the past also and in certain negatives, I find the fiction monosyllable+ useful. For example, the comparison of the phonological structure of the following groups seems to me clearer if we adopt the following approach:

> *cat* – monosyllable
> *cats* – monosyllable+

Similarly, *fish, fishes; pass, passes; talk, talked; want, wanted.* Paradoxically enough, though *want* I regard as a monosyllable, *won't* I regard as a monosyllable+ along with *shan't, don't, can't, aren't;* and those which sound like two, *couldn't, didn't, wouldn't* are in the same classification as monosyllable+.

You will now appreciate the importance of regarding the elements of structure as prosodically interdependent and mutually determined. The prosodic approach is very different from the American procedure by segmentation or succession of unit segments, each to be occupied by a phonemic unit. The prosodic approach is especially useful in dealing with longer stretches of speech, from the phrase to the sentence. As I have said, I am not going to define the sentence. I will, however, say that by sentence I do not intend a judgment expressed in words or a logical proposition consisting of a predicate, that which is not the predicate being the subject. All this logical or psychological analysis we have abandoned. There may be many one-word sentences; there will be a large number of verbless sentences. We shall need such descriptive classes as nominal pieces, verbal pieces, adverbial phrases, particle phrases, among others.

Returning to the point I have previously made on the importance of recognizing the prosodically interdependent items of the piece or sentence, take a common nominal piece such as *the Head of the School, a Member of Parliament.* The particles such as the articles and prepositions are prosodically dependent on the whole piece, and noticing the elements of structure which have vowels such as the *V* in *Head* and the *V* in *School* and relating them to other syllabics enables us to state the prosodic characteristics of the piece as a whole. Verbal pieces similarly are to be dealt with as wholes, the elements of which are prosodically as well as grammatically interdependent. For example, *I shan't be seeing him until tomorrow; he wrote and told me that all the previous correspondence had been lost; he didn't tell me he was going to ask you; I shall have written to him by the time you get there; I should've*

thought you might; I haven't been to see him for weeks; he's going to be
teaching when you want him; he's the man you said you'd bought furniture
from.

May I draw your attention to the careful distinction drawn between
structure and system. Structure, whether it be phonological or grammatical, is a syntagmatic relationship. It is an interrelationship of
elements within the text or part of the text, whereas a system such as a
system of vowels or a system of grammatical forms is in the nature of a
paradigm. The values of a paradigm are determined by the interior
relations within the paradigm itself. This is a necessary principle to
grasp before we turn to the grammatical level of analysis as applied to
the study of English. We have all seen and taught the paradigm of the
English verb. I have considerable difficulty in using the traditional
paradigms in stating the verbal characteristics of the verbal piece or
sentence in contemporary English. Since, as I have said at the outset, I
regard the sentence or whole clause as the essential object of study, it is
important to look for verbal characteristics in the sentence and the clause
as a whole. These characteristics may be discontinuous and distributed
in such a way as not to correspond with what you are accustomed to find
in the traditional paradigms. In this matter, I am at one with Professor
Louis Hjelmslev of Copenhagen who has often stressed this point,
namely that the verbal characteristics of the sentence are rarely in
parallel with what you find in tabulated conjugations in the grammar
books. This is certainly true of contemporary English. To give you a
difficult example to work on, *he kept popping in and out of my office all the*
afternoon. I suggest that the verbal characteristics of this sentence
require notice of a pronominal form (*he*), which provisionally I will
term nominative and of a post-transitive nominal piece (*my office*) after *of*.
It is clear that the indications or exponent of tense are in the word *kept*
and that this word *kept* is an auxiliary of aspect in association with the
ing-form *popping*. *Popping* itself would undoubtedly find a place in the
word-scatter or paradigm of the verb; that is to say, it would be one of
four (*pop, pops, popped, popping*). In that sense, *popping* marks one of the
verbal characteristics of the sentence and is associated with the verbal
particles *in* and *out*. A paradigm could be completed for *to pop in* and
to pop out. Undoubtedly, there is another verbal characteristic of the
sentence which is associated with the adverbial phrase *all the afternoon*.
One could not very well say *he kept popping in and out of my office at ten*
o'clock or *at once*. And, therefore, there is justification for my statement
that *he kept popping in and out all the afternoon* is grammatically close

knit as a verbal piece. The elements of structure are also prosodically interdependent.

In describing the English verb, I would only set up two tenses, present and past. This one would be in the past, but I would also require a large number of aspects and a certain number of modes. *To keep*, in this sense, is an aspectival auxiliary associated with the imperfective *-ing* form. You will see, therefore, that in one sense verbal characteristics and verbal paradigms, though connected, are not by any means identical expressions. You will all recognize this use of *keep*, paralleled by *to go on*, and the opposite aspect, the auxiliaries of which are *to begin* and *to stop*.

You will appreciate that the first step in understanding the verbal characteristics of English sentences is to grasp the use of the twenty-four operators—*am, is, are, was, were, have, has, had, do, does, did, may, might, can, could, shall, should, will, would, must, need, ought, dare, used to*. I stress the importance of the technical term operators since it is their central syntactical functions which I am emphasizing. They must not be regarded as part of the verb *to be* or the verb *to have* and they must all be considered as finites, having no infinitive form whatever. These twenty-four words operate in the main function of negation, interrogation, emphasis in the verbal piece and are also what I call code verbs. A negative piece in English is characterized by the one exponent of negation, the negative particle *not*. This particle is used with all classes of words, but in the finite verbal piece always with one of the twenty-four operators, and with them constitutes a negative conjugation quite distinct from the affirmative conjugation. The association of the negative particle with the operators is so close that they become prosodically one in such monosyllables + as *don't, won't, shan't* and *can't*. It is not possible to regard *won't* as built upon the phonetic basis of *will* and *not*. Similarly, *don't* cannot be considered as a union of *do* and *not* in any phonetic sense.

The exponent of interrogation in English may be intonational, but when we employ inversion or front-shifting, the twenty-four operators are the finites affected by the inversion, for example, *are you going?; may I have one?; need I ask him?; dare you go?* Three of the operators are specifically emphatic—*do, does, did*, e.g. *I do like it; he did say so.* All the other operators, similarly, may take the main stress in the verbal piece.

Lastly, there is the characteristic use of the operators as code verbs. For instance, I will employ some of these operators as code verbs in the following conversation: 'I don't think so, because his two younger

brothers have gone.' 'Do you think he will?' 'I don't know, he might.'
'I suppose he ought to, but perhaps he feels he can't.' 'Well, his brothers
have. They perhaps think he needn't.' 'Perhaps eventually he may. I
think he should and I very much hope he will.' You will see very little
meaning could be attached to this as it stands. I will now put it in what
I call an extended collocation, which would suggest the situation. Let us
suppose we are discussing three brothers, two of whom have joined
the army in a National Emergency. 'Richard hasn't joined the army,
has he?'. . .

The characteristics of the non-finite verbal piece also involve grammatical categories other than that of the base verb which would appear
in a paradigm. For example, *not having seen him, I can't tell you.* In the
verbal piece *not having seen him* you will find the negative particle *not*
with the *-ing* form, coupled with the past participle *seen*, in the perfective,
followed by a post-transitive nominal. *Your having got married last week
has altered everything.* Here, similarly, you have the perfective *-ing* form
with preceding nominal and the adverbial *last week*. The verbal
characteristics of the infinitival form involve the use of what one might
call 'different cases' and the infinitival particle *to*. *For you to say so
would be wrong; for me to have said so was a mistake; I told him not to
say anything; do you want to?; you'd better not; you've got to; I warned
him not to.*

Referring to grammatical analysis in more general terms, I think it is
necessary to distinguish between philosophical time, solar time, clock
time, and what I may call grammatical time which is none of these.
Every language has its own grammatical time system which is not
always exhibited in the verbal systems. In fact, in English I suppose
fiancé is future and *the ex-Kaiser* and *grandfather* past. It is misleading to refer to the verb as the time word, which I know you do in
German, but I hope you will not attach undue importance to its etymological meaning.

Similarly, one must be careful to distinguish between *number* covering
single, dual, trial, plural (Fijian); *numbers* such as six, half a dozen, a
dozen, score; *numerals*, 1, 2, 3, first, second, third; and *figures* which are
international with different names in different languages. These may
seem to you trivial details of nomenclature but they raise fundamental
problems and indicate how careful we must be in the use of language
about language—that is to say, one must establish with the greatest
care what I have called the language of description.

I have used the expression 'restricted language' and have said that descriptive linguistics is at its best when dealing with such languages. The material is clearly defined, the linguist knows what is on his agenda and the field of application is sufficiently circumscribed for him to set up *ad hoc* structures and systems. Such restricted languages would be those of science, technology, politics, commerce, a particular book, a particular form or *genre*, a characteristic type of work associated with a single author or a type of speech function with its appropriate style. A restricted language can be said to have a *micro-grammar* and a *micro-glossary*. This is of some interest to teachers, since in foreign countries they have first to decide what restricted languages they should begin with at the various stages of schooling. A young schoolboy would be given training through a different restricted language from a science student in a technological college. In promoting European unity and in advancing international European co-operation, it might be useful to promote such restricted languages as would allow colleagues in various professions and occupations to understand one another's languages. It is a more helpful approach than to set out to learn English in general—whatever that may mean.

For the scientists, there are books available, but I suggest micro-grammars and micro-glossaries of restricted languages with suitable texts should be seriously considered. Incidentally, such work has a direct bearing on mechanical translation by electronic computers.

Moving on now to other levels of analysis, I should claim stylistics as one of the levels of linguistic analysis. If the style of the text or of an author can be said to have lineaments and physiognomy, then these features or elements of style can be stated in linguistic terms. I have made an attempt to show a method of approach in this sort of work in *'Modes of meaning', which handles the stylistics of Swinburne's lyrical poems. A certain amount of work of this kind has been done in America where they refer to it as 'discourse analysis'. It is not altogether new and Bally in Geneva produced two volumes which you may know on *Stylistique française* (similar works also appeared in German), which are mainly linguistic in principle. What I am suggesting is a much more systematic linguistic analysis of what is called 'style', avoiding value judgments and making no attempt at aesthetic appreciation.

In this connection, I would like to put forward the concept of *collocation* which I have introduced in my own work. This is the study of key-words, pivotal words, leading words, by presenting them in the company they usually keep—that is to say, an element of their meaning is indicated when their habitual word accompaniments are shown. The collocations presented should usually be complete sentences and, if it is conversation, the collocations should be extended to the utterances of preceding and following speakers. It is also useful to notice the collocational compounds and collocational phrases in which common words appear. For example: *safety—safety match, safety first,* etc.; days and months (i.e. *March hare*); *1914—before 1914, 1914-18 war, after 1914,* etc. (and other leading dates); *English—the English people, English literature, English reserve, English manners, English countryside,* the short phrase *the English and all that can be said about them, the English Public Schools, English Universities*; *British—British Army, British Commonwealth, British Empire* (fading out), *British way of life, British Isles, British Foreign Policy.*

When we turn to lexicography, we have to say that *British scholars* have excelled in this field since Scottish scholars contributed much to the success of the Oxford Dictionary, the official name of which is the *New English Dictionary.* In the Philological Society of Great Britain, of which I have the honour to be President, we refer to it as the Society's Dictionary since it was a project launched by the Society in 1858 and which took over seventy years to finish. This Dictionary has given rise to sons and grandsons, as you know. There is the two-volume Dictionary, the Concise Dictionary and the Pocket Dictionary. The study of the principles involved in making all the various statements of meaning in a full dictionary entry, say in the *Oxford English Dictionary* would draw upon the whole range of linguistic theory. What sort of statements of meaning do you expect to find in a good dictionary? First, the established orthography and, in addition to that, an indication of pronunciation either by the use of key-words which is the usual practice, or by means of a systematic phonetic transcription such as you find in Professor Daniel Jones' *Pronouncing Dictionary.* No dictionary entry is complete without a grammatical designation for each item of entry. The grammatical designation contributes an element of meaning which is described as the grammatical meaning. It is only when the grammatical meaning is clearly stated that a suitable definition can be made. This definition involves a special definition language, carefully considered, and is in a sense, even in a unilingual dictionary, a sort of translation. But the definitions never provide an equipollent or equal value for the word, since they may not be substituted one for the other. The formal history, derivation, etymology, is usually added and then citations must be provided in historical order in support of a definition given, providing attested occurrence in that sense. If I give you a common collocation for the word *ass*, it would be *don't be such an ass, he's a silly ass anyway*. These are collocations of the word *ass* and show the sort of company a word keeps. They are not citations in the dictionary sense. I have not given a definition nor have I sought written authority in a recognized work for this use. This difference is important since a dictionary citation must always be keyed to the definition which in turn directly depends on the grammatical designation and is related to the whole form of entry. At this stage, I submit that the last place where you find the conceptual or generic meaning of a word is in a dictionary. Though a dictionary may be theoretically very imperfect, it is none the less practically indispensable, but, from my point of view, it should be kept in its place.

The statement of meaning of words and sentences and, indeed, of whole texts is the concern of descriptive linguistics as a whole. To deal with this vast subject it is necessary, rather in the manner of the dictionary itself, to split up the problem of meaning into its components or elements. The process may be compared, metaphorically speaking, to the dispersion of white light into a *spectrum* by means of a prism. The prism in our case is descriptive linguistics and the spectrum is the multiple statements of meaning at various levels of analysis. This approach was first stated in my *'Techniques of semantics', and has developed steadily since in association with my departmental colleagues in London.

The essential social basis for the study of meaning of texts is the *context of situation*. A most important forerunner of situational theory was Philipp Wegener whose *Untersuchungen über die Grundfragen des Sprachlebens* was published in 1885 in Halle. His theory of the situation included psychological and logical references as providing possible end-points in relations with texts. He sub-classified the main situations to include recognition in present experience and organized knowledge connected with it. This is really quite unlike our present-day approach which is restricted to a limited number of end-points in the situation to be related to the text. They are the personalities of the participants, their verbal behaviour, non-verbal behaviour, relevant events and objects in the situation and the observed effective result. The whole approach is a study of the creative process of which language is the main force.

I could elaborate the study of the situation but I feel I have said enough to lead me to a subject to which I think all linguists should turn with renewed interest, taking the fullest advantage of all the recent advances in linguistics theory and mechanical invention. I refer to translation. Pedants frequently pride themselves on the observation that translation from one language to an entirely different one is impossible, and, in English at any rate, 'untranslatable' is quite a common word. On the subject of untranslatability I should like to refer back to the context of situation which I have just described. It is frequently impossible to translate, so to speak, into words what is communicated by the non-verbal elements of the situation. The English which is embedded in characteristically English social life, in typical English situations, is of course difficult to translate say into German and vice versa, and in order to get a similar effective result situational elements have to be, so to speak, transferred or translated into language. This is a commonplace of all translation requirements if fullest information is to be provided.

I am sure I could think of many untranslatables, both in English and in German. What is to be done, for instance, with the English expression *all right*, with all the possibilities of punctuation with it? Though the little German words such as *jetzt, schon, mal, noch* may be indirectly translatable, they have no word-for-word equivalents in any other language. As I know they are extremely difficult to be sure of in use.

The fact is that translation, far from being impossible, is being achieved on an ever-widening scale in an ever-increasing number of languages and, perhaps, at more frequent intervals for the same text. One of the reasons why Shakespeare holds the theatre in Germany perhaps better than in England is the modern translation. In England, producers have tried *Hamlet* and *Macbeth* in modern dress, Hamlet in a dinner jacket with a revolver and Macbeth in khaki. *We* cannot get the text, however, into linguistic modern dress and so give it modern meaning in linguistic terms. *You* can!

What is it in the modernity of the language which makes the difference in the effective result? A very difficult question to answer. The fact is that though there are wonderful human translation machines, no one really knows how they work. Do you really know what you do when you translate? The questions 'how do we translate?' and 'what in fact do we translate?' are a challenge both to linguistic theory and philosophy.

I have earlier referred to what I call 'restricted languages'. The difficulties of translation between two discrepant languages are not so great if the situations are to some extent common. It is easier to build the bridge from the *source* language to the *target* language if the situational context is mutually assimilated by cultural convergence.

The dispersion of the problem of meaning into a number of levels of analysis must recognize different modes of meaning corresponding to the statements made at each of the levels. It is part of the meaning of a German word to sound like one. So that the study of German phonetics and, it must be added, phonology, report findings on this aspect of the meaning of German and you will readily agree that some of this phonological mode of meaning can be translated into English more easily than into French or Italian, for example. One of the most difficult modes of meaning to translate, I should say, is the *phonaesthetic* mode which I can best illustrate from English. For example: (*'Modes of meaning', Swinburne):

Ah the banner-poles, the stretch of straightening streamers
Straining their full reach out!

And prince that clogs, and priest that clings.

At the morphological level, there are many difficulties. An Indian authoress who writes in Urdu announced the other day that she had great difficulty writing Indian fiction in English on account of the limited pronominal system for address and reference, since in Urdu her resources would include at least two more—second person singular, both familiar and contemptuous, and also the second person singular and plural honorific. In Japanese and Korean, similarly, the personal status of all participants in a situation finds verbal expressions in speech. Social status is not left to speak for itself merely by implication.

Grammatical meaning is often translated and we know how grammatical categories and structures can be borrowed—the article, for instance, certain Romance elements in Maltese, and one must not forget the influence of Latin prose on European languages. It is most difficult to find parallels for collocations of a pivotal word in any other language and, as we all recognize, one-to-one relations are not common in the dictionary. That is one reason why newer types of dictionaries are required, which would cope with recurrent pieces and sentences in important restricted languages.

With this emphasis on the importance of focusing attention within a circumscribed field on a restricted language, I should like to conclude. I have little or nothing to say about English in general or how to tackle the English universe or, indeed, the whole universe through English.

The approach to the study of restricted languages in English depends upon whether interest is concentrated upon English in England—in modern jargon, English in the British way of life—or whether English is being regarded first of all in a European setting for European purposes or as a world language. Basic English should, I think, be placed in the second category and though a language with limitations, especially of vocabulary and syntax, it is not really in my sense a restricted language. A restricted language is limited by its use and its micro-glossary may be rich and its micro-grammar specialized.

The study of such languages in literature has scarcely begun. In British universities, there has been of recent years some decline in what may be called English philology of the traditional type. The Cambridge English tripos does not recognize it and in other universities too there is a good deal more emphasis on literature than language. Some of my colleagues in the English Departments suggest that the place of Old English and Germanic philology should be taken by courses of study such as have been suggested in London—e.g. the development of English as a means of literary expression. Since the study of development and evolution is not characteristic of the intellectual climate of today, I am not enthusiastic about that suggestion. There is, however, a great opportunity for the application of general linguistics in the study of the mother tongue as well as in the study of English as a foreign language.

Summary[1]

I. *Descriptive linguistics* is one aspect of General Linguistics, that is to say it is one of the applications of the theory of language. Its main concern is to make statements of meaning in purely linguistic terms. Such statements are made in terms of structures and systems at a number of different but congruent levels of analysis, e.g. at the levels of phonetics, phonology, grammar (mainly syntax), stylistics, glossaries and situational contextualization. The attestation and establishment of the texts of the *corpus inscriptionum* is a first duty.

The structures of words, phrases or other 'pieces' and of sentences are stated in terms of interrelated elements assigned to phonological, grammatical and other mutually determined categories. These elements are in syntagmatic relation with one another and if grammatical, are said to constitute a colligation. In English, the pronoun third person singular masculine may be in a colligation with a simple singular third person verb and a pronoun objective third person singular feminine.

In German it is advantageous both to study and teach the nominal colligations of articles or other determinatives with all the nominals, i.e. adjectives and nouns as whole pieces.

Systems either of phonematic or prosodic units or parts of speech are in the nature of paradigms. Such units, e.g. vowel, consonant and prosodic units, or grammatical systems such as gender, number, case, tense, aspect, etc. derive their values from mutual commutation, within each separate system.

2. *The study of English* is a very vague expression referring to a whole universe of possibilities which must be reduced and circumscribed to make exact study and disciplined teaching possible. Hence the notion of a *restricted language*. Restricted languages function in situations or sets or series of situations proper to them, e.g. technical languages such as those operative in industry, aviation, military services, politics, commerce or, indeed, any form of speech or writing with specialized vocabulary, grammar and style.

Descriptive linguistics of the structural kind is at its best when dealing with a restricted language. The restricted language, which is also called the *language under description (beschreibene Sprache)* must be exemplified by texts constituting an adequate *corpus inscriptionum*.

In order to promote clarity and firm guidance of theory in practical application the following distinctions must be kept constantly before us:

(a) The language *under* description (l.u.d. *beschreibene Sprache?*) which should whenever possible be a restricted language;

(b) The language *of* description (l.o.d., *beschreibende Sprache, Aussagesprache?*). The l.o.d. includes the technical terms and expressions and all forms of notation, phonetic, phonological and formulaic, grammatical and lexicographical;

(c) The language of translation (l.o.t., *Übersetzungssprache?*). This is not always a foreign language—the English of a restricted language may be presented in what may be rightly called a translation. It should be remembered that so-called translation equivalents between two languages are never really equivalent and the use of the expression 'translation-meaning' is now accepted not to imply more than providing an identification name.

Meaning is handled by splitting up the problem and making multiple statements. The statements of meaning are dispersed at a series of levels, e.g. phonological and grammatical. Syntactical statements are statements of the interrelations between elements of structure. These elements are grammatical categories—not words. Grammatical relations subsist between categories in *colligations*, not between words. Cf. *collocations*.

Collocation states the habitual company a key-word keeps. Words must at some level or other be taken at their face value in their common and usual verbal environment. The word *ass* in present-day spoken English is usually collocated with such other words as *you silly . . ., don't be such an . . ., only an . . . like Bagson would do such a thing*, etc.

The meaning of *Friede* and *demokratisch* in Eastern and Western Germany can first be differentiated by contrasting collocations. Even the meaning of the word *Berlin* since 1946 must similarly be stated first in characteristic contemporary collocations differentiating it from pre-war usage. It is, for example, frequently collocated with *Insel* in the West, as well as with *Weltstadt, Congressstadt*, etc.

At the grammatical level, it is important to look for verbal characteristics in the sentence as a whole and these characteristics are rarely in parallel with what you find in the tabulated conjugations in the grammar books. The first step in understanding the verbal characteristics of English sentences is to grasp the use of the twenty-four operators. The infinitival particle *to* is also a syntactical operator, e.g. *for you to say so would be wrong; for me to have said so was a mistake; I told him not to say anything; do you want to?; you'd better not; you've got to; I warned him not to.*

The essential social basis for the study of the meaning of 'texts' is found in the abstraction 'context of situation'. The difficulties of translation even between two discrepant languages are not so great if the abstracted situations are to some extent congruent. It is easier to build the bridges from the source language to the target language if the situation contexts can be regarded as mutually assimilated by cultural convergence.

Note

1. [This does not appear to be so much a summary as a restatement in slightly different terms of ideas expressed in the main paper. In its original form some paragraphs were identical with sections of the paper and have now been excised. F.R.P.]

Eight

A new approach to grammar†

The title of my lecture immediately suggests three things: first, that there is such a subject as general grammar, and, secondly, that it is to be approached as a problem, not rehearsed as collective doctrine, and, thirdly, that the approach is new.

There is nothing new under the sun. Yet the sun rises anew every day and spring comes round every year with new life. Grammar is especially ancient. It is as old as letters in Sanskrit, Greek and Arabic, and the special grammars of these three classical languages have understandably enjoyed traditional permanence over the centuries. These grammatical traditions have been carried by the learned to enable them to fulfil their obligations, often under religious sanctions, as servants of the continuity of culture, both by word of mouth and through the heritage of literature.

Widely scattered societies have treasured the classical sources of Sanskrit, Greek, Latin and Arabic over long periods, and the special grammars have been many and various, but they have not in any one tradition been utterly unlike one another, and rather suggest a constellation of systems held together by the source of light.

We in the West must concede the claim often made by Indian scholars that 'in no other country has the science of grammar been studied with such zeal and carried to such theoretical abstractions as in India' and Sanskrit still lives there, even in speech. In that country, there are current today at least a dozen different schools of Sanskrit grammar. Hundreds of writers and over 1,000 separate treatises, original as well as explanatory, may also be regarded as current. Scholars in the

---

† Read as the 'Stevenson lecture' to an audience at Bedford College London in 1956. The latter part of the paper was in hand-written form and clearly little more than lecture notes. I have omitted a few passages that seemed to me either obscure or not wholly relevant to the argument.

universities of the West are not ashamed to own their obligations to Indian grammarians of 2,000 years ago. But, the scholars in the schools of England, even in grammar schools, have poor English grammar or none at all.

I have just mentioned—almost in passing—a generalized science of grammar, and have referred to the considerable variety of special grammars. Here is the core of what the English Association recognized as the *problem of grammar*, in a pamphlet under that title first published in 1923. The title had been taken from the Report of the Departmental Committee on the teaching of English. On page 4 of the pamphlet it is stated that the first Annual Conference of the English Association, after the publication of the English Report, was devoted to the problem of grammar, and that it was held in this College on the 27th May 1922. The pamphlet recognizes the connection between the problem of grammar, the teaching of English and the classical tradition.

As an Elizabethan preface has it—'A schoolmaster liketh that he knoweth, and seeth not the use of that he knoweth not.' Grammar must, therefore, be taught to the schoolmaster. But what are the languages necessary to the good life, requiring good manners in speaking and in writing? Latin, French, German, English? Is not good English necessary for a good life? And a good grammatical knowledge of English the necessary basis for the serious study of foreign languages? And how many kinds of English? Good manners in the good life extend to the many parts a person must play, and to a wide variety of vocations and professions. The problem of establishing a common grammar of the main languages of life, which are varieties of English, must first be dealt with at the level of science—that is by general or theoretical linguistics. And so also must the special grammars of restricted English and school grammars.

The dominance of Latin grammar in England since the work of Aelfric in the tenth century is proportional to the importance of Latin in the Christian way of life and, later, to the place of the humanities in the life of scholarship. A comparison of Latin in the Middle Ages with English today is arresting. Latin in the life of Western Europeans of any period is dwarfed by the magnitude and diversity of the uses of English today in the lives of Indians, Pakistanis, Sinhalese, and men, women and children of many other races in Asia and Africa. With the rapid development of technology, now to be liberally endowed by government, English in science and technology becomes international, both in a general sense and also in the English of specialized sciences. To approach these problems anew requires both general and special grammars formulated in the light of contemporary linguistic theory. And, with the rapid development and extension of English, the urgency of translation both from and into English requires grammar to help build the inter-lingual bridges.

When Latin was the language of the good life in Western Europe, grammar, dialectic, rhetoric, music, arithmetic, geometry and astronomy formed an organized curriculum and, even as late as William Lily's *Short introduction of grammar* and other works published between 1529 and 1537, figures representing the seven arts and sciences of the Trivium and Quadrivium surround the title pages. Lily's works dominated school grammar in the sixteenth and seventeenth centuries and he was reprinted in the eighteenth. His formal approach to the articles and the seven genders of Latin disappeared at the end of that century.

Although Medieval Christian Latin is not susceptible of description within the compass of one grammar, and it is clear there can be no one lexicon, the general principles of concord and construction were agreed and taught to guide those who used Latin, in recognizing the right word in the right place at the right time in reading, and in approaching some sort of norm in writing and speaking Latin.

There are many specialized languages called English and to establish a common grammar for all styles and specializations of contemporary English is a much bigger problem than for Medieval Latin. And yet, surely it is just as important to get the right word in the right place at the right time in the English of its many specialized international uses as it was in the Latin uses of the Church or the Latin of the laws. In the grammar schools and universities after the Revival of Learning the grammar and rhetoric of classical literature continued to be obligatory and authoritative. Professors of English Literature might do worse than encourage new approaches to grammar and rhetoric, taking into consideration the development of the linguistic sciences during the last thirty years. In developing linguistic research in Medieval Latin and, in my opinion, in Middle English, the notion of restricted languages, even limited to one author and sometimes to one manuscript, must be applied to circumscribe the field of inquiry sufficiently for the statement of coherent grammatical structures and systems. Since grammar must, almost by definition, concern itself with letters and marks, systematically used in spelling, a similar restriction is to be applied to spelling and writing as the first level of structural analysis in sorting out the grammatical meaning of texts in ancient and medieval languages. Where palaeography ends such a study begins and I have tentatively given it the name of graphematics, that is the structural study of systems of writing. It might prove especially interesting in Old and Middle English.

A senior American Rhodes scholar who is spending some time in Oxford told me the other day that the fairly uniform standards of the English language in use in Oxford in his student days seemed to have been swept away or, at any rate, had been supplanted by bewildering variety—and not only accent. In the University of London recently Convocation has heard significant warnings of the dangers of reducing the requirements in English for the General Certificate of Education. Amid all these circumstances, I cannot refrain from repeating an appeal for more disciplined modern linguistic studies in the English schools of the universities. For large numbers of students linguistic discipline in English must be developed to equal the standards of the classical languages without copying them. What has been described as English philology, excellent though it is in its historical setting, is not quite the discipline I have in mind. But to abandon it for non-linguistic studies is a form of relaxation which I deplore. The switch-over to science and technology just ahead of us must include a place for the linguistic sciences as understood today, and grammar is one of them.

A new approach to grammar requires a new approach to meaning. The older classical grammatical tradition was associated with logic and was based on the logical meaning of sentences. Rhetoric recognizes other meanings. More recently psychological meaning, a sort of rough-and-ready analysis of thought, has been drawn upon to supply additional criteria for grammatical categories. English grammars of this sort are eclectic, both in materials and method, in theory and practice, and it is not surprising that they satisfy nobody nowadays and lead to frustration in attempts at formal linguistic studies of English.

The American phonemic approach looks for the minimum number of phonological units in phonemes and distinctive features and, having found them with the help of meanings of a sort, usually naïve, goes on to state the occurrences and distributions of the units, employing statistical techniques in accordance with the logic of distributional relations. They then claim to have excluded meaning altogether by a mechanistic method, avoiding what they denounce as mentalism. This approach is now being severely criticized. I believe the mechanist-mentalists, as I describe them, have had their day.

The Swiss, French and Scandinavian linguists still base all linguistic analysis on the duality of the sign, the meaning of which is for them always arbitrary. In phonology and grammar they regard a language as a system, generally one system of code signs. But linguists, even in America, are beginning to be aware of almost exclusive pre-occupation with meaningless signalling systems, and social anthropologists are offering more meaningful approaches.

Grammar after all is a study of meaning in generalized terms. The essential thing about our sentences and sequences of sentences is that they are multi-evental. Only by generalization can we avoid the appalling consequences of the continuous change of content in all expressions of a living language and of the belief that meaning can only be real in individual instances of human invention.

This new approach to grammar requires first the abandonment of the dualist view of meaning involving such phrases as word and idea, thought and its expression, form and content, and the adoption of what I may call a psychosomatic attitude to meaning and finding it in the statement of the internal relations of the structures and systems in a language, and the extended relations of these within generalized contexts of situation.

Two topics I have already mentioned: first, the place and nature of general theoretical grammar and its relation to special grammars; secondly, the need to limit and circumscribe the field of investigation in special grammar in two ways—(a) by dispersing grammatical inquiry and resulting statements at a series of congruent levels of analysis such as graphematics, phonology, morphematics and syntax, and (b) by applying the above spectrum of grammatical analysis in the first instance to restricted languages.

From this point of view, it is not just a question of the differences between spoken and written language. There are many specialized languages called English, both spoken and written, and many different styles. A common grammar for all styles and specializations of contemporary English would have to be generalized to a high degree of abstraction and would require not just a new approach to general grammar, but the production of special grammatical studies of restricted forms of English and of studies in stylistics.

As examples of restricted languages I have recently looked at mathematical treatises in English, French and German, concentrating on the grammatical meaning and noticing the vocabulary and styles of the three languages employed. I found the terse and sharply pointed German of Landau extremely restricted, and this appeared in the English translation. The French I found similarly restricted, but something could be said about what appears to be a traditional classical style. You can imagine how restricted the pronominal and verbal systems are in such works.

If next you will consider for a moment the restricted languages of meteorology, and I am sure you will approve of the description 'restricted' in this case, you will realize that special studies would show how different the internal relations of the structures and systems are in English and French. Further, in the second set of relations, the extended relations, the weather situations and the reading public are so different in England, Canada and Australia, and in France, Algeria and Quebec.

The American phonemic approach to all linguistic analysis is one way of dealing with all styles at once. Some American scholars, by stating combinations formed with a minimum number of phonemic units, seek to establish morphemes which exhibit patterns of occurrence and distribution. This is called morphemics and deals, in the words of the two most unreadable writers on this sort of analysis, 'with the recurring patterned partials in utterances'. Nothing is said about written texts. These authors also use what they call 'meanings' of the fractions of utterances as a general guide and short cut. Extremely naïve or even quite impossible meanings are to be expected in such work. The lexicon which results from this sort of grammar, based on what is termed 'morphophonemics', is a list of all the morphemes. No contribution is made to syntactical analysis in this phonemic procedure, and the authors confess the treatment is uneven and inadequate.

By basing all this so-called grammar on phonemic analysis of American English and by relying on studies of distribution of the minimum units in General American English, nothing of any great value in the learning of English or other languages results and, in my view, nothing even for the machine translators. For the study of language as a medium of literary expression they have no syntax to offer and the distribution of units in all styles tears stylistics to shreds. And yet amid a set of unattractive new terms they find it possible to regard the term 'possessive case' as self-explanatory and a large number of traditional terms are used without definition—and I do not see how they can mean anything in the context of morphemics.

I have just mentioned terminology. In the new approach I propose many of the traditional terms survive, but their meanings are determined by the new contexts in which they are used. In this connection, may I quote a letter from Sir Richard Temple to Sir George Grierson of the Linguistic Survey of India. Both these great men were members of the Oriental Advisory Committee on the Terminology and Classifications of Grammar which met in 1918. Sir Richard Temple had interested himself in exotic languages of all types and, incidentally, attempted a sketch of Universal Grammar. Writing in 1907 he said:

> The question of terminology in my Theory resolves itself thus; is it a smaller strain on the brain to put new definitions on to old words or have new words? I thought the latter is the best, but if the former is the best, it is all one to me.

I am sufficient of a traditionalist to take over the bare words of the available grammatical vocabulary, and derive other words from them. Scientific terminology is in no sense self-explanatory, and cannot be so in grammatical description. It is relative and functional.

The day of the Report of the Joint Committee on a Common Grammatical Terminology for Greek, Latin, French, German and English is gone. Even the revised report of 1911 was out of date and useless when it first appeared and little attention has ever been paid to it. I have nothing to say on the standardization of terminology nor do I consider nomenclature in itself of primary importance. Never quarrel about words for other words or about letters for other letters. But we must have orderly language to discuss language, which is obviously based on ordered relations.

Many school-teachers deliberately avoid the use of well-known grammatically descriptive words which, like other common words such as matter, motion, force, energy, have also technical meanings. It seems to me that children should be shown how interesting it can be to talk in an orderly way about their use of language in speech, reading and writing. After all, the language games they have to learn at school and play for the rest of their lives have their rules. In most traditional school grammars the rules are not factually formal, but are based on value judgments usually deprecatory. The rules of a game must penalize foul play, but they are really designed to regulate the game for the enjoyment of both players and spectators, while allowing endless variety.

Elementary phonetics and grammar at school level could even be used for a child's early lessons in science. Thinking and talking about language could, for some children, be an intellectual experience of great value. Children should not be pedagogically robbed of words for it. A lecturer in this university once protested to me that you shouldn't use such a term as *preposition* for words which behaved so contradictorily to its real meaning. The notion of real meaning was based on the etymology of the word *etymology* as understood in the days of Trench and Skeat. In those days, however, boys at any rate knew enough Latin to know that prepositions in that language could be *inter* and *post*, as well as *pre*. I find it easy to defend the use of a preposition to end a sentence with.

We have perhaps left behind the custom of labelling words as really belonging to one part of speech, though occasionally used in another. In the old style a preposition could be used as an adverb, or sometimes the two could be crossed in adverbial prepositions, or preposition-like adverbs. Grammatical nonsense of this sort is still common.

The categories of grammar are abstractions from texts, from pieces or stretches of discourse spoken or written. Syntax itself is concerned with the interrelations of some of these categories, not of words as such. So that many words in English can be exponents of several categories. *Back* may be a substantive, an adjective, a verb or an adverb. Taken at its face value, it has orthographic form and nothing else. *In, out, up, down, on, off*, may function as prepositions, adverbs or aspectival particles. As aspectival particles they are exponents of one of the possible verbal characteristics of the sentence. May I illustrate this by quoting one of my well-known examples which I first used at a colloquium on machine translation. Somehow or other the game of finding the verb had been mentioned. And, pressed for material, I suggested the sentence *she kept on popping in and out of the office all the afternoon.* Where's the verb? *Kept? Popping? Kept popping? Kept on popping? Kept on popping in* and *kept on popping out* (with forms, as they say, understood), or *kept on popping in and out*, or *kept on popping in and out of?* Is there a tense here? What conjugation does it belong to? How would you set it out?

If you look at the various ways in which what is called the English verb is set out in tabulated paradigms, you will get nowhere at all. It is useful here to distinguish between the verb in English as a part of speech, and what may be called the verbal characteristics of the sentence. The exponents of these characteristics in the sentence I have quoted, *she kept on popping in and out of the office all the afternoon*, are distributed over the sentence structure, are not co-terminous—in fact, have no termini and are not in any time sequence. The order is not even one of words but of grammatical relations and it need not be continuous and is certainly not in parallel with the words as such. In noticing such verbal characteristics as person, tense, aspect, mode and voice, I do not expect to find them in any single word to be called the verb, drawn from a book conjugation. The exponent of tense I find in *kept* which is in this use a verb of aspect. I need only two tenses, past and present, remembering that I am not dealing with clock or solar time, but with grammatical time marked in tense. The aspectical use of *kept* which is in the formal scatter of a four-form verb *keep, keeps, kept, keeping*, requires the *-ing* form of the verb *popping*. The finite structure of the verb in the matter of person is marked by the pronoun, and the aspectival category of the two verbal forms is supported by relations with verbal and aspectical particles *on, kept on*, and also *in* and *out* in *popping in and out*. Adverbials are sub-classified and this one, *all the afternoon*, is in a group that accords with the aspects I have mentioned in connection with *kept* and *on*, and *popping* and *in* and *out*. Other adverbials such as *suddenly* or *at ten o'clock* would accord with different generalized verbal characteristics.

Though I do not look for any single word named the verb in which to find accumulated verbal characteristics, i.e. in languages which recognize institutionalized words, an economical way of stating an element of generalized meaning is to classify them into parts of speech. It is felt by some scholars that there are perhaps wordless languages, in which case the method of stating characteristics would still apply. There are from this point of view wordless symptoms here and there in French and even in English. If I say in rapid colloquial *aiʃtʃθɔːt sou* there would be some difficulty with *aiʃtʃ*. Or again if I say *aiŋənə bai wʌn fə miself*, what sort of word is *aiŋənə*?

At present I should use fourteen parts of speech in a common grammar of careful polite English that can be written in orthography. The class called *verb* among others would sub-divide and all told there might be twenty classes including sub-classes.

In this way we are able to classify as verbs such binomials as *go and see, come and get*, and we provide for those who *stand and stare* as well as those who *sit and think*.

In addition to the part of speech and the more specialized categories distributed over the sentence, or rather abstracted from the longer pieces, we must continue to classify the longer pieces themselves, especially in so-called wordless languages.

The basic syntactic classification distinguishes as always between affirmative and negative and states the forms of interrogation and emphasis, noting the prosodies of intonation, stress, quantity, etc. among the exponents of these categories in all texts bearing the implication of utterance. In English it is best to use the three negative particles *not, neither, nor*, as the principle criteria of negation, supported by extended relations in the situational context, and to abstain from any search for a logical negative or negative idea. I find some pleasure in classifying the sentence *Nobody never tells me nothing round here* as strongly affirmative with an alliterative emphasis reminiscent of Bantu.

The interpolation of *don't* here is unusual but would undoubtedly be classed as negative—*nobody don't never tell me nothing round here*. That doesn't sound right somehow. It might be better without *never*.

What I regard as a useful test with negative particles is helpful with binomial verbs, as in *I wrote and asked him* but *perhaps you didn't write and ask*. This is very different from *perhaps you didn't write and didn't ask him* or *if you did write, perhaps you didn't ask him*.

Again our grammatical analysis must not require us to supply missing words understood. The infinitival particle *to* is a very independent operator for example, and is capable of taking the negative particle itself. Consider the following material: *I told him to; I didn't tell him to; I told him not to; I didn't tell him not to*. The more I consider the negative in English, the more I find that comparisons with other languages, for example French, carry me further and further away from universal grammar and from any hope of one-to-one equivalents in the grammatical analysis of different languages. For the comfort of machine translators, if they need it, which I doubt, there are promising parallels in some restricted languages which are cognate and mutually assimilated in cultural situations.

In presenting the features of the verbal phrase, or, if you like, the verbal characteristics of certain phrases, the negative is again useful since there is the implication of the affirmative.

The following are non-finite verbal forms: *seen him?; just seen him!; not seen him; seeing him?* and more often constituent clauses of sentences. They also suggest the need for infinitival formulae in English: *not to see him, not to have seen him, not to be seeing him, not to have been seeing him, not to be seen, not to have been seen*, and there are others.

Reverting to the binomials, we can also give a grammatical account of such sentences as *he never forgave me for not having written and asked him to come and see me*. As a whole the sentence is affirmative with one negative clause including a dependent binomial in the affirmative. That generalized description would cover thousands of cases in received English.

In the list of verbs of aspect in English I should include *to keep, to go, to get*—without aspectival particles, and *to begin* and *to start*, but I hesitate to accept *to commence* in this category. *To stop* and *to finish* I would include, but not *to cease*. Aspectival particles go well with *to start* and *to finish* but not with *to commence* and *to cease*. Taking examples at lower levels of style does not as a rule strain this sort of analysis, for example—*get cracking!; he's been and got drunk; just look at what she's been and gone and done*. In the older Latin grammars *Hic, Haec, Hoc* were described as articles and used singly or in groups as exponents of the seven genders in the nominal phrase. A similar approach is essential in German, especially in teaching English pupils. The article, the adjective and substantive, held together in the nominal phrase, present the nominal characteristics of gender, number and case. In French the articles have similar grammatical weight, but not of course in parallel. The demonstratives of French are in no way parallel to the words *this, these, that, those*, since in that language there is really only one article-like demonstrative *ce*, with gender and number forms. For the rest French uses double words.

Theories are inventions, or better, constructions, and are useful if they correctly predict the phenomena giving rise to them. Under otherwise equal circumstances we prefer that theory which covers a larger field of phenomena, or which from some points of view appears clearer though not necessarily simpler. I do not believe myself that even words for detergents and toilet preparations are really invented. I coined the word *phonaesthetic* myself. It is a new word perhaps, but I didn't invent it.

The span of useful life for a strict scientific theory is about thirty years. Theory succeeds theory. The approach I have suggested is new only in that sense.

Summary

The language of grammatical description, both general and special, should arise from general linguistic theory as we now know it, taking the fullest advantage of the great advances of the last thirty years.

In the theory I have represented I have suggested a new approach to the statement of the meanings of language from a non-dualist point of view and in purely linguistic terms. The statement of meaning at the grammatical level by dispersion at a series of levels of analysis is perhaps at its best when applied to what I have called *restricted languages*.

The separation of the study of grammatical relations from the study of the patterns and designs of words, sentences and the longer elements of discourse which is properly called *discourse analysis* or *stylistics,* also helps in the characterization of such restricted languages. This strengthens both studies and not only provides a firmer bridge for translation, but a much more disciplined approach to the study of language in literature.

Nine

Applications of general linguistics†

The subject of my Address arises from my experience as a teacher of general linguistics in London. My colleagues will agree that in London we have developed general linguistic theory in close application to particular descriptions of a variety of languages at a number of different levels of analysis. Though these descriptions have, in the main, been phonological, they have been more comprehensive than traditional morphological word studies, as a result of the prosodic approach. They have carried over some of the rigorous methods of comparative philology and have perhaps gone further in austerity. The title of my Address suggests an analogy with science, pure and applied. In some respects, the analogy—if not pressed too hard—might help to separate applied linguistics from general linguistic theory. Linguistic analysis is impossible without the guidance of theory and skill in the methods and procedures of its application. The expression 'linguistic analysis' was used by Malinowski to describe his treatment of ethnographic texts. His theory was more ethnographic than linguistic, but he does show skill in its application. Some of our philosophers offer what they also call linguistic analysis, but the theory is philosophical and skill in its application is a form of dialectic. Perhaps the term 'linguistic analysis', shared by different disciplines, should not be interpreted too technically, unless the other disciplines concede it to linguistics. In linguistics, it seeks to establish elements of structure by delimiting both the structures and the elements and stating their values. This process necessarily leads to the statement of functions. It will be seen at once, therefore, that general linguistics is mainly a study of relations. This is in a large measure also

---

† *TPS* 1957, Presidential Address delivered to the Society on Friday, 3rd May 1957.

true of contemporary comparative studies of the Indo-European family of languages.

The general linguistic theories of de Saussure and of all his real descendants, including Hjelmslev, are best stated in French, employing a characteristic phraseology and nomenclature which are essentially *dichotomic*. Such a dichotomic framework multiplies binary oppositions of all kinds, in all branches of applied linguistics, beginning with the *langue-parole* distinction requiring theories of speech and of language, proliferating in dichotomies, synchronic or diachronic, of form and substance, of content and expression, and eventually binary oppositions in phonology, morphology, and even syntax, nowadays supported by binary mathematics.

All the successors of de Saussure have reproduced and extended dichotomic theory. The most successful applications of Saussurean theory are probably those of his first successor in the Chair at Geneva, Charles Bally. The present incumbent, Professor Henri Frei, is an ardent disciple, but has not specialized in applied linguistics. In France, there has been some falling off in Saussureanism since the great days of Meillet. In England, Sir Alan Gardiner is perhaps the only well-known Saussurean, but he is not truly orthodox. Perhaps the most highly developed Saussureans are to be found in Copenhagen and Oslo. The Copenhagen group, led by Professor Louis Hjelmslev, has concentrated on theory of such an abstract nature that the special name 'glossematics' has to be used in referring to it. Hjelmslev is a logico-mathematical theoretician who has made much more of the principles of de Saussure than can be found in the master's treatise. Nevertheless, glossematics is clearly French in inspiration—if French in this connection can be taken to include the Geneva School. Though I do not share Hjelmslev's fundamental assumptions and am in no sense a Saussurean, I find Hjelmslev's quasi-mathematical approach excellent in that general quality. It is comprehensive in its implications and possible range of application to language. But it is only fair to point out that no thoroughgoing glossematic analysis of any language whatever—not even Danish —has yet appeared. It is precisely this lack of application which suggests that perhaps it is best regarded as a kind of pure mathematics, to be applied by those who understand it, when they think fit. I was recently at a social gathering of scientists and happened to overhear a small group of mathematicians discussing an interesting practical example of applied mathematics, when one of them remarked, 'Well, that's not mathematics, anyway'. It rather looks as though Professor Hjelmslev has often said, 'That's not glossematics, anyway!' I personally look forward to the first complete application of glossematics.

There have been various amendments and corrections to the original dichotomy of *langue* and *parole*. I have not forgotten *langage*—de Saussure affirmed there was no *linguistique du langage* to parallel *linguistique de la langue* and *linguistique de la parole*. *Discours* has been inserted between *langue* and *parole*, and in addition to the dichotomy of *signifié* and *signifiant* in *signification*, there is also the possibility of *désigné* and *désignant* in *désignation* and *référé* and *référant* in *référence*, and so on in exploitation of the resources of French etymology. My own interpretation of the glossematic approach to the study of signs on two planes of content and of expression would run very briefly as follows.

The substance of the content of signs, what some might call 'meaning', would in French be *signification*, and the relation between content (*signifié*) and expression (*signifiant*) would in the system of *langue* be termed *désignation*. The study of the sign in *langue* would be by 'sememics' concerning itself with the 'sememe', on the plane of content, by 'phonemics' concerned with the 'phoneme' on the plane of expression. In studies of *parole*, 'semics' would state 'semes' and 'phonics' would represent 'phones', and the two combined would deal with *référence* by relating the *référé* in terms of 'semes' with the *référant* in terms of 'phones'. Further, *référence* would be normalized in *désignation*, 'semes' in relation to 'sememes' and 'phones' to 'phonemes'. These indications could be schematized in very broad generalizations, but in the last resort, they would come very near the familiar nineteenth-century dualisms of language and thought, thought and its expression or communication, and we are not much nearer an empirical and objective science of language. There is however a great advance in clarity.

The principles and methods of the old Prague Circle, including the great work of Trubetzkoy, were also profoundly influenced by de Saussure, though the Slavonic components are there, reaching back to Baudouin de Courtenay.

In the Soviet Union, all this has counted for little or nothing. Russian linguists first enjoyed and afterwards worried about Marr, then came other misapplications of Marxism, including the view that language was to be considered an ideological superstructure on an economic basis. This Stalin denounced since it apparently interrupted the essential continuity of Russian and the Slavonic group of languages. The linguists of the Soviet Union have always been kept busy in applied linguistics over a great variety of languages, and for many social and political purposes from alphabetization to the organization of propaganda, not forgetting education.

The theory to be applied is therefore of the highest political importance. Saussurean formalism and idealism have been uniformly denounced in Soviet Russia, and the recent tendency to devote more attention to historical and comparative linguistics not only looks like international co-operation, but emphasizes the importance of Russian as the main language of the Slavonic group and of the whole Union.

The Chinese will keep phonemics in its place for obvious linguistic reasons—it is difficult to conceive the Chinese tradition leading to a theory of the ABC. In any case, there is a mass of Russian work available and, in the absence of parallel works in English, it looks as though neither Saussurean theories nor phonemics will find ready application in China. Saussurean dichotomic theory does not in any case readily find application in renewal of connection with linguistic and social experience. I think it will command less respect in applied linguistics as the years go by.

There are probably more students of linguistics in the United States than anywhere else in the world. The majority of these, whatever particular school they belong to, will be following a structuralist line of approach. From Sapir to Bloomfield and his successors, methods and procedures have been developed, especially in phonological analysis, leading to the present position of phonemics as the dominant technique. The origins of phonemics are to be found in ethnographic studies of the American Indian. One of the practical needs of the ethnographer is to reduce to writing the language of the people he is studying. In this, Sapir was the great master. Though he wrote the first of a number of books appearing under the simple title *Language*, it was not in any real sense a theoretical work, though there were suggestions of an approach to the theory of the phoneme. Phonemics has moved a long way from its sociological beginnings and has now become one of the established techniques for reducing languages to writing in the roman script. There have been signs that phonemics for its own sake, as a kind of linguistic game, has been treated as a theoretical discipline. This is rather like generalizing pure mathematics from practical arithmetic. Phonemics is essentially a technique with a limited objective attainable in a limited time. Some phonemicists make use of logical and statistical theories,

9

but this—I take it—justifies my description of phonemics as applied—that is to say, the application of the logic of distributional relations,[1] of elementary statistics and, more recently, of communication theory in setting up phonological units for any given language. The amazing thing is that a phonemicist need not be a phonetician. In fact, a phonemicist should be able to phonemicize or rephonemicize suitably recorded materials from any source. In his last book on language, Professor Kenneth Pike[2] has generalized from the nomenclature and phraseology of phonetics and phonemics and differentiates the 'etic from the 'emic approach—'etics from 'emics. When phonemicists have cleared up the mess that has been made of *juncture* and of *zero*, they can begin afresh with a much wider range of abstractions, and a more clearly defined nomenclature.

Before turning to applications of General Linguistics, I would like to recapitulate by mentioning the following points. (1) General linguistic theory is invented for application in the description of particular languages and in dealing with specific language problems. It is not a theory of universals for general linguistic description. It should serve as a guide for the descriptive analysis of languages, especially of restricted languages, and also provide the necessary principles of synthesis to deal not only with the longer pieces of language, but also with the useful results of linguistic studies of the past. (2) Linguists should be prepared to produce the main structural framework for the bridges between different languages and cultures. (3) Not all general linguistic theories are however equally suitable for practical application and that is perhaps the principal reason for bearing in mind the two aspects—general linguistics and applied linguistics.

It is only quite recently, say during the last forty years, that linguistics in Europe has become an autonomous discipline, at any rate on the theoretical side. And it is something of a revolution in status. One of the greatest handicaps in the advance of the linguistic sciences has been dependence on other prior disciplines. Instead of producing linguistic theory for application, linguists often enough were condemned to apply the theories of logic, rhetoric, philosophy and later on, of psychology, even of pedagogy. Today, some linguists strive to apply theories of distributional relations originating outside the discipline, others play second fiddle to cybernetics, communication theory, digital computers, speech machines, or telecommunications engineering.[3] Again and again, linguistic scholarship has served the formal education of the time. Aelfric wrote his Latin Grammar in English to help teach Anglo-Saxon boys in the cloisters. In the Middle Ages, there were some advances in independent grammatical invention, but even these were for schooling. Although language theory had a place in scholastic philosophy, it was within a Catholic theology. And after the voyages of discovery, the mission fields needed alphabetic studies and the multiplication of grammars and dictionaries leading to translations of the Gospel and devotional literature. The theory was derived from logic, rhetoric, teaching and educational practice. The study of grammar and rhetoric, of elocution and phonetics, the teaching of composition and all forms of linguistic exercise in English and foreign languages were all based on applied notions derived from a variety of sources—a miscellaneous set of applied notions, often ill-assorted and probably unrelated except in the form of classroom procedure. There are still remnants of this sort of thing in our Institutes of Education. Indeed, in an earlier edition of *Chambers's Encyclopaedia*, the article on Linguistics, written by an old friend of mine, the late H. O. Coleman, dealt with the teaching of languages. Phonetics in this country and in France was pedagogical in origin and in purpose. The organ of the International Phonetic Association is still called *Le maître phonétique*.

Now I think the tables are turned and general linguistic theory is sufficiently developed for it to be clearly applied to suitable language problems all over the world. In other words, from its newly won place in the University curriculum, it should find reapplication in various faculties and in the institutes and schools.

Now let us turn to some of the wider fields of possible and indeed desirable applications of General Linguistics. Within the Commonwealth, we have the Colombo Plan for economic and technical aid for development in South Asia. One of the catchwords of the day is development for what are called under-developed countries. *Development for free Asia* is the title of a competent book by Maurice Zinkin who, after service in the I.C.S., went into industry and commerce. He summarizes a good deal in the following sentences—first about education. 'Each new development means a new educational curriculum.' 'What has been done for clerking must be done for every job which matters in development.' 'To give practical jobs the same prestige as desk jobs, most of them must be taught academically.' 'The model must be nineteenth-century Germany or twentieth-century America, with their courses in everything from journalism to carpentry—not England or France with their belief that the academic must be really academic.' 'The University's job (in these countries) therefore, is not so much to turn out double firsts, who can in any case only be a few, but to mass produce the equivalent of American junior college graduates.' 'Scientific research institutions in India are being founded outside the Universities and the brilliant people can always go abroad.'

As you will at once realize, this leads to all manner of linguistic difficulties, especially since nationalism leads people to a longing for linguistic equality, which has particularly complex effects.

Once upon a time, the educated classes of the world conducted their affairs and performed their duties in very few languages—Latin, Arabic, Sanskrit, Chinese. The educated were few, the audience small and the scholarly traditions concentrated. All this has fallen more and more into desuetude. The number of languages used by the popular presses, by broadcasting and all manner of services increases steadily. The ambition of most Asians is to develop every language which is spoken by an appreciable number of people until it becomes a possible instrument of scholarship—say in physics or in history. It is clear that the tasks in which linguists have jobs to do are considerable and increasing in responsibility. Translations and original writing in the rising national languages involve the consideration of the place of English in most of these societies. English as an expression of English life is of little importance—what matters is English in relation to the national languages in the changing Asian ways of life. 'Once people can educate themselves in their own language, it will be much easier to create good overseers and foremen and electricians—all the people indeed of whom Asian societies are so deplorably short' (Zinkin). A society in which there are no officials, or works managers, or professors who do not really understand the people under them, is clearly able to change much more quickly than one in which there are severe barriers to downward communication. One can neither inspire nor easily teach those whose lives are conducted in an altogether different idiom. The linguistic problems of Asia are largely concerned with making the leadership of the educated effective—both in English and in the rising national languages. The practical applications of linguistics in the West must act in parallel with developing Asia and so raise the standard of proficiency in contemporary Asian languages, that we can take part in the new leadership or at least understand it. Scholarship in Asian languages and in general linguistics in the West must be related in some way to the new language situations, if we are to take part in cultural development alongside our participation in economic development to our mutual advantage and profit.

The teachers of the modern languages of Asia in this country must obviously take notice of these matters. They must take heed of due warning given.

I have just been in Pakistan, including a short visit to Delhi, and have found great scope for applied linguistics in both countries. Both in Pakistan and India, Americans are very much in evidence, as experts, advisers and teachers. They often descend on their assignments in teams with all the necessary equipment and books, and the language which carries all this is American.

India has taken up American linguistics, including large doses of phonemics, in the hope of carrying out new linguistic surveys with a view to the enrichment of the national language from dialect sources, and to promote some convergence at any rate in vocabulary of the principal languages. They have worked on technical terminology in the sciences and on nomenclature and phraseology for the administrative and defence services. My impression is that they still have a long way to go even in the preliminary exploratory and learning period. And phonemics, like patriotism, is not enough. In Pakistan, the language problems are not so vast or so intricate, and they are not yet committed to any extensive programme of linguistic research. But at a recent Conference in Karachi which I attended, along with American representatives, a special Committee composed of two Vice-Chancellors, two senior educationists and three Pakistani linguists, decided to recommend the gradual establishment of at least two University departments of general linguistics, and strongly urged the training of suitable young scholars abroad.

In a message to the language teaching conference at Karachi, the Prime Minister, Mr Suhrawardy, directed our attention, and in my opinion that of all serious linguists interested in South Asia, to the new pattern of English indicated by the present-day developments in the rising national languages which must be taken into account, so that at certain points in the educational streams where English and the national languages meet, balances may be struck. Whatever the media of instruction, auxiliary English or plain contemporary English with a practical bias would be desirable in schools and other institutions at the pre-University stage and possibly also in the Universities. Several leading Pakistani delegates called for intensive research in applied linguistics bearing on the Bengali, English and Urdu languages in use in all walks of life, and especially in science and technology. Research was also needed in the matter of selecting reading materials and adapting language courses to the ends in view in the present age. It was generally

felt that very few teachers of any grade had any training in the study
and teaching of language as language, independent of literature. It was
in this connection that the need for general linguistics in the Universities
was emphasized with the intention that applied linguistics might be
directed towards the language problems of the two wings of Pakistan.

There are similar problems in Malaya and Singapore where the
Government and the University are endeavouring to promote research
towards some solution of their own language triangle, Malay, Chinese
and English. Everywhere in South Asia national aspirations are directed
towards partnership with the Americans and ourselves in this developing
scientific and technological civilization.

National leaders and the ambitious educated classes realize they can
only move their own languages into these uses in well-directed effort at
the highest levels. In this atmosphere it is not difficult to imagine their
reaction to our concentration on good old rather quaint Oriental
languages. They rather feel there are no modern *Oriental* languages—
only modern languages. A real change of direction is needed in Great
Britain in all specialized institutions dealing with modern Asian and
African languages, and applied linguistics must mean something for
the future of the national languages and of English in those continents.

The language problems of India are overwhelming. The enormous
difficulties of social, political and economic problems are aggravated
by the tangle of diversity of languages and of stages of development. No
wonder the tendency is to promote convergencies of various kinds.
Normalization in Hindi is one of these. Problems of terminology vex
them, and they have not so far understood that nomenclature is not
enough and that research in phraseology and grammatical resources
must be brought in too. Moreover, English has to be regarded as a
'classical' source, alongside the traditional classical languages. The
treatment of all these problems in South Asia will have to be specialized
at least to the extent to recognizing the characteristics of the Dravidian,
Sino-Tibetan and Mon-Khmer languages.

Much more interesting to the reading public and to those intending
to become technicians, are the two great developments likely in the
immediate future—translations into and creative writing in the languages of India and Pakistan. Narrow academic or sectional dogmas
should be kept out of translation projects because experience has shown
that such translations are apt to date very quickly and are usually more
ephemeral than spontaneous translations. The Osmania translations
into Urdu provide a case in point. Wherever possible, original writing

on a subject, however elementary, is much to be preferred to translation from an English text specifically written for the purpose.

It will be readily agreed that the fields of research for applications of general linguistics in South Asia cannot be fully exploited, even if all the linguists of the world were to unite. Beginnings can be made in the restricted languages calling for steadily increasing use in science, technology, defence, law and civil administration. In some countries the administration of the law requires the official use and constant recourse to a number of languages; for example in Malta, West Africa and other societies which have developed in close partnership with Britain. A good deal of field research is necessary into the English actually in use in multi-lingual countries in law, industry, commerce, science and technology, and in pursuing these enquiries it should be constantly borne in mind that the new patterns for English in these countries involve the rising national languages.

If we turn to a greatly neglected subject, the science and art of translation, a world-wide range for experiment lies before us, and valuable opportunities for inter-cultural co-operation. In addition to translations into Asian and African languages for education and for regular use in specialized occupations, there is the duty of collecting and collating the traditional oral literature and other creative compositions of Africa and the Pacific, to be translated into English for the use of all the peoples of Africa and the Pacific as well as the rest of the world.

The needs of the Asian and African peoples constitute a call to all those in a position to promote or carry out useful language work. Let this call be loudly heard so that we may see a certain amount of de-classicization both in East and West. This is bound to follow the waking up of linguistic scholarship.

The number and diversity of languages discovered by recent research all over the world plainly exhibits the futility of such distinctions between languages as primitive and civilized. No simple classificatory scheme can adequately measure the linguistic social and political problems involved, nor can it be held that any language is in itself a bar to cultural advance. It is becoming increasingly apparent that we can and must learn to build bridges between any two languages whatever their cultural matrix. This gives a general description of the multitude of tasks and the enormous scope in the application of general linguistics, especially for the development of the free countries of Asia and Africa. The leaders of those countries are quick to realize the value of linguistics and are asking for the help of linguists in furtherance of their national aims. They turn to the United States which has the books, has the men, and has the money too, to Russia which has a gospel and creed and also to England—I hesitate to summarize what we have got nowadays—but we may have a little of something the others haven't got, so that all of us may help.

The interpenetration and interaction of linguistic forces and the forces of nationalism are to be observed all over the world and one of the obligations of a general linguist is not only to be aware of this, but to offer what help and guidance he can.

Notes

1. Language isolates are described by naming them in accordance with a framework of categories and nomenclature. This is in effect by distribution in groups and classes, in structures and systems. The structures and systems are also grouped and distributed. Distribution of this kind is a distribution in the abstract categories of linguistics which can indeed be said to have places and order, but not in any spatio-temporal sense. Distribution of entities in sequential or successive segments, of time or of space for that matter, like telling beads on a string, is an entirely different matter. There is considerable confusion and inconsistency in the use of the word *distribution* in contemporary linguistics. Distribution of *what? where?* and *how?*

2. In the concluding paragraph of a recent article in *Language* 33.1, 35 (1957), he writes—'The theoretical implication of these studies is that the analysis of languages requires a treatment of structural phonological units larger than the phoneme, with contrastive types on each level of the hierarchy. A phonological theory is inadequate to portray the structure and functions of these units, with their various contrastive features, if it attempts to squeeze such data into one non-hierarchical linear sequence of chopped up disparate segmental phonemes and quasi-segmental juncture phonemes.'

3. As Professor W. S. Allen has reminded us, de Saussure long ago warned us not to 'faire de la linguistique la caricature d'une autre discipline'. (Frei, *Word* 10.2–3, 145).

Ten

Ethnographic analysis and language
with reference to Malinowski's views[†]

In the field of linguistics, it has been said with some truth that the English have excelled in phonetics and in lexicography. They have always been interested in the spelling of their language, which has the longest literary tradition in Western Europe. The English were the first to make use of their native language in law, chronicle and translation. The first grammar of Latin in a Western European language was written by the Anglo-Saxon Aelfric in the tenth century. I have elsewhere (1946) given some account of the English interest in spelling and pronunciation, culminating in an appreciation of our greatest philologist, Henry Sweet.

It is, therefore, a matter of some satisfaction to an Englishman, writing an appreciation of the linguistic work of Bronislaw Malinowski, to be able to quote him as follows (1923, 495n.): 'I quote from H. Sweet (*Introduction to the history of language*), because this author is one of the cleverest thinkers on language'. Malinowski notices Sweet's statement that language and logic 'often diverge from one another' and that they are constantly at loggerheads. In Section 4 of the same Supplement, he mentions his concern with the

> definition of single words and with the lexicographical task of bringing home to a European reader the vocabulary of a strange tongue. And the main result of our analysis was that it is impossible to translate words of a primitive language or of one widely different from our own, without giving a detailed account of the culture of

† *Man and culture: an evaluation of the work of Bronislaw Malinowski* ed. R. W. Firth, London, 1957, 93–118.

its users and thus providing the common measure necessary for a translation (1923, 470).

Malinowski faces the crucial problem of definition throughout his work. It should be remembered that all definitions of the 'meanings' of a word are arbitrary and that authoritative citations collected by the lexicographer or ethnographer are usually keyed to these selected uses of the word under description. Throughout Malinowski's ethnographic work, from his account of the natives of Mailu (1915)[1] to his *Coral gardens* (1935), it can be said that he makes every effort to give the native words the fullest cultural context of ethnographic description in English. There is one notable exception which he learnt to abandon in later years. In his account of the Mailu classificatory terms of kinship (1915, 532-4), he gives English terms first, even when the Mailu equivalents are often repeated for different entries.

In the nature of our history, British scholars have been faced with the necessity of offering some account of the exotic languages they have had to live with all over the world. Most of these accounts are, by modern standards, amateurish and inadequate, but the pioneer work was there. Malinowski's contribution in English to the advancement of the study of such languages from the point of view of a professional anthropologist is a brilliant enhancement of the English tradition and we can be proud to include him as one of the makers of linguistics as we now understand it in this country.

Having dealt first with the definition of single words in his Supplement on 'The problem of meaning in primitive languages', we next find him looking at language in an ethnographic perspective, using the concept of context of situation in order to give an outline of a semantic theory useful in the work on primitive linguistics and throwing some light on human language in general. He goes on to describe language, in its primitive function, as a *mode of action*, rather than as a *counter-sign of thought*.

All this is truly in the tradition of British empiricism and of the philosophic radicals and utilitarians, whose influence was far-reaching and is obvious in the works of the Vienna Circle. It finds echoes in Wittgenstein, who would probably have endorsed Malinowski's views on meaning. 'The meaning of words lies in their use' (Wittgenstein, 1953, 80). 'One cannot guess how a word functions. One has to look at its use, and learn from that' (Wittgenstein, 1953, 109). He likens the practice of various types of language in speech behaviour to games with rules. 'A language is a set of games with rules or customs' (Wittgenstein, 1953, 47, 81). The publication of Malinowski's essay on the problem of meaning as the first Supplement to a work largely inspired by C. K. Ogden is itself significant in this connection. Malinowski himself refers to his own *ethnographic empiricism* (1923, 481).

Among the linguists mentioned in the Supplement, the leading German comparatists are missing but W. von Humboldt, Sweet and Jespersen are there, and notably Wegener (1885), to whom Malinowski owed his early notions of the Situation. Wegener was one of the first to propound what he called the *Situationstheorie*.

Malinowski explicitly informs us that he was not acquainted with the technicalities of Indo-European comparative linguistics. 'Of Brugmann-Delbrück's treatise, I tried to understand only the main outlines and the general theoretical parts' (1920, 37, n. 1).

Of his outstanding ability as a practical linguist, we have abounding evidence. To begin with, it is perhaps enough to notice his mastery of English as a vehicle for his original thought. He tells us of what he calls his facility, in his introduction to his work on the Mailu:

> I am afraid I must explicitly boast of my facility for acquiring a conversational command of foreign languages, since I understand that the time in which I learned to speak the Motu would have been normally too short a period for acquiring a foreign, and especially a native, tongue. I wish also to state that the ability to speak Motu and to follow a conversation was of no small advantage in my work. Over and over again, I was led on to the track of some extremely important item in native sociology or folklore by listening to the conversation of my boy *Igua* with his Mailu friends, who used to come from the village to see him.   (1915, 501).

In associating him with Anglo-American rather than Continental traditions of linguistic scholarship, the further point might be made that he explicitly dissociated himself quite early from Durkheim's philosophical basis of sociology (1913; 1916, 423, n. 1). He would have nothing to do with a collective soul and presumably had no interest in the French conception of *langue* as a function of the *collectivité*. It is well known that leading French scholars, notably Meillet, held Durkheimian views in their sociological approach to language. This was reflected in their contributions to *L'année sociologique* (Meillet, 1926). I know from personal association with Malinowski that those parts of de Saussure's general linguistic theory which led in that direction, he found not only unattractive but of little practical value in the study of meaning, which was his principal interest. In order to make way for his own approach, he declared that the postulate of a collectivity was barren and absolutely useless for an ethnographical observer. He wished to see his 'social ideas' embodied in institutions or traditional texts formulated on the basis of work with competent informants (1916, 424).[2]

As a social anthropologist and ethnographer, he was primarily interested in the analytical and functional study of culture, and throughout his work he made the fullest use of language possible to him in stating and commenting on his facts. The linguist, however, must keep the language text in the focus of attention and his main work is the linguistic analysis of the language data collected in his *corpus inscriptionum*.

The London group of linguists associated with my own work have accepted the notion of the institutionalized word in the broadest sense and have always kept to the text as the point of departure. Throughout his ethnographic work, Malinowski had stressed the importance of the institution[3] viewed from the native point of view and interpreted by the scholar, and he makes copious use of native expressions almost as loan words in his descriptive writing. The importance of applying his idea of the institution to language and the liberal recording of textual material is fully recognized in present-day linguistics in England. The procedure is explicitly stated in his *Argonauts of the Western Pacific*:

The best ethnographical writers—here again the Cambridge school with Haddon, Rivers and Seligman rank first among English Ethnographers—have always tried to quote *verbatim* statements of crucial importance. They also adduce terms of native classification; sociological, psychological and industrial *termini technici*, and have rendered the verbal contour of native thought as precisely as possible. One step further in this line can be made by the Ethnographer, who acquires a knowledge of the native language and can use it as an instrument of inquiry. In working in the Kiriwinian language, I found still some difficulty in writing down the statement directly in translation which at first I used to do in the act of taking notes. The translation often robbed the text of all its significant characteristics—rubbed off all its points—so that gradually I was led to note down certain important phrases just as they were spoken, in the native tongue. As my knowledge of the language progressed, I put down more and more in Kiriwinian, till at last I found myself writing exclusively in that language, rapidly taking notes, word for word, of each statement. No sooner had I arrived at this point, than I recognized that I was thus acquiring at the same time an abundant linguistic material, and a series of ethnographic documents which ought to be reproduced as I had fixed them besides being utilized in the writing up of my account.

(1922, 23–4)

In a footnote, Malinowski recognizes the encouragement given him by Dr A. H. Gardiner, now Sir Alan Gardiner, in collecting and interpreting his *corpus inscriptionum Kiriwiniensium*. It is a considerable satisfaction to me to remember Malinowski's association with Sir Alan Gardiner at that time, to be followed by my own association with both these distinguished scholars, since it provides a further illustration of Malinowski in his English setting and his part in the development of linguistics in this country. This is further borne out by his reference to

> Sir Richard Temple's most interesting attempts at a semantic theory adapted to the study of primitive languages. His outlines of a Universal Grammar and their application, although very condensed and carried out only in very broad outlines, seem to me of extreme importance: the problems are set forth in an excellent manner, and the solutions offered are undoubtedly correct in all essentials.
>
> (1920, 74, n. 1—with reference to Temple, 1899a)

The placing of Malinowski in the English tradition links him with the work of distinguished amateurs, so characteristic of scientific leadership in England in the nineteenth century.

He tells us that during his first stay in Kiriwina, from 1915 to 1916, he had no linguistic preparation, but on his return to Melbourne he undertook a good deal of linguistic reading which enabled him to write on linguistics (1920, 73–4). He appears to have studied Sir Richard Temple's 'A theory of universal grammar' carefully and especially Temple's detailed examination of Portman's *Notes on the languages of the South Andaman group of tribes*. Temple reproduces Portman's texts of the Andaman fire legend with inter-linear word-for-word equivalents, followed by a rendering in running English with somewhat crude syntactical notes. Temple described this procedure as the analysis of the language in which the story is couched and, in a good deal of Malinowski's own linguistic work, little more than this is attempted. His reading of Temple reminded him of the difficulties of grammatical description in dealing with exotic languages. As he says, 'there is no universally acknowledged set of definitions and no consistent body of views about the various linguistic categories, everyone is compelled to use his own discretion and to coin his own terminology' (1920, 74).

Sir Richard Temple devotes some time to the consideration of a new set of grammatical categories coupled with an original nomenclature in contrast with traditional terminology. This he summarized in 'The skeleton of a theory of universal grammar' (1899*b*). Sir George Grierson of the Linguistic Survey of India must have taken some interest in this matter since I have in my possession a letter addressed to him by Sir Richard Temple in November 1907, in which he says:

> The question of terminology in my 'Theory' resolves itself thus:— is it a smaller strain on the brain to put *new* definitions on to old words or have new words? I thought the latter was the best, but if the former is the best, it is all one to me. Of course, to a man immersed in a set terminology, a new one is a trouble—but for the learner at large, it may be best to discard what is old and give him something new for new notions. At any rate you avoid confusion in teaching by so doing.

Malinowski expressly approves of the main essentials of Temple's approach. I certainly agree with some of the general principles myself. For example, Temple says:

> Of course, grammarians will know that all this is syntax, and I will now explain why I consider that it is far more important to study function than form as essential to the correct apprehension of words, and how to my mind accidence arises properly out of syntax and not the other way round, as we have all been taught.
>
> It is obvious that any given word may fulfil one or more or all the functions of words, and that therefore words may be collected into as many classes as there are functions, any individual word being transferable from one class to another and belonging to as many classes as there are functions which it can fulfil. The functions a word fulfils in any particular sentence can be indicated by its position therein without or with variation of form, and, because of this, the form which a word can be made to assume is capable of indicating the class to which it belongs for the nonce. It is further obvious that words transferable from class to class belong primarily to a certain class and secondarily to the others, that a transfer involves the fulfilment of a new function, and that a word in its transferred condition becomes a new word.   (1899*a*, 4–5)

Again, Temple is on the right track when he says:

> I found myself, in building up the theory, compelled, in order to work out the argument logically, to commence where the accepted Grammars ended, viz. at the sentence, defining the sentence as the expression of a complete meaning, and making *that* the unit of language.   (1899*a*, 2)

It is not surprising, in the light of the development of linguistics since, that Malinowski found Temple's approach attractive. He did not, however, pay much attention to functional grammar or move in the grammatical directions suggested by Temple. He remained reasonably traditional, but grammatically unsystematic.

In developing a school of social anthropology in London, Malinowski gave all his emphasis to the need for linguistics, especially in connection with the establishment of sound ethnographic texts. It may safely be said that he was among a very few scholars who actively promoted descriptive linguistics both by the example of his own work and by what may be called propaganda. He realized the need for the development of linguistic theory different from the one prevailing, the main orientation[4] of which was the study of historical change and evolution. He even regarded his important article on Kiriwina as

> an example of a general proposition, namely, that there is an urgent need for an Ethno-linguistic theory,[5] a theory for the guidance of linguistic research to be done among natives and in connection with ethnographic study. It was stressed above, in the introductory paragraph, that as there can be no sound theory which is not based on an extensive study of facts, so there can be no successful observation of facts without the guidance of a sound theory. A theory which, moreover, aims not at hypothetical constructions—'origins', 'historical developments', 'cultural transferences' and similar speculations—but a theory concerned with the intrinsic relation of facts. A theory which in linguistics would show us what is essential in language and what therefore must remain the same throughout the whole range of linguistic varieties; how linguistic forms are influenced by physiological, mental, social and other cultural elements; what is the real nature of Meaning and Form, and how they correspond; a theory which, in fine, would give us a set of well-founded plastic definitions of grammatical concepts.   (1920, 69)

The field-worker relies entirely upon inspiration from theory.

(1922, 9)

Jespersen's book *Language*, published in 1922, opens with the sentence—'The distinctive feature of the science of language as conceived nowadays is its historical character'.[6] In 1931, Malinowski found it necessary to say that 'many linguists realize the importance of studying the language of living rather than dead specimens, and everyone would probably admit that the study of native languages is of paramount importance'. He brings in, as he says, 'even Delbrück' in support of the view that 'a finer analysis of given linguistic phenomena could be achieved on living languages only' (1920, 71).

Sweet, in his Presidential Address to the Philological Society of Great Britain in 1887, pointed out the special English interest in the observation of the phenomena of living languages:[7]

> Our tendency is not so much toward the antiquarian philology and text-criticism in which German scholars have done so much, as towards the observation *of the phenomena of living languages* . . . the real strength and originality of English work lies . . . in phonology and dialectology. Our aim ought clearly to be, while assimilating the methods and results of German work, to concentrate our energies mainly on what may be called 'living philology'. The vastness of our Empire, which brings us in contact with innumerable languages, alone forces us incessantly to grapple with the difficulties of spoken, often also unwritten, languages. We ought to be able to send out yearly hundreds of thoroughly and specially trained young men.

As I have pointed out earlier, Malinowski in a sense joined this especially English trend and was unaware of the developments in the United States, as he says himself (1920, 72, n. 1).[8]

While emphasizing by example and precept the importance of general linguistics in theory and practice, Malinowski clearly appreciated the value and importance of comparative and historical studies and goes out of his way to notice them. Furthermore, he points out that:

> So-called functionalism is not, and cannot be, opposed to the historical approach but is indeed its necessary complement. The functional method, if I understand it rightly, is interested primarily in the processes of culture as an explanation of its products. It introduces thus the time element, at first on a smaller scale, but

none the less in the real historical sense. I myself have advocated the biographical approach in the study of kinship. In my work on language, I have attempted to show that the study of meaning should start with observations on infant speech and the growth of linguistic expression within the context of culture. In the study of law, I have tried to point out that the consideration of transactions in the long run, as the extensive and enduring balancing of interests, is the only way to understand primitive jurisprudence. The context of time as well as the context of culture essential to the functional approach are, on the one hand, historical concepts, and, on the other, they lead to the formulation of general laws of process so necessary to any reconstructive work. Here again, therefore, I do not see that functionalism and historical reconstructions stand in antithesis. I agree with Professor Kroeber that 'basically a functional approach is rather close to the historical approach'.   (1939, 43)

This view accords with my own approach which emphasizes the mutually complementary nature of historical and descriptive studies in linguistics though I am inclined to the opinion that the development of descriptive linguistics on a large scale is an essential preliminary for the reformulation of problems in comparative and historical work. This could only be the case if, as I have frequently emphasized, linguistics recognizes that its principal objective is the study of meaning in its own terms (Firth, 1950, 8–14; 1951a, 82–4; 1951b, 118).

Malinowski's functionalism extended to language, as is clear from his Supplement to *Meaning of meaning*: 'The lack of a clear and precise view of Linguistic function[9] and of the nature of Meaning has been, I believe, the cause of the relative sterility of much otherwise excellent linguistic theorizing' (1923, 471).

By no stretch of imagination could he be described as a 'structuralist', nor would I, myself, accept the appellation, if it be narrowly interpreted to require adherence to basic phonemic 'structures' or with 'alterations' in 'sub-structures' and 'super-structures', the main reason being that 'the structure of all this linguistic material is inextricably mixed up with, and dependent upon, the course of the activity in which the utterances are embedded' (1923, 473). He gets nearer the structural approach— which I distinguish from 'a structuralist approach'—in Section VI of the Supplement (1923, 495) in which he faces the problem of the structure of language:

Every human tongue has a definite structure of its own. . . . This

10

body of structural rules with their exceptions and irregularities, the various classes into which the elements of the language can be ranged, is what we call 'the grammatical structure' of a language.

It is not easy to assess his contribution to linguistic analysis as understood today because his language material is closely wedded to his ethnographic work. Yet there are, throughout his work, indications that he appreciated the bearing of function and structure in linguistics. In approaching his study of the classificatory particles in Kiriwina, he indicated his awareness of

> the general features of linguistic structure, rules of syntax, parts of speech and word formation. Everybody agrees that in an ethnographic work these should be recorded, that all essential linguistic facts should be collected. But all collection of facts requires the guidance of definite theoretical principles.   (1920, 34)

Again, in his concluding paragraphs, he reiterates what seems almost like a wish unfulfilled—the need for a theory:

> We need a Theory, devised for the purpose of observation of linguistic fact. This theory would give a recast of grammatical definitions, based on an analysis of meaning. It would analyse the nature of syntax, parts of speech, and formation of words, and besides giving adequate and plastic definitions would open up vistas of problems and thus guide research.   (1920, 78)

And here, I cannot refrain from repeating a favourite quotation from Goethe: 'Das Höchste wäre zu begreifen, das alles Faktische schon Theorie ist.'

It is clear that Malinowski contributed very little towards such a theory for the statement of linguistic facts in terms of phonetics, phonology, the various branches of grammar or stylistics. This we shall appreciate by a close study of his linguistic work following the indications here given. His main interest, as he indicates in his Supplement, was in the problem of meaning, and such theory as he developed arose from his study of primitive societies. The key concept of the semantic theory he found most useful for his work on native languages was the notion of *context of situation*. He read widely in linguistics,[10] always looking for the kind of theory which could find a place and prove useful in his ethnographical work. He was always eager to discuss theoretical questions with linguists of his acquaintance, as I well know from personal experience. It is no accident that both he and Sir Alan Gardiner acknowledge their indebtedness to Dr Philipp Wegener. In dedicating his book *The theory of speech and language* to Wegener, Gardiner (1932) calls him 'a pioneer of linguistic theory'.

Malinowski and Gardiner[11] both make great use of the situation theory, and I, too, have developed its application in descriptive linguistics, though in a more abstract and general form as one of several levels in linguistic analysis, all of which should be congruent.[12] In Wegener's original work (1885), the concept of the situation is related to his distinctions between the logical and grammatical subject and predicate, and there is much which has to be abandoned. Nevertheless, a good deal survives which has, with modifications, been incorporated into subsequent work by later theorists.

Wegener's theory requires three types of situation: (a) die Situation der Anschauung; (b) die Situation der Erinnerung; (c) die Situation des Bewusstseins (1885, 21–7).[13] He recognizes both speakers and hearers, objects and events as possible end-points in sets of relations set up to state the meaning of language. In other words, if language is studied in context of situation, mutual comprehension and co-operation is not by language only. Even using logico-grammatical terms, he would maintain that the predicate or the subject of a situational communication might be in the relevant objects and events of the situation. The situation is the basis, the environment for all the facts or data and we see the effective process of speaking and listening therein displayed. The presence of the persons and relevant objects, he regarded as providing essential environmental relations which may be thought of within the three sub-situations above mentioned. First, the objective situation as presented and observed; second, the immediately associated memorial elements or the factor of retentiveness; and, thirdly, the situation of the whole state of mind (with special reference to the consciousness of self or of personal identity in all participants) in which the content of the specific language finds its meaning completed.

In some respects, this analysis has links with my own point of view though I do not require his trinity of situations, nor do I wish to introduce a reference to retentiveness nor to consciousness of self or of personal identity. A serious confusion of the analysis of the context of situation with the other levels of analysis such as the grammatical level has been one of the main weaknesses of early attempts to relate statements of meaning to other social and psychological factors. Nevertheless I place a high value on Wegener's realization that the context of situation provided a valid configuration of elements comprising persons, objects, non-verbal events as well as language between which significant relations obtained, thus constituting a set of functions as a whole.

This reshaping of the most interesting features of Wegener's theory, if related to other levels of linguistic analysis in terms of interior relations, would accord with the practice of a number of present-day linguists in this country. It should be borne in mind, however, that Malinowski and others who have used the situation approach did not grasp the full theoretical implications of Wegener's hints, though he has been frequently quoted.[14]

A general theory such as this must include similar approaches in other branches of linguistic analysis. Naturally, the sentence and syntactical analysis finds a central place. Even the origins of all speech, considered biographically in the nurture of the young and in the history of the race, are to be found in sentences: 'Alle Sprachelemente sind ursprünglich Sätze' (Wegener, 1885, 181). It is not surprising that Wegener pays special attention to imperatives, interrogatives, demonstratives and pronouns. No wonder Malinowski found all this attractive in his search for concepts likely to assist him in developing a technique for the elucidation of ethnographic texts. He had found similar notions in the work of Sir Richard Temple.

Ranging himself with the primitive man's pragmatic outlook and regarding language as a mode of action rather than as a counter-sign of thought (1923, 459, 479), Malinowski selected for notice only such features of his languages as were essentially bound up with his contexts of situation in trading, fishing (1923, 474), gardening and similar pursuits. There, he noticed direct indications of these activities, references to the surroundings, words of command, words correlated with action (1923, 473), the expressions of feeling and passion bound up with behaviour, many of them stereotyped in form, such as spells, chants and narratives.

It is language material of this kind which he presents throughout his ethnographic work with little or no development of formal description as understood by linguists. The linguistic treatment of ethnographic texts, from *Argonauts of the Western Pacfic* (1922) to *Coral gardens and their magic* (1935), is fundamentally the same though in *Coral gardens* we are given a 'full treatment' of the 'language of agriculture'.[15]

In substantiation of the above criticism of his linguistic technique, it is sufficient to notice his chapter on 'Words in magic' in the *Argonauts of the Western Pacific* (1922, 428–63).[16] In the course of this chapter, he makes repeated use of the expression 'linguistic anlaysis' (428, 433, 442, 459) with reference to his ethnographic texts, but it must be pointed out that the expression as used by linguists refers to highly abstract analyses of a given language—usually a restricted language—at the phonological level, at various grammatical levels and in the summary entries of dictionaries. Malinowski fully realized his short-comings in linguistic analysis, as we now understand it, and said so explicitly: 'The analysis to which I now proceed can be given only in an approximate manner, for, in a full one, a long disquisition on grammar would have to be given first' (1922, 433). He never managed to realize what may have been his secret ambition—a technique of analysis satisfying the demands of linguistic science.

The main features of his textual method can be summarized as follows: having placed the text functionally, from the sociological point of view, let us say, as a particular kind of spell tabulated in his systematic magic, linguistic statements of 'meaning' are to be made—first, by an interlinear word-for-word translation, sometimes described as a 'literal' or 'verbal' translation, 'each expression and formative affix being rendered by its English equivalent', secondly, a free translation in what might be described as 'running English', thirdly, by the collation of the interlinear and free translations, leading, fourthly, to the detailed commentary, or 'the contextual specification of meaning'.

The commentary relates the free translation to the verbal translation and deals with the 'equivalents' and adds phonetic and grammatical notes.

First, then, he no doubt intended really to suggest *an* English equivalent for ethnographic purposes. When I was associated with Malinowski in his Linguistics Seminar in the early 1930s, he often referred to this word-for-word translation method, and even employed the expression 'fixed term equivalent' [17] for the English counters that he placed against the elements of native texts. He states as his fundamental principle that for each native word we adopt one English 'fixed meaning'. Unfortunately, in this connection, he reverts to notions characteristic of early work by such etymologists as Skeat, and makes an attempt to establish what he calls the 'primary meaning' [18] of a word, numbering derived meanings in the text. But he found that it was not 'always feasible or convenient to use primary meanings as the fixed equivalent'.

In my opinion, the concept of primary and derived meanings must be abandoned, and even in Malinowski's work it served no useful purpose. I well remember discussing with him the primary meaning of the word 'ass' in familiar, colloquial English. To bring in the animal, we had to place the word in another 'language'. Such difficulties are met by applying the concept of meaning by collocation, which I have dealt with elsewhere (Firth, 1951*b*; see also Mitchell, 1952 and 1953). The word 'ass' in colloquial English is usually collocated with expressions of personal reference and address and the plural is not very common.

Moreover, 'fixed term equivalents' or counters are of doubtful value in the structure as I define it, that is to say, taken together in sentences and longer pieces.[19] The notion of a fixed term equivalent, arbitrarily chosen to cover systems of words, is another matter. Systems of units or terms, set up by the linguist, provide sets of interior relations by means of which their values are mutually determined. In order to have validity, such systems must be exhaustive and closed, so far as the particular state of the language, suitably restricted, is under description.

Malinowski's lists are rich in information and testify to the excellence of his field-work. But, as he says himself, not all of his lists are exhaustive and the reader is left to judge for himself (1935, II, 5). There is one example, however, of what a linguist would accept as a system to be found in his treatment of the six[20] Trobriand words for 'garden'. That they can be regarded as a lexical system on the evidence supplied is clear from his own statement that they 'are defined by placing them within a series of terms with mutually exclusive uses' (1935, II, 16).

We now turn from the verbal translation to what Malinowski calls a 'free translation' (1922, 457):

> Comparing the free translation with the literal one, it is easy to see that certain additions have been made, sentences have been subordinated and co-ordinated by various English conjunctions which are either completely absent from the native text, or else represented by such very vague particles as *boge* (already) and *m'tage* (indeed).
>
> (1922, 458)

Occasionally, the comparison of the interlinear version with the free translation is held to be sufficient. Indeed, a great deal of the method of statement depends upon this double-entry procedure in giving what is nowadays technically described as the 'translation meaning'.[21]

Throughout his work, he uses the double translation method of stating 'meaning'. He was in the habit of accumulating large numbers of texts and he even uses the method in dealing with native definitions provided by informants.[22]

The third and fourth features of his textual method, namely, the

collation of the interlinear and free translations, must be considered
together, since what is called 'the contextual specification of meaning'
(1935, II, 37) is with reference to the text (and not the situation) and
to the two translations requiring a full miscellaneous commentary.

In doing this, a great many words 'have to be reinterpreted when
we pass from the interlineal word-for-word rendering to the free translation'. He claims that this transition is not arbitrary and that his
commentaries on the texts illustrate definite principles. In the *Argonauts
of the Western Pacific* (1922, 457) he makes the astonishing claim
that 'the verbal translation renders word for word the individual meaning of every particle and root, according to a definite grammatical and
lexicographical scheme which has been adopted for this text in common
with a few hundred more'.[23] In spite of the above statement, he confesses that he had not made any distinction in the verbal translation
between the inclusive and exclusive first person, dual and plural. It is
difficult to imagine the definite grammatical and lexicographical scheme,
presumably expressed in the translation, and not easy to agree that the
opening sentences of the formula given (1922, 440) 'are so clear that
the translation word for word explains itself without any closer commentary'. Malinowski's notion of 'translation' extends to his whole
method of

> *defining a term by ethnographic analysis*, that is, by placing it within
> its context of culture, by putting it within the set of kindred and
> cognate expressions, by contrasting it with its opposites, by gram-
> matical analysis and above all by a number of well-chosen examples
> —such translation is feasible and is the only correct way of defining
> the linguistic and cultural character of a word.   (1935, II, 17)

He did, however, deal explicitly with 'the translation of untranslatable
words' (1935, II, 11).

'The contextual specification of meaning' includes phonetic, grammatical and lexical observations, many of which are of doubtful value
and would not be technically recognized as useful in descriptive linguistics today. To say that the real difficulty of the Trobriand language is
'not in the complexity of the grammatical apparatus but rather in its
extreme simplicity' may be an amusing paradox, but it fails to satisfy
the sophisticated reader, and we get very little further when we are told
that:

> Its structure is on the whole what might be described as telegraphic;
> the relation of the words, as well as the relation of the sentences,

has mainly to be derived from the context. In many cases the subject remains unmentioned, is represented merely by a verbal pronoun and has to be gathered from the situation.

(1935, II, 36)

Grammar is concerned with the interrelation of categories, not of the words as such, and cannot be derived from any context other than that of grammatical analysis. In referring to the subject of the situation, Malinowski goes back again to Wegener.[24]

Most linguists would regard his grammatical treatment of texts (1935, II, 30–7) as unsatisfactory. To begin with, most of the grammar is notional, of the traditional pattern. We find for instance that 'this sound *b* changes the character of the verb'. He connects it with what he calls the 'future tense' but 'very roughly' and adds that it 'conveys the idea of potentiality, past, present or future; or at times it is simply emphatic'. The confusion of all levels of analysis is well exemplified in his summary sentence: 'As a fixed meaning distinguishing verbs thus modified by the potential *b* I have chosen the English auxiliary verb "might"' (1935, II, 31). Levels are again confused and vagueness reigns supreme in the following:

> This sound imparts a tinge of definiteness; at times it places the action into a regular past, accomplished state; at times it only gives emphasis. On the whole it is best to regard it as an implement of definiteness and accomplishment. The letter *l* I have rendered by the fixed meaning 'did', *luku-gis*, 'thou didst see'.   (1935, II, 32)

Traditional grammatical categories are obviously accepted as universals as is shown by his remarks (a) that the distinction between the transitive and intransitive verbs is not easy to make, and (b) that the passive does not exist. He is much better on the classificatory particles, to which he gave special attention in an article previously quoted, and in his introductory note to Part v[25] of *Coral gardens* he specifically refers those grammatically interested to this article (1935, II, 78). He did not develop any precise forms of lexical entry, but attempted more or less systematic glossaries (1935, II, 115, 150–5).[26]

He appears to be acutely conscious of his shortcomings in phonetics as a basis for what he calls his transliterations of the texts—they are certainly not phonetic transcriptions—and confesses that his phonetic distinctions probably do not go as far as they ought to, and he very often finds in his notes two or three transliterations of what he calls 'the same word'. He dismisses the difficulty by saying that perhaps phonetics carried too far is unprofitable. However, he appreciated the need to connect sound of the language in some way with what he regarded as meaning but had no technique of analysis at his command nor language of statement. He had to be content with such observations as 'alliterative symmetry so dear to Kiriwinian magic'; 'a heavy thumping rhythm indicated by sharp and circumflex accents'; 'the manner of reciting these parts is more perfunctory, with fewer melodic modulations and phonetic peculiarities'; 'this phonetically very expressive word is used with very great sound effect'; 'this sentence, giving the vowels a full Italian value, such as they receive in the Melanesian pronunciation, does certainly have an impressive ring' (1922, 441, 444, 447, 450).

The abundance of the linguistic materials would justify revision in the field by a linguist since, as Malinowski says, 'belief in the efficiency of a formula, results in various peculiarities of the language in which it is couched, both as regards meaning and sound' (1922, 451). It would be of considerable linguistic interest to know more of the 'effects of rhythm, alliteration and rhyme, often heightened and accentuated by actual vocal accent' (1922, 452; 1929, 304).

The use of synoptic tables in presenting at a glance the consecutive progress of work and magic as inseparables, is a useful example of the ethnographic method of analysis and justifies the expression 'systematic magic' with its formulae, rites and spells (1922, 414 ff.).

As I have already pointed out (p. 148, n. 15), Malinowski was fully aware that as his work became better known, it was easier for him to expand his linguistic documentation to great lengths. But he was also apparently conscious of the possible danger of his ethnographic apparatus becoming too obvious and wished to get beyond the field-worker's notebook (1935, II, 45).

A critical appreciation of his contribution to linguistics may be summarized under the following four heads:

1. General theory, especially his use of the concepts of context of situation and of types of speech function (1935, II, 53; 1923, 475–7).
2. The statement of the meaning of a word by definition with reference to culture context.
3. The statement of meaning by translation.
4. The relations of (i) language and culture; and (ii) linguistics and anthropology.

1. As we have seen, the situational approach in linguistic theory can

be regarded as beginning with Wegener's work (1885), which has the merit of general theoretical abstraction with no trace of 'realism'. My own development of the situational approach has been of this kind.

In the work of Gardiner[27] and Malinowski there are distinct traces of the realist approach, which is in strange contradiction, in Malinowski's case, to his repeated insistence on the need for theory. He seems to imagine that there is such a thing as the 'existence' of the brute 'fact', independent of and prior to any statement of fact. 'To us', he says, 'the real linguistic fact is the full utterance within its context of situation.' There is belief in the 'concrete situation', the 'situation of action' in which the utterance is 'directly embedded' and he even used the phrase 'environmental reality' (Malinowski, 1935, II, 57). The word 'utterance' seems to have had an almost hypnotic suggestion of 'reality' which often misleads him into the dangerous confusion of a theoretical construct with items of experience. The factors or elements of a situation, including the text, are abstractions from experience and are not in any sense embedded in it, except perhaps in an applied scientific sense, in renewal of connection with it. In one place, however, he seems to have realized that if a sound film could be taken of a Trobriand gardening activity, so that the 'visual part of it would be self-explanatory', 'the accompanying sounds would remain completely incomprehensible' and would have to be explained by a long and laborious linguistic analysis (1935, II, 10, 26).

It was perhaps in order to avoid giving 'a disproportionate amount of space and attention' (1935, II, 10) to language that he adopted the not altogether satisfactory methods we have just reviewed.

In my own work, I first turned to the context of situation in 1930[28] and, more recently, have held to the view that the context of situation and the notion of types of speech function are best used as schematic constructs to be applied to language events and that they are merely a group of related categories at a different level from grammatical categories but of the same abstract nature. The linguist sets up interior relations[29] of three main kinds:

(a) the interior relations of elements of structure, words and other bits and pieces of the text;
(b) the interior relations of systems set up to give values to elements of structure and the bits and pieces;
(c) the interior relations of contexts of situation.

The interior relations of the context of situation may be summarized as follows (see Firth, 1950, 7):

1. The relevant features of participants: persons, personalities.
   (a) The verbal action of the participants.
   (b) The non-verbal action of the participants.
2. The relevant objects.
3. The effect of the verbal action.

The situational approach, I believe, requires also the classification of types of speech function, in which Malinowski pioneered the way in his Supplement[30] and in *Coral gardens and their magic*.[31]

A great deal of the linguistic work we have noticed deals with studies of the magical word in the sociological sense; but language can be regarded as magic in the most general sense. Malinowski's treatment suggests many possibilities of research for all students of words in action. It was perhaps this magic which led him to regard speech in infancy and childhood as sources of magical meaning for all of us (1935, II, 62). The creative functions of language which he always emphasized are indeed miraculous.

These aspects of his general theory, which were first sketched in the Supplement, are more clearly stated in *Coral gardens*[32] and are his weightiest contributions in the sociological approach to the statement of meaning.

He pointed out the 'richest field of modern verbal magic'—advertisements—and his amusing parallel of Trobriand beauty magic and the advertisements of Helena Rubinstein and Elizabeth Arden he commends to any young anthropologist interested in modern as well as primitive savagery. He concludes this interlude in a light vein with the remark: 'In my opinion, the study of modern linguistic uses side by side with those of the magic of simple peoples would bring high rewards.'[33]

2. His attitude to words as such is curiously unsatisfactory when we remember his concern with institutions[34] and customs. There is no doubt that, in literate societies such as our own, words and other elements of language are institutionalized, and statements about them in dictionaries and even in common talk are treated with a respect felt to be due to some sort of authority. He says, for instance, that words do not exist in isolation and adds that they 'have no independent existence in the actual reality of speech' (1935, II, 23). The descriptive linguist does not work in the universe of discourse concerned with 'reality' or what is 'real', and is not concerned with the ontological question

of whether his isolates can be said to 'have an existence' or 'to exist'. It is clear that one cannot deal with any form of language and its use without assuming institutions and customs. It has long been a commonplace of linguistics, as Malinowski himself says (1935, II, 22), that the sentence and not the word is its main concern, but it is not the lowest unit of language, nor is it a 'self-contained or self-sufficient unit'. Let us again emphasize that 'facts' do not 'exist', they are *stated*, and it may indeed be a better guide to the handling of facts to regard them as 'myths' in which we believe, and which we have to live with.

I should agree that 'the figment of a dictionary is as dangerous theoretically as it is useful practically' and, further, that the form in which most dictionaries are cast, whether unilingual or bilingual, is approaching obsolescence, partly on account of the arbitrariness of the definitions and preoccupation with the historical value of the citations. In his method of definition (see above, pp. 138–9), Malinowski makes some approach, though rather vaguely it is true, to the tendencies in modern linguistics to use contextual definitions and make statements of meaning at a series of levels. He does, however, pay great attention to systems of words having mutually exclusive uses in a given field of application— for example, the six words for 'garden' in Kiriwina. He fully appreciates what we might describe in technical linguistic terms as 'distinctive meaning' (see below, p. 165, n. 36). Throughout his work he is at great pains to describe in English sociologically important distinctions in use (see 1929a, 58, 388, 422).

Perhaps the most interesting full-length commentary on the use of a common word is to be found in his *Freedom and civilization*, which is an analysis of the 'multiple meanings' of 'freedom in its universe of semantic chaos'. The whole work he himself describes as the semantics of freedom, and his treatment I find not only more sophisticated but more stimulating than similar general semantic studies which have appeared in the United States. Two remarks in this work are of central importance: first, 'all mental states which are postulated as occurrences within the private consciousness of man are thus outside the realm of science' (1947, 84); and secondly, 'we have completely to throw overboard any meek acquiescence in dictionary meanings, in the dictates of epigram, metaphor and linguistic vagary. We have often stressed that in science we must run counter to linguistic usage. This is even more important in social science than in the study of matter or organism' (1947, 80).

There are signs that in this work his general theory had so developed as to make consideration of primary meaning and fixed equivalents obsolete. While recognizing, as a social fact, that most people do take up attitudes towards words, he sounds the very necessary warning that the 'physicist does not inquire through universal suffrage or a Gallup Poll what the meanings of his concepts are' (1947, 81).[35] We know how obsessive is the desire to define the 'core of meaning' (1947, 68) of such a word as 'freedom'. His final decision is a 'complete rejection of this core of meaning'. At the same time, as we have already pointed out, he recognizes the influence of such beliefs on human behaviour. In science, however, as he rightly warns us, we are to beware of the tendency to reify and hypostatize such general words as representing valid general concepts (1947, 77). Such words are often conceived anthropomorphically. In the language of description in linguistics, we refer chiefly to structures, systems and relations. Our task is observation, analysis, synthesis and renewal of connection. Words such as 'freedom' and 'law' he regards—in accordance with sound tradition in linguistics —as polysemic and the words themselves as summaries of homonyms and homophones.

3. Whatever shortcomings we may find in Malinowski's analysis of texts, we must concede his realization of the central importance of the statement of meaning by what may be termed 'systematic transla-tion'. He presents in his synoptic tables the consecutive progress of work and linguistic magic as inseparables (see above, p. 153). His state-ments by double translation with commentary bring into the focus of attention the whole question of what may be called 'translation mean-ing'[36] in linguistics.

Comparative linguists have perhaps not fully realized the technical implications of the translation meanings by means of which they identify words, let us say, by employing in English such translation equivalents as 'horse', 'sheep', 'father', etc. Translation meanings as identification names require careful consideration in all descriptive work. Translation meanings consisting of pieces of phrases in analytical languages, set against words in other types of languages, are all too often carelessly conceived and often quite haphazard in application. But translation meanings, however systematic, do not in themselves constitute linguistic analysis.

It is perhaps useful in this connection, to apply the two words 'use' and 'mention' to our procedures. A distinction must always be main-tained, even in unilingual descriptions, between the word, piece or sentence in *use* and a reference to these by using the same words as autonyms in *mention*. What Malinowski calls an equivalent, especially in such cases as the six Kiriwinian names for 'garden' (see above, p. 150), should be specifically noted as such, so that the translation meaning does not masquerade as analysis, but serves its identification function in linguistic description. It is in no sense to be regarded as a sociological equivalent.

This leads me to the triple distinction of (a) language under description, (b) the language of description and (c) the language of translation. The language of translation subdivides into word-translation meanings, and translation meanings offered as a means of identifying longer pieces or as names for other native categories supplied by informants. What Malinowski calls free translation, though it may be regarded as contributing to the general statement of meaning, might be referred to simply as 'translation' to distinguish it from the more formal apparatus which we have referred to as systematic translation meanings. The rest of the language of description, being both technical and general, may incorporate translation meanings and translations as part of the description, alongside the necessary technical nomenclature and phraseology of the statement of the analysis proper.

4. The subject of this essay, 'Ethnographic analysis and language', which arises from the consideration of Malinowski's work between 1915 and his death in the United States of America in 1942, has been very much on the agenda of anthropologists and linguists among others in recent years. In 1951, a Commission was set up by the International Council for Philosophy and Humanistic Studies of Unesco, of which I am a member, to promote a number of linguistic investigations to serve as the basis for an examination of the relationships between language and the other aspects of culture, undertaken by linguists, cultural anthropologists and philosophers (Firth, 1951a). May I repeat Malinowski's warning in this connection:

> But there is nothing more dangerous than to imagine that language is a process running parallel and exactly corresponding to mental process, and that the function of language is to reflect or to duplicate the mental reality of man in a secondary flow of verbal equivalents.
>
> (1935, II, 7)

In 1953, the results of a Conference of anthropologists and linguists were published as a Supplement to the *International journal of American linguistics*. This has been previously referred to. Although the Conference did not actually face the problems stated by Lévi-Strauss (1953), his clear summary of the position should be noted. He distinguished the relations between (1) *a* language and *a* culture; (2) language and culture; (3) linguistics as a scientific discipline and anthropology. He also remarked on something I have often experienced myself, namely, the dangers which beset scholars of different disciplines when they meet to discuss what they consider to be common problems, often employing similar language. In recent conferences on communication theory, scientists and humanists have imagined that, when they employ the same words, they mean the same things. A far more healthy state of affairs was indicated by my namesake, Raymond Firth, when he remarked, in a humorous vein at a meeting in which we both took part, that the audience should not allow themselves to be confused by the identity of the patronymic but should remember that though we were colleagues working in similar fields, neither of us really knew, in any technical sense, what the other fellow was talking about. Lévi-Strauss expressed it as his belief that one of the main teachings of the Conference was that whenever they tried to express linguistic problems and culture problems in the same language, the situation became tremendously complicated and they would always have to keep this in mind (1953, 3).

If it be admitted that linguistics is a social science of some sort, it is certainly true that it is ahead of the others in theoretical formulation and technique of statement. The coming together of anthropologists and linguists in recent conferences may have the highly desirable effect of, first, convincing anthropologists that they need to look not only to their theories but also to their technical language of statement, including systematic nomenclature, and secondly, to demonstrate to the linguists that they are concerned with the statement of meaning in linguistic terms and that 'linguistics limited to the signal factor' was a 'necessary but fragmentary stage' (1953, 59). As Lotz remarks, linguists should not feel so pessimistic about statements of meaning in linguistics.

In a paper at the same Conference, Roman Jakobson, summing up his impressions of the Conference, declared, 'One of the most symptomatic features of this Conference was that we lengthily and passionately discussed the questions of meaning', and concluded, 'Thus, meaning remains a No Man's land. This game of Give-away must end. For years and decades we have fought for the annexation of speech-sounds to linguistics, and thereby established phonemics. Now we face a second front—the task of incorporating linguistic meaning into the science of language' (1953, 19, 21).

It is my personal opinion that linguistics is suffering from a surfeit of phonemics and that our energies must turn to the second front. As we have seen in our review of the work of Malinowski, approaches to the problem in Great Britain go back over three-quarters of a century. In my own work, associated with my colleagues in London, I have indicated a strictly formal study of meaning at all levels, in linguistic terms, without poaching either on the sciences of the mind or of society.

It is of considerable interest, therefore, to notice the published results of still another Conference in the United States on the interrelations of language and other aspects of culture. Even Hockett, who places semantics outside linguistics as he understands it, finds it possible to say that ethnography without linguistics is blind: linguistics without ethnography is sterile (1954, 225). From my own point of view, I should move a drastic amendment to the last phrase and say that linguistics without 'meaning' is sterile. I do, however, find myself in agreement with Hockett that 'it had better be the linguists who work on this systematic end of semantics' (1954, 250).

I should like to suggest once more that linguistics at all levels of analysis is concerned with meaningful human behaviour in society and that the structures and systems and other sets of abstractions set up enable congruent statements of meaning to be made in exclusively linguistic terms.

Let us now turn to Malinowski in this connection. His approach, as one might expect, was practical and concerned itself with teaching. 'A close co-operation between linguistic teaching and anthropological training seems to me of the greatest importance' (1929b, 29). Even earlier, he had pleaded 'for a more intensive interest in linguistics on the part of the student of man, and at the same time for a study of language more thoroughly correlated with investigations on other aspects of human culture' (1927, 157). He encouraged the linguist in setting up his grammatical categories to look to other levels of linguistic analysis which would take note of the situation, including the personalities, institutions and customs:

A grammar of a primitive language cannot be fully stated without reference to further analysis.

The various pronouns of possession[37] in Melanesia, some modifications of verb and noun, are deeply correlated with the practice to which the language is put within its various cultural contacts, and to separate the study of language from the study of culture means merely a waste of time and an amateurishness in most aspects of the work. (1929b, 29)

I think it is a fair criticism to say that Malinowski's technical linguistic contribution consists of sporadic comments, immersed and perhaps lost in what is properly called his ethnographic analysis. As he says himself, 'I was able to incorporate a great deal of my linguistic information into the analysis of magical texts and into the ethnographic descriptions, so that not very much is left to purely linguistic commentary and etymological speculation' (1935, II, 170). There is a need to separate the two techniques of ethnographic and linguistic analysis and, at the same time, to correlate the results so that the trend towards a statement of meaning in linguistics shall be made clear at all levels. Linguistic analysis I reserve for statements about language data in terms of phonetics, phonology, grammar, stylistics, lexicography and textual analysis in a background of statements of collocation and of contexts of situation as I understand these terms.[38]

In conclusion it may surely be taken as a tribute to Malinowski that we have found it possible to discuss the wide subject of ethnographic analysis and language, still very much before us as the recent conferences show, largely in terms of his published work.

His outstanding contribution to linguistics was his approach in terms of his general theory of speech functions in contexts of situation, to the problem of meaning in exotic languages and even in our own.

Notes

1. It is of some interest to note that a copy of this work was presented by the author to the Library of the School of Oriental and African Studies on Malinowski's return to England and is one of many indications of his appreciation of the work of his British colleagues in exotic languages.
2. Malinowski's procedures and techniques with *informants* are fully described, and of high importance both in ethnographic and linguistic analysis. See especially: (1935) II, 5, 23–6, 84, 95, 100–1, 119–21, 127, 129, 135, 156–7, 158, 175, and (1922), 396, 398, 400, 409, 429, 433, 453–5, 483, 490–1.
3. cf. Wittgenstein (1953), 108, para. 337. 'An intention is embedded in its situation, in human customs and institutions. If the technique of the game of chess did not exist, I could not *intend* to play a game of chess. In so far as I do intend the construction of a sentence in advance, that is made possible by the fact that I can speak the language in question.' See also above, p. 138 and n. 1.

4. See Malinowski, 1920*b*, 55. The establishment of texts in living languages by the descriptive linguist may prepare the way for studies of such subjects as the degree of obsoleteness of words and grammatical forms. 'It is extremely astonishing that, although this is the only way of gaining an insight into the historical changes of a native language, and although historic change and evolution have been the main orientation of linguistics, yet, to my knowledge, very little attention has been paid to the degree of obsoleteness of words and grammatical forms.'

5. Eventually in Vol II of *Coral gardens and their magic* (1935), Malinowski stated what he there describes as an ethnographic theory of language.

6. cf. Firth, 1951*a*.

7. cf. Firth, 1951*a*, 218. 'In the session 1950–1 the School of Oriental and African Studies was able "*to send out*" seven "*thoroughly and specially trained young men*" whose whole task was "*the observation of the phenomena of living languages*" and both they and at least a score of others are "*concentrating their energies mainly on what may be called 'living philology'*". In America there is a similar history to report since the foundation of the American Philosophical Society [1838], the American Oriental Society [1842], and the Smithsonian Institution [1846]. Today there is the Linguistic Society of America which supports the annual Linguistic Institute; also the Linguistic Circle of New York, the *International journal of American linguistics*, and the Summer Institute of Linguistics for the training of missionaries for linguistic work in the mission fields of the world (see ***"Atlantic linguistics").'

8. 'There has been much, and as it seems excellent, work recently done on the American native languages, but with that I am completely unacquainted.' Present-day American linguists return the compliment by remaining unacquainted with Malinowski's contribution to the subjects of their concern.

9. In the same Supplement, Malinowski uses the expressions 'speech function', p. 476, 'linguistic uses', p. 474 (cf. Wittgenstein, 'Meaning is use'—see above, p. 138).

10. Malinowski, 1935, II, xi. 'Since I regard it as of the greatest importance always to stress the fact that only theoretical training enables us to see a sociological fact and to record and interpret it correctly, I should like to say that in no other branch of Anthropology has my reading been as extensive as in Linguistics.'

11. See Gardiner, 1932. For *Situation*, see pp. 49, 51, 194. Gardiner's book was published in 1932, nine years after Malinowski's Supplement in which the phrase 'context of situation' is first used. For his reference to Wegener's *Situationstheorie*, see pp. 60, 124, 127, and refer to the Index, where there are sixteen entries. Gardiner points out that his own terminology is different from Wegener's—so is his whole theory.

12. See Firth, 1935, 23, 33; 1950, 181–2; 1951*a* 225; 1951*b*, 192–6.

13. This philosophical use of the word *consciousness* in English really begins with Locke's *Essay concerning human understanding*. His French amanuensis and translator, M. Coste, found great difficulty in rendering Locke's thought in this connection. Wegener's use of *Erinnerung* and *Bewusstsein* is also traceable to Locke. Under the entry *Personality* in Dr Johnson's Dictionary, the following quotation from Locke is cited: 'This personality extends itself beyond present existence to what is past, only by consciousness, where it imputes to itself past actions just upon the same ground that it does the present.' See Firth, 1950.

14. Let Wegener speak for himself in the following extract from his work, pp. 21–3. 'Die Situation ist der Boden, die Umgebung, auf der eine Thatsache, eine Ding u. s. f. in die Erscheinung tritt, doch auch das zeitlich Vorausliegende, aus dem heraus eine Thätigkeit entsprungen ist, nemlich die Thätigkeit, welche wir als Prädicat aussagen, und ebenso gehört zur Situation die Angabe der Person, an welche die Mitteilung gerichtet ist. Die Situation wird bei der sprachlichen Mitteilung nicht blos durch Worte bestimmt, viel gewöhnlicher und ausgedehnter durch die umgebenden Verhältnisse selbst, durch die unmittelbar vorhergegangenen Thatsachen und die Gegenwart der Person, mit der wir sprechen. Die durch die umgebenden Verhältnisse und die Gegenwort der angeredeten Person gegebene Situation kommt uns durch die Anschauung zum Bewusstsein, wir nennen sie daher die Situation der Anschauung.

'Stehe ich mit Jemandem vor einem Baume, so genügt vollständig das Wort *Linde*, um zu sagen: *dieser Baum ist eine Linde*. Der vor uns stehende Baum bildet, auch unbenannt, das Subject des Satzes. Oder sage ich bei dieser Situation: *das ist eine Linde*, so erhält doch das Pronomen erst durch die gegenwärtige Anschauung seinen Inhalt.—Stelle ich Jemanden in einer Gesellschaft vor, so wäre es gradezu unpassend zu sagen: *dies ist Herr Müller*, ich weise nur mit der Hand auf ihn hin, um ihn von den übrigen anwesenden Personen zu unterscheiden und sage: *Herr Müller*. Die lebendige Anschauung, präcisiert durch den Gestus, ist die Situation und das Subject. Es ist klar, dass ein gegenwärtiges Anschauungsbild nicht so einfach ist, dass alle Teile desselben das Subject sein könnten, noch auch das gesammte Anschauungsbild. Neben jener Linde im Parke steht veilleicht auch eine Eiche, und vieles Andere ist sichtbar, die angeredete Person ja auch. Der Gestus und die Richtung der Augen geben Anhaltepunkte für die Ausscheidung eines Teiles aus dieser complicierten Masse, doch auch ohne diese Illustration bleibt ein derartiges Prädicat beziehbar. Ja, der Gestus selbst ist ja eine Thätigkeit, die Hand, der Arm, ein Finger wird dabei gezeigt, warum bezieht der Hörende das Prädicat nicht anf diese Teile der Anschauung? Es muss ein Schluss von dem Hörenden aus der Natur des Prädicats sowohl wie aus dem Inhalte der Anschauung gewonnen werden, um die Beziehung richtig zu machen. Ich deute hier diese Frage nur an über welche die zweite Abhandlung einigen Aufschluss geben soll.

'Setzt Jemand ein Glas Wein vom Munde und sagt: *vortrefflich!*, so zweifle ich keinen Augenblick, dass en den eben genossenen Wein so nennt; selbst wenn ich nur das leere Glas sehe, so ergänze ich den Ausruf zu dem Satze: *der Wein ist vortrefflich*. Also die Situation wird auch bestimmt durch vollendete Handlungen, die noch im Vordergrunde unseres Bewusstseins stehen. Und das zu denkende Subject ist nicht blos die gesammte Handlung, wie hier das Weintrinken, sondern ein Moment dieser Handlung, der Wein,—also auch hier liegt ein Schluss des Verstehenden vor, von dem später die Rede sein wird. Diese Situation wird passend genannt werden Situation der Erinnerung. . . . Hört der Jäger von *Löffeln*, so ist er wenigstens ebenso geneigt an die Ohren des Hasen zu denken, als an die Suppenlöffel bei Tisch, selbst wenn er einen solchen bei Tisch in der Hand hält. So hat der Militär seine besonderen Gruppen der grössten Associationsfähigkeit, andere der Jurist, andere der Seemann, andere der Philologe, andere der Geistliche u. s. f. Daher die hübsche Anecdote, welche Steinthal erzählt, dass ein Menschenkenner sich anheischig macht, aus den Antworten, welche verschiedene ihm unbekannte Personen auf eine Rätselfrage geben, ihren Stand zu bestimmen. Diese verschiedenen Interessenkreise haben daher ihre eigenen Ausdrucksweisen, die bekannten termini technici, welche ihren Inhalt aus der Situation des Bewusstseins, d. h. aus den fest gewordenen Interessen ergänzen, so *die Löffel*, *der Lauf* des Hasen, *der Schweiss* des Wildes, die vielen juristischen Termini und die grosse Menge der Handwerkerausdrücke; *testudo* bei den Römern kann die Schildkröte, das militärische Schilddach, die Leier sein.'

15. Malinowski, 1935, I, xi. 'For the first time I am able here fully to document my ethnographic contribution from the linguistic point of view. This is not due to the absence from my field notes of the same, or of a reasonably comparable quantity of texts, commentaries, sayings and terminologies to validate the statements which I have made in *Argonauts of the Western Pacific* or in *The sexual life of savages*, in my booklet on *Myth* or in *Crime and custom*. The reason is, that earlier in my career there would have been no chance of publishing as full a linguistic documentation as has become possible now, when the interest in the Trobrianders and in more detailed ethnographic accounts has on the whole increased. I trust that the theoretical parts of this book, the Introductions to the Linguistic supplement and to the Magical formulae (Parts IV and VI), will add to this interest and to the understanding that such full documentation is necessary, and that they will justify the methods here adopted.'

16. 'These three texts will be quite sufficient to give an idea of the method of dealing with linguistic evidence, and of the documentary value of immediately recorded native opinions.'

17. This notion he adheres to in *Coral gardens and their magic*, in which he formulates rules of interlinear translation. 'The fundamental principle here is that for each native word we adopt one English *fixed meaning*' (II, 28). My comment here is that such 'fixed meanings' are of value in stating systems but difficult to apply in interlinear translation. Such systems of differentiated words might be technically referred to as *distinctive meanings* in the relative sense of mutual exclusiveness.

18. cf. Malinowski, 1947, 86. 'Social science is still burdened with the superstition that words contain their meanings.'

19. My own theory of analysis requires that the terms 'structure' and 'system' be kept distinct in technical use. Structures are abstractions from utterances or parts of utterances recorded textually. Thus CVCVC and Noun-Verb-Noun might each constitute a structure specifically defined in a particular language, at the phonological and grammatical levels respectively. A *structure* is said to comprise *elements* or categories in mutual syntagmatic relation. At any given level of analysis closed systems of categories, units or terms are set up to give mutually determined values to the elements of structure. The terms of a *system*, or of a *sub-system* within it, *commute*, thus enabling account to be taken of the elements, constituents and features which are given order and place in structures. See my **'Synopsis of linguistic theory', also Robins, 1953, 109.

20. 1935, II, 15. 'For they really have no word corresponding to our general term "garden". Instead they have a series of words: *bagula, buyagu, tapopu, kaymata, kaymugwa, baleko*, each of which describes a certain type or kind, aspect or phase of "garden". But to "translate" any of these native terms by equating it to an English word would not merely be wrong, but impossible; or rather it would be impossible to find an English word exactly corresponding to any one of the native ones. Furthermore, to label the native term by even a combination of English words is at least misleading.'

21. 1935, II, 38. 'In any case, comparing the interlineal version with the free translation, the text becomes quite clear.'

22. 1922, 460–1. The 'two versions will give an inkling of how I was able to obtain from my native informants the definition of unknown and sometimes very involved expressions and how, in the act of doing it, I was given additional enlightenment on obscure details of belief and custom'. Further, on p. 463, he comments 'these three texts will be quite sufficient to give an idea of the method of dealing with linguistic evidence, and of the documentary value of immediately recorded native opinions'.

23. Leading American ethnographic linguists are still using this somewhat primitive method of so-called 'equivalents', confusing at least three levels of analysis, and mixing up translation with grammatical and collocational statements. 'A point by point morphemic transformation of kwteletiiwena = *advise-animate-reciprocal-inanimate thing-plural* = *laws*; hence, saawanwa kwteletiiwena = *Shawnee Laws*.' See Voegelin, Yegerlehner and Robinett, 1954, 32. Even Harris makes use of translation meanings, though not systematically. See Harris, 1951, 165–7, 182–4, 211, 213, 216–7, 223–4, 285–9, 339–44.

24. See above, p. 139, and pp. 147–8.

25. *Corpus inscriptionum agriculturae Quiriviniensis;* or 'The language of gardens'.

26. The following example is typical of the entries: '*kwanada:* yam growing in *odila*; eaten in *molu*'.

27. Gardiner, 1932, 49–52, 127 and especially 193 for the expression 'the present situation of the utterance'.

28. See Firth, 1930; 1950; 1937, Chapter X; 1951a, 83–4, 87.

29. See above, p. 150 and note 19.

30. 1923, see especially 476–7.

31. 1935, II, Part IV and Part VI, Division V.

32. 1935, see especially II, Part IV, Division I, 52–62, and Part VI, Division V, 236–7. Cf. 1929a, 296–7, 299.

33. 1935, II, 238. See also Harold Lasswell and Associates, 1949, in which quantitative methods are attempted in the study of key symbols, slogans and the *credenda* and *miranda* of politics.

34. See 1916, 428. 'If you examine the "broad masses" of a community, the women and children included, you will find that, whenever they grasp your questions, their answers will not vary.' See also 1935, II, 172. 'These three texts are a good example of how time after time one receives the same answer from different informants belonging to different communities. Perhaps unfortunately, I did not usually take down statements which I found merely duplicated information already noted.'

35. See also Voegelin, E., in which notice is taken of certain words of power as traditional language symbols evolved in the social process.

36. This has also been dealt with, though less satisfactorily, by American linguistics. See the Supplement to *IJAL* 19 (1953), *Results of the conference of anthropologists and linguists*, 58–9. Malinowski has covered in detail the three kinds of meaning for linguistics suggested by Professor A. A. Hill: (1) differential meaning (distinctive meaning); (2) translation meaning; (3) structural meaning. Such multiple, yet congruent, statements of meaning at different levels are characteristic of the approach of the London group of linguists. See also the examination of inferences from linguistic to non-linguistic data by Greenberg (1954, 13–4).

37. In the Bauan dialect of Fijian, for example, the following expressions may

serve as illustrations: (1) na nona *waqa*, 'his canoe'; (2) na mena *ti*, 'his tea'; (3) na *yava*-na, 'his foot'; (4) na mena *yaqona*, 'his kava'; (5) na kena *uvi*, 'his yam'. The noun bases are italicized.
38. See my **'Synopsis of linguistic theory'.

References

FIRTH, J. R. (1930). *Speech*, London.
FIRTH, J. R. (1935). *'Technique of semantics.'
FIRTH, J. R. (1937). *The tongues of men*, London.
FIRTH, J. R. (1946). *'The English school of phonetics.'
FIRTH, J. R. (1950). *'Personality and language in society.'
FIRTH, J. R. (1951a). *'General linguistics and descriptive grammar.'
FIRTH, J. R. (1951b). *'Modes of meaning.'
GARDINER, A. H. (1932). *The theory of speech and language*, Oxford.
GREENBERG, J. H. (1954). 'Concerning inferences from linguistic to non-linguistic data', *Language in culture* (see Hoijer, H.), 3–19.
HARRIS, Z. S. (1951). *Methods in structural linguistics*, Chicago.
HOCKETT, C. F. (1954a). 'Chinese versus English: An exploration of the Whorfian theses', *Language in culture* (see Hoijer, H.), 106–23.
HOCKETT, C. F. (1954b). 'The problem of the Whorf Hypothesis', *Language in culture* (see Hoijer, H.), 225.
HOIJER, H. (ed.). (1954). *Language in culture: Proceedings of a conference on the interrelations of language and other aspects of culture*, American Anthropological Association memoir 79. Menasha, Wis.
JACOBSON, R. (1953). Chapter Two in *Results of the Conference of anthropologists and linguists*, Supplement to *IJAL* 19 (Memoir 8), 11–21.
LASSWELL, H. and associates (1949). *The language of politics*. New York.
LÉVI-STRAUSS, C. (1953). Chapter One in *Results of the conference of anthropologists and linguists*. Supplement to *IJAL* 19 (Memoir 8), 1–10.
MALINOWSKI, B. (1913). Review of Durkheim, E., *Les formes élémentaires de la vie religieuse*, *Folk-lore* 24. 525–31, London.
MALINOWSKI, B. (1915). 'The natives of Mailu: Preliminary results of the Robert Mond research work in British New Guinea', *Transactions and proceedings of the Royal Society of South Australia* 39. 494–706, Adelaide.
MALINOWSKI, B. (1916). 'Baloma: Spirits of the dead in the Trobriand Islands', *Journal of the Royal Anthropological Institute* 46. 353–430. Reprinted 1948. London.
MALINOWSKI, B. (1920). 'Classificatory particles in the language of Kiriwina' *BSOAS* 1.33–78.
MALINOWSKI, B. (1922). *Argonauts of the Western Pacific*, Studies in Economics and Political Science, No. 65, London.
MALINOWSKI, B. (1923). 'The problem of meaning in primitive languages', *The meaning of meaning* by Ogden, C. K., and Richards, A. I. International library of psychology, philosophy and scientific method, 451–510, London.
MALINOWSKI B. (1927). Review of S. H. Ray, *A comparative study of the Melanesian Island languages*, *Man* 99.
MALINOWSKI, B. (1929a). *The sexual life of savages in North-western Melanesia*, London.
MALINOWSKI, B. (1929b). 'Practical anthropology', *Africa* 2. 23–39.
MALINOWSKI, B. (1935). *Coral Gardens and their magic*. London.

MALINOWSKI, B. (1939). 'The present state of studies in culture contact: some comments on an American approach', *Africa* 12. 27–47.

MALINOWSKI, B. (1947). *Freedom and civilization*, London.

MEILLET, A. (1926). *Linguistique historique et linguistique générale*, La Société de Linguistique de Paris, Paris.

MITCHELL, T. F. (1952). 'The active participle in an Arabic dialect of Cyrenaica', *BSOAS* 14.11–33.

MITCHELL, T. F. (1953). 'Particle-noun complexes in a Berber dialect', *BSOAS* 15.375–90.

ROBINS, R. H. (1953). 'Formal divisions in Sundanese', *TPS* 109–42.

TEMPLE, R. (1899a). 'A theory of universal grammar, as applied to savage languages', *The Indian antiquary* 28. 197–208, 225–35, Bombay.

TEMPLE, R. (1899b). 'The skeleton of a theory of universal grammar', *Journal of the Royal Asiatic Society* 597–604.

VOEGELIN, C. F., YEGERLEHNER, J. F. and ROBINETT, FLORENCE M. (1954). 'Shawnee laws: perceptual statements for the language and for the content', *Language in culture* (see Hoijer, H.), 32–46.

VOEGELIN, E. (1952). *The new science of politics*, Chicago.

WEGENER, P. (1885). *Untersuchungen über die Grundfragen des Sprachlebens*, Halle.

WITTGENSTEIN, L. (1953). *Philosophical investigations*, Oxford.

Eleven

A synopsis of linguistic theory, 1930–55†

'Das Höchste wäre zu begreifen, das alles Faktische schon Theorie ist.
GOETHE

I

The theory of general linguistics here presented in outline, has some of its roots in India[1] but it also has links with the laboratory of today. It is anticipated that the elements of the theory will be found consistently interrelated though the building-up process has been gradual during the last twenty-five years, and however idiosyncratic it may appear, owes much to constant collaboration with my colleagues at the School of Oriental and African Studies in the University of London, especially during the last seven years.

Though retrospective in genesis, the theory as a whole starts from the present situation, taking into account the amplitude of our empirical knowledge. Again it must be pointed out that the excessive use of method and procedures is avoided so that theoretical relevance may not be hidden or obscured. The passion for the accumulation of so-called 'facts', the piling-up of trivialities to be treated statically, perhaps with defective theoretical principles, are all too common symptoms among the 'scientistic technicians' multiplying in our midst. It is the view of the writer that linguistics must not be allowed to become more deeply engaged in methodology, but that a special effort is needed to keep it to theoretical order.

A theory derives its usefulness and validity from the aggregate of experience to which it must continually refer in renewal of connection.

---

† *Studies in linguistic analysis* (Special volume of the Philological Society, Oxford, 1957, 1–31).

'Under otherwise equal circumstances one will prefer that theory, which covers a larger field of phenomena, or which from some points of view appears to be simpler'—or as I should prefer—clearer. There is no doubt that 'intuition' or 'hunch' is the kind of 'common sense' that best serves the scientific theorist, but it has very little to do with the workaday common sense of our common sensual life. Dr James Conant[2] employs a very useful notion of *the degree of empiricism* to indicate the extent to which our knowledge can be expressed in broad conceptual terms. According to this view, science may be considered as an attempt either to lower the degree of empiricism or to extend the range of theory.

'Every scientific discipline must necessarily develop a special language adapted to its nature, and that development represents an essential part of scientific work.'[3] It is especially to be emphasized that 'the meaning of a technical term in the restricted language of a theory cannot be derived or guessed at from the meaning of the word in ordinary language. What in mechanics is called *force* or *work* can in no wise be derived from the meanings these words carry in everyday language'.

In the following exposition, such technical words in linguistic theory include the expressions *level or levels of analysis, context of situation, collocation* and *extended collocation, colligation, structure, system, element, unit, prosody,* and *prosodies,* to name a few of the pivotal terms. Moreover, these and other technical words are given their 'meaning' by the restricted language of the theory, and by applications of the theory in quoted works. 'Many people think that if they can define words they are being scientific, as though science were merely a warehouse of dictionary definitions.'[4] Where would mechanics be if we were to use as point of departure an explanation of what *motion* 'really is'?

In linguistics, as in other social sciences, we start with man's active participation in the world we are theorizing about. And we are all participants in those activities which linguistics sets out to study. Speaking and listening, writing and reading, are simply accepted as 'meaningful' in human life in society. In brief, linguistics accepts speech and language texts as related to the living of, and therefore to the 'meaning' of, life, and applies its theory and practice as far as it is able, to the statement of such 'meaning' in strictly linguistic terms—that is by employing the restricted language of linguistics[5] set in its own theoretical framework.[6]

In the most general terms, the approach may be described as monistic:

If we regard language as 'expressive' or 'communicative' we imply that it is an instrument of inner mental states. And as we know so little of inner mental states, even by the most careful introspection, the language problem becomes more mysterious the more we try to explain it by referring it to inner mental happenings that are not observable. By regarding words as acts, events, habits, we limit our inquiry to what is objective and observable in the group life of our fellows.[7]

As we know so little about mind and as our study is essentially social, I shall cease to respect the duality of mind and body, thought and word, and be satisfied with the whole man, thinking and acting as a whole, in association with his fellows. I do not therefore follow Ogden and Richards in regarding meaning as relations in a hidden mental process, but chiefly as situational relations in a context of situation and in that kind of language which disturbs the air and other people's ears, as modes of behaviour in relation to the other elements in the context of situation. A thoroughgoing contextual technique does not emphasize the relation between the terms of a historical process or of a mental process, but the interrelations of the terms—set up as constituents of the situation itself.[8]

A similar point of view had been put forward in 1930 in *Speech*[9] from which the following passages with minor alterations are quoted as relevant:

Ability to extract the fullest advantage from such properties of sound as propagation by refraction from heights—e.g. the tops of trees and rocks—even in high winds, and also by diffraction round and over obstacles and through openings, must have been of the greatest value in self-protection in the evolution of the race. Voice leaves the hands and eyes free, travels well, has characteristic quality conveying identity, and can become a characteristic function of a situation. Noises come to be used for concerted action, and then follows the confidence of group power. Perhaps those families in which the young quickly understood and responded to speech had the best chance. So that for the all-important family group, and later for other social groups, the successful use of speech, or systematic use of sound in relation to the sense of hearing, came to have a high survival value. Then came the descent from the trees. Liberated from the tyranny of smell, these animals walked upright with their arms free. They opened their eyes and, most important of all, opened their mouths. Their most important actions were systematic noises.

Nothing succeeds like success. Man became at once more social and more linguistic. In time 'words', 'signs', were made permanent, tangible, portable. And so language comes to function in specialized ways. Besides the word spoken, the word heard, the written word and the word which is seen, there is the word felt by the blind, signalled by the deaf-mute, the African talking drums and developments like the Morse code.[10]

The older conceptions of language as 'the expression of thought by means of speech sounds', or 'outward manifestations of inward workings of the mind', or 'expression for the sake of communication, thought made apprehensible', are based on a now somewhat discredited psycho-physical dualism, speech being only an external manifestation of inner psychical processes. The American behaviourist, Watson, on the contrary, says there is no such thing as thinking. There is only 'inner speech' or the incipient activity of laryngeal and other speech processes. A healthy conflict of views! Bertrand Russell in his *Outline of philosphy*, while not necessarily agreeing with Watson, realizes how little we really know about speech and language, and advocates a thoroughgoing behaviouristic method in linguistic research. 'I think myself', he adds, 'that "meaning" can only be understood if we treat language as a bodily habit.'[11]

This study of what people say and what they hear and in what contexts of situation and experience they do these things is properly the province of linguistics.[12]

One of the first to envisage the problem from the social point of view in the present century was Professor Bally, of Geneva, who wrote in 1913: 'The problem of linguistics of the future will be the experimental study of the social functioning of speech.'[13]

Again, in 1937,[14] the following sentences re-emphasize the essential basis in abstractions from total behaviour:

Let us begin by regarding man as inseparable from the world in which he lives. He is just part of it. He is not here primarily to think about it but to act suitably, which must be taken to include the ability to refrain from acting when the situation requires it. This

applies to man's most important social action, the disturbance of the
air and other people's ears by means of bodily utterance.

Your speech is not merely tongue-wagging, larynx-buzzing and
listening. It is much more the result of the brain doing its job as a
manager of muscle to keep you going in your situation. Similarly
it would be misleading to use the word 'listen' in describing the
function of the ears in everyday speech. We do not 'prick up' our
ears just to catch a few sounds. Our ears are actively interested in
what is going on.

In dealing with the voice of man we must not fall into the prevalent habit of separating it from the whole bodily behaviour of man
and regarding it merely as a sort of outward symbol of inward
private thoughts. Neither should we regard is as something apart
from what we all too readily call the outside world. The air we
talk and hear by, the air we breathe, is not to be regarded merely
as the outside air. It is inside air as well. We do not live just within
a bag of skin, but in a certain amount of what may be called living
space, which we continue to disturb with some success. And the
living space of man is pretty wide nowadays. Moreover, we never
really live in the present. In any situation in which we find ourselves
there is a hang-over of the past, and, as Sir Charles Sherrington
said, the 'shell of our immediate future surrounds our heads which
are fraught most with a germ of futurity!' In any situation, the
normal human being and his environment are one; the past merges
in the present in which the future is always on the point of being
born. To be really alive you must feel this active personal interest
in what is going on, and your speech must serve your natural
familiarity with your surroundings.

It will be obvious that such a philosophy has no particular use for
the traditional duality of mind and body, idea and word. The voice
of man is one component in a whole postural scheme, is part of a
process in some sort of situation. And in this sense a man speaks
with his whole body, and in particular with his breathing apparatus,
his body, muscles and his head ... The brain gives us a grip on
our world, and the world a grip on us. Sherrington regards the
brain as a manager of muscle, 'the restless world outside' giving it
the word go, caution or stop; it has great co-ordinating power
amounting to a sort of general vigilance. If our voices and written
words do not serve this mutual grip in some clearly demonstrable
way there is something wrong somewhere. Parrots and other talking

birds apparently manage some of the phonetics, but nothing of speech.[15]

The voice of man is dependent on the medium in which we have our being—the air . . . It is almost as if our postures and movements were determined by disturbance in the air, as those of fishes are in water. We balance our behaviour, so to speak, by give and take on the air.[16]

II

In dealing with language in the matrix of experience as the above approach requires, the actual language text duly recorded is in the focus of attention and two main sets of relations are set up, *firstly* the interior relations connected with the text itself. These sub-divide into (a) the syntagmatic relations between elements of structure considered at various levels, e.g. elements of grammatical structure in colligations, and phonological structure. In these structures, one recognizes the place and order of the categories. This, however, is very different from the successivity of bits and pieces in a unidirectional time sequence.[17] (b) The paradigmatic relations of terms or units which commute within systems set up to give values to the elements of structure. For example, a five-term vowel system giving possible values for V in the first syllable of a CV^5-CV^7-CCV^2 structure.

The second main set of situational relations again sub-divides into two: (a) the interior relations within the context of situation, the focal constituent for the linguist being the text. The text is seen in relation to the non-verbal constituents and the total effective or creative result noted. (b) Analytic relations set up between parts of the text (words or parts of words, and indeed, any 'bits' or 'pieces'),[18] and special constituents, items, objects, persons or events within the situation.

Relations are set up between the text and the other constituents of the situation, grouped and selected in attention as relevant. The linguist decides what is relevant and must be clear, in the light of his theory and practice, about what is on his agenda for the formulation of his statements of meaning in terms of linguistics.

The central proposal of the theory is

to split up meaning or function into a series of component functions. Each function will be defined as the use of some language form or element in relation to some context. Meaning, that is to say, is to be regarded as a complex of contextual relations, and phonetics, grammar, lexicography and semantics each handles its own components of the complex in its appropriate context.

'No semantics with morphology'—therefore, I must briefly sketch the technique for the description of the forms, and indicate what is meant by phonetic, morphological and syntactical functions, as component functions of the whole complex of functions which a linguistic form may have. Our knowledge is built up as the result of previous analysis. The study of the living voice of a man in action is a very big job indeed. In order to be able to handle it at all, we must split up the whole integrated behaviour pattern we call speech, and apply specialized techniques to the description and classification of these so-called elements of speech we detach by analysis.[19]

Even in historical semantics and certainly in lexicography

scholars have split up meaning into components or sets of relations in order to describe the facts.[20]

Throughout our review of the study of meaning we have seen how it has been split up and regarded as a relation or system of relations:[21]

We are accustomed to the subdivision of meaning or function. Meaning, then, we use for the whole complex of functions which a linguistic form may have. The principal components of this whole meaning are phonetic function, which I call a minor function, the major functions—lexical, morphological and syntactical (to be the province of a reformed system of grammar), and the function of a complete locution in the context of situation, or typical context of situation.[22]

Let us therefore apply the term linguistics to those disciplines and techniques which deal with institutionalized languages or dialects as such. A statement of the meaning of an isolate of any of these cannot be achieved at one fell swoop by one analysis at one level. Having made the first abstraction by suitably isolating a piece of 'text' or part of the social process of speaking for a listener or of writing for a reader, the suggested procedure for dealing with meaning is its dispersion into modes,[23] rather like the dispersion of light of mixed wave-lengths into a spectrum. First, there is the verbal process in the context of situation.[24] Social and personal commentary is especially relevant at this level. The technique of syntax is concerned with the word process in the sentence. Phonology states the phonematic and prosodic processes within the word and sentence, regarding them as a mode of meaning. The phonetician links all this with the processes and features of utterance.[25]

To make statements of meaning in terms of linguistics, we may accept the language event as a whole and then deal with it at various levels, sometimes in a descending order, beginning with social context and proceeding through syntax and vocabulary to phonology and even phonetics, and at other times in the opposite order, which will be adopted here since the main purpose is the exposition of linguistics as a discipline and technique for the statement of meanings without reference to such dualisms and dichotomies as word and idea, overt expressions and covert concepts, language and thought, subject and object. In doing this I must not be taken to exlude the concept of mind,[26] or to imply an embracing of materialism to avoid a foolish bogey of mentalism.[27]

Descriptive linguistics handles and states meaning by dispersing it in a range of techniques working at a series of levels.[28]

The above extracts are conveniently arranged to present the main principles of the theory, embracing a series of congruent analyses at a range of abstracted levels, which has been well tried since 1930. The use of the term *levels* in the phrase *levels of analysis* is not to be confused with other uses—for example, its use by Bloomfield in *Language*.

III

The basic assumption of the theory of analysis by levels is that any text can be regarded as a constituent of a *context of situation*[29] or of a series of such contexts, and thus attested in experience, since the categories of the abstract context of situation will comprise both verbal and non-verbal constituents and, in renewal of connection, should be related to an observable and justifiable grouped set of events in the run of experience.

The important thing to remember in this approach is the abstract nature of the context of situation as a group of categories, both verbal and non-verbal, which are considered as interrelated. Instances of such context of situation are attested by experience. The context of situation according to this theory is not merely a setting, background or 'backdrop' for the 'words'. The text in the focus of attention on renewal of connection with an instance is regarded as an integral part of the context, and is observed in relation to the other parts regarded as relevant in the statement of the context.

Malinowski[30] regarded the context of situation as a sort of behaviour matrix in which language had meaning, often a 'creative' meaning.[31] The context of situation in the present theory is a schematic construct for application especially to typical 'repetitive events' in the social process. It is also an insurance that a text is attested as common usage in which the occasional, individual and idiosyncratic features are not in the focus of attention.

Nonsense can, of course, be repetitive and referable to generalized context. Such nonsense language may be referred to literary, didactic or pedagogical context, treated serially—that is quasi-historically.

The present writer illustrates what is termed 'grammatical meaning' by concocting such sentences as 'My doctor's great grandfather will be singeing the cat's wings',[32] or 'She slowly rushed upstairs to the cellar and turned the kettle out to boil two fires'. Lewis Carroll's nonsense provides excellent illustrations of grammatical meaning, but it is now met with so frequently that it can be referred to quotation situations. Grammatical and 'prosodic' meaning in German is similarly amusingly exemplified by such lines as[33]:

> Finster war's, der Mond schien helle, schneebedeckt die grüne Flur, als ein Wagen blitzesschnelle langsam um die Ecke fuhr, . . .
>
> Da sah ich vier Stühle auf ihren Herren sitzen, da tat ich meinen Tag ab und sagte: 'Guten Hut, meine Damen.'

To make statements of meaning in terms of linguistics, we first accept language events as integral in experience regarding them as wholes and as repetitive and interconnected, and then we propose to apply theoretical schemata consisting of a consistent framework of categories which are given names in a restricted language and in which all such specialized terms and expressions have their setting. The 'meaning' in this sense is dealt with at a mutually congruent series of levels, sometimes in a descending order beginning with the context of situation and proceeding through *collocation*, syntax, including *colligation*, to phonology and phonetics, even experimental phonetics, and sometimes in the opposite order.

Such an analytic dispersion of the statement of meaning at a series of levels, taking the fullest advantage of all our traditional disciplines and techniques consistent with the theory, and drawing on the aggregate of experience, does not imply that any level includes or constitutes a formal prerequisite of any other. The levels of abstraction are only connected in that the resulting statements relate to the same language texts in the focus of attention in experience, and the theory requires them to be congruent and consequently complementary in synthesis on renewal of connection in experience.

No hard and fast lines can be drawn at present to form a strict classification for contexts of situation. Some might prefer to characterize situations by attempting a description of speech and language functions with reference to their effective observable results, and perhaps also with reference to a linguistically centred social analysis.

The technical language necessary for the description of contexts of situation is not developed, nor is there any agreed method of classification. At this level there are great possibilities for research and experiment. It will be maintained here that linguistic analysis states the interrelations of elements of structure and sets up systems of 'terms' or 'units' and end-points of mutually determined interior relations.[34] Such interior relations are set up in the context of situation between the following constituents:

1. The participants: persons, personalities and relevant features of these.
   (a) The verbal action of the participants.
   (b) The non-verbal action of the participants.
2. The relevant objects and non-verbal and non-personal events.
3. The effect of the verbal action.

No linguist has yet set up exhaustive systems of contexts of situation such that they could be considered mutually determined in function or meaning. There is some approximation to this, however, in Malinowski's *Coral gardens and their magic*, and here and there in special studies of contexts of personal address and reference, and of well-defined technological activities such as fishing or weaving or making war, and of rituals of various kinds.

In classifying contexts of situation and in describing such contexts as wholes, a language of 'shifted-terms', that is to say a vocabulary and phraseology of descriptive definition involving notional elements is probably unavoidable. It is, however, a clear scientific gain if such notional language only appears at this level and is rigidly excluded from all other levels such as the collocational, grammatical and phonological levels. But even the use of such notionally descriptive terms as *deictic*

12

situations, or *onomastic situations* or *situations of personal address* or of *personal reference*, either in the presence or absence of the person mentioned, does not involve the description of mental processes or meaning in the thoughts of the participants, and certainly need not imply any consideration of intention, purport or purpose.

The description of the context of situation by stating the interior relations of the constituents or factors,[35] may be followed by referring such contexts to a variety of known frameworks of a more general character such as (a) the economic, religious and other social structures of the societies of which the participants are members; (b) types of linguistic discourse such as monologue, choric language, narrative, recitation, explanation, exposition, etc.; (c) personal interchanges, e.g. mentioning especially the number, age and sex of the participants and noting speaker-listener, reader-writer and reader *or* writer contexts, including series of such interchanges; (d) types of speech function such as drills and orders,[36] detailed direction and control of techniques of all kinds, social flattery, blessing, cursing, praise and blame, concealment and deception, social pressure and constraint, verbal contracts of all kinds, and phatic communion.[37]

Statements of contexts of situation may be presented in tabular form under headings selected from the above list. One method of tabulation would comprise ten entries as follows: (i) type of context of situation; (ii) type of speech function; (iii) the language text and language mechanism; (iv) the restricted language[38] to which the text belongs; (v) the syntactical characteristics of the text (colligation); (vi) other linguistic features of the text and mechanism, including style and tempo; (vii) features of collocation; (viii) the creative effect or effective result; (ix) extended collocations and (x) memorial allusions, providing serial links with preceding or following situations.

Situations in which the text is egocentric are not without formal interest. Diaries, engagement books, personal notes and memoranda and perhaps most manuscripts are egocentric in this sense. If a man finds nothing worth saying to himself, in monologue or soliloquy, he has nothing to say to anyone else. The reading situation[39] is full of interest and has been dealt with by Wittgenstein.

Choric contexts of the 'Sieg heil' type were terrifying to listen to in Nazi Germany, but they are pleasant enough in 'Are we downhearted?' 'No!!!' Chorus is a very common linguistic form in phatic communion or 'sharing'. Contextual studies of the linguistic recognition of social differences, of social hierarchy, of inferiority or superiority, of feelings of conformity and non-conformity, of class, religion, nationality or race, gain in force by more precise formulation.

A vast field of research in 'biographical' linguistics[40] still lies unexplored. The language of social control in the whole of education, including all forms of apprenticeship, and not only schooling, might well be systematically studied and stated by situational formulation. The *do* and *don't* texts and all the interrogatives and jussives of childhood and adolescence lend themselves to such analysis. In this connection, a plea must be entered for the restoration in schools of a suitable language in which children can talk about their language as a vital part of their experience.

The contextualization of narrative is another obvious case for formulation. Traditional narrative employing 'fixed' or 'correct' language or having other characteristic formal features as in fairy tales, traditional forms less fixed, news, fiction, free narrative within customary observance and finally free personal invention[41] can be exemplified in almost all societies.

Even in the study of vocabulary[42] when ordered series of words are presented, such as kinship terms, parts of the body, terms of orientation in time and space, numerals, calendrical terms, names of social units, proper names of persons as well as of places,[43] it is essential that they be separately and severally attested in contexts of situation. It is, however, necessary to present them also in their commonest collocations.

IV

The *placing* of a *text* as a constituent in a context of situation contributes to the statement of meaning since situations are set up to recognize *use*. As Wittgenstein says, 'the meaning of words lies in their use.'[44] The day-to-day practice of playing language games recognizes customs and rules. It follows that a text in such established usage may contain sentences such as 'Don't be such an ass!', 'You silly ass!', 'What an ass he is!' In these examples, the word *ass* is in familiar and habitual company, commonly collocated with *you silly—, he is a silly—, don't be such an—.* You shall know a word by the company it keeps! One of the meanings of *ass* is its habitual collocation with such other words as those above quoted.[45] Though Wittgenstein was dealing with another problem, he also recognizes the plain face-value, the physiognomy of words. They look at us! 'The sentence is composed of the words and that is enough.'

From the preceding remarks, it will be seen that collocation is not to be interpreted as *context*, by which the whole conceptual meaning is implied. Nor is it to be confused with *citation*. When a lexicographer has arbitrarily decided how many 'meanings' he can conveniently recognize in the uses of a given word, he limits his entries accordingly and, after definitions of the 'meanings' in *shifted terms*, he supports them by *citations*, usually with literary authority. Lexicographical citations are keyed to the definitions, intended to exemplify a series of different 'meanings' arbitrarily selected and defined, and also to illustrate changes of meaning. The habitual collocations in which words under study appear are quite simply the mere word accompaniment, the other word-material in which they are most commonly or most characteristically embedded. It can safely be stated that part of the 'meaning' of *cows* can be indicated by such collocations as *They are milking the cows, Cows give milk*. The words *tigresses* or *lionesses* are not so collocated and are already clearly separated in meaning at the *collocational level*.

Situations of calendrical reference in which, for example, the names of the days of the week and of the month are a feature would attest the systematic use of the series of seven and twelve. But that is not by any means the complete cultural picture. In English, for instance, typical collocations for the words Sunday, Monday, Friday and Saturday furnish interesting material and would certainly separate them from the corresponding words in Chinese, Hebrew, Arabic or Hindi. The English words for the months are characteristically collocated: March hare, August Bank Holiday, May week, May Day, April showers, April fool, etc.

It is true that *Alice in Wonderland* is a world classic but foreigners must allow it to remain in English. An Italian colleague, commenting on the Italian attempt to render 'March hare', felt embarrassed by *lepre marzaiolo*—'non si usa!' And though there is *marzolino*, it is not collocated with *lepre*—'ma non significamente, unito a lepre'.

Statements of meaning at the collocational level may be made for the *pivotal* or *key words* of any *restricted language* being studied.[47] Such collocations will often be found to be characteristic and help justify the restriction of the field. The words under study will be found in 'set' company and find their places in the 'ordered' collocations.

The collocational study of selected words in everyday language is doubly rewarding in that it usefully circumscribes the field for further research and indicates problems in grammar. It is clearly an essential procedure in descriptive lexicography. It is important, however, to regard each word separately at first, and not as a member of a paradigm. The collocations of *light* (n.s.) separate it from *lights* (n.s.) and *light* n.adj.) from *lighter* and *lightest*. Then there are the specific contrastive collocations for *light/dark* and *light/heavy*.

The collocational study of such words as *and, the, this, for, one, it,* is only of profit in that it dictates the necessity of a more generalized treatment of words and raises the problem of the general and grammatical classification of words. Grammatical generalization of word classes and the setting up of categories for the statement of meaning in terms of syntactical relations is clearly indispensable.

Collocations of a given word are statements of the habitual or customary places of that word in collocational order but not in any other contextual order and emphatically not in any grammatical order. The collocation of a word or a 'piece' is not to be regarded as mere juxtaposition, it is an order of *mutual expectancy*. The words are mutually expectant and mutually prehended. It is also an abstraction, and though the name of a collocation is the hearing, reading or saying of it, its 'meaning' at other levels must not be directly taken into consideration. The statement of collocations and extended collocations deals with mutually expectant orders of words and pieces as such, attention being focused on one word or one piece at a time.

In the study of selected words, compounds and phrases in a restricted language for which there are restricted texts, an exhaustive collection of collocations must first be made. It will then be found that meaning by collocation will suggest a small number of groups of collocations for each word studied. The next step is the choice of definitions for meanings suggested by the groups.[48]

V

The statement of meaning at the grammatical level is in terms of word and sentence classes or of similar categories and of the interrelation of those categories in *colligations*.[49] Grammatical relations should not be regarded as relations between words as such—between *watched* and *him* in 'I watched him'—but between a personal pronoun, first person singular nominative, the past tense of a transitive verb and the third person pronoun singular in the oblique or objective form. These grammatical abstractions state some of the interrelated categories within an affirmative sentence. Different categories of the negative conjugation with operators would be necessary to deal with 'I didn't watch him'.

In order to state the facts of negation in contemporary English, it is necessary to set up a class of from twenty-two to twenty-four syntactical operators which function not only in negation but also in interrogation with front-shifting of the first nominal element of the verbal phrase, in emphatic affirmation and also as code verbals. These twenty-four operators are not to be regarded as items of the verbal conjugations of *to be* or *to have* but are grouped as separate terms of the ordered series of operators. They are: *am, is, are, was, were, have, has, had, do, does, did, shall, should, will, would, may, might, can, could, must, ought, need, dare, used* (*to*).

These operators are then to be sub-classified and related to sentence structure. They are essential in negation when a finite verb is used with the negative particle and they form an element of structure in the negative conjugation. All the twenty-four operators are colligated with the negative particle without exception and all negative finite verbs are colligated with one of these operators. It is interesting that some of the actual *word* forms or exponents of the colligation operator-negative cannot be suitably divided with reference to the affirmative forms, thought of course they must have phonetic and phonological shape—e.g. *ʃal/ʃaːnt, wil/wownt, kan/kaːnt, duw/downt.* Note the interrogative negative *aːnt ay?*

When, say in Latin, a preposition is said to govern the accusative case or, even more loosely, is said to be used with or joined with the ablative case of nouns or pronouns to define their relations with other parts of speech, for example, the verb, the statement refers to the interrelation of a set of grammatical categories transcending the actual words which may fall into those categories. Syntactical analysis must generalize beyond the level of the word isolate, since in many languages the exponents of the grammatical categories may not be words or even affixes. In colligations of grammatical categories constituting the elements of a sentence structure in such very different languages as Latin, Hindi and Swahili, the exponents of gender and number are discontinuous. This is traditionally referred to as 'concord' or 'agreement' between actual word isolates. Words are said to 'agree'.

Collocations are actual words in habitual company. A word in a usual collocation stares you in the face just as it is. Colligations cannot be of words as such. Colligations of grammatical categories related in a given structure do not necessarily follow word divisions or even sub-divisions of words. Segmental analysis of the phonemic type cannot therefore correlate with such colligations. A colligation is not to be interpreted as abstraction in parallel with a collocation of exemplifying words in a text.

A single word isolate such as Latin *pedibus* might have to be considered in a sentence structure in which the categories in colligation would include gender, number and person, and the noun-substantive itself. But where are all these if the grammarian looks at the word *pedibus* itself? The exponents of the categories are 'cumulative' in the word and also discontinuous in the sentence.

A consideration of what has been written around the word 'morpheme' since Vendryès' *Le langage* in 1921 [50] leads me to the opinion that all analyses of phonic and graphic materials having in view the statement of grammatical categories usually considered morphematic, and also the description of their exponents, should be applied to the piece, phrase, clause or sentence. 'Morphematics' at the grammatical level is thus congruent with prosodic studies at the phonological level. It follows that the distinction between morphology and syntax is perhaps no longer useful or convenient in descriptive linguistics. No valid theory of the morpheme built on the phoneme has yet been framed. Systems of grammatical categories are not to be confused either with lists of phonic or graphic exponents, or with phonological systems. 'Morphological' categories are to be treated syntagmatically and only appear in paradigms as terms or units related to elements of structure. This approach emphasizes the need for prosodic analysis at the phonological level. The exponents of articles, deictic particles, pronouns and all manner of so-called verbal auxiliaries in English, French and German, for example, are obviously prosodically dependent on the nominal or verbal piece or phrase. The mutually expectant relations of the grammatical categories in colligation, however, cannot be regarded as necessarily having phonological 'shape'.

VI

In discussing the concept of colligation as the interrelation of grammatical categories in syntactical structure, the term *exponent* has been introduced to refer to the phonetic and phonological 'shape' of words or parts of words which are generalized in the categories of the colligation. It may be that such bits, pieces or features may be adequately referred to in terms of the orthography with additional prosodic, including punctuative, marks. Indeed, the consideration of graphic exponents is a companion study to phonological and phonetic analysis, unfortunately not always harmonious but often of provocative interest. Arising out of this is the need for a reconsideration of the categories of descriptive phonetics and the necessary notation to state them.

The setting up of phonological elements of structure and of the systems of units or terms from which their values may be known results in ranges or sets of interior functional relations. Renewal of connection with the language under description in experience requires that recognizable phonetic and possibly graphic shape shall be given to what have been termed the exponents of the phonological categories. Not all the phonic data need, or indeed can, be given. From such data, the characteristic features only need be described and new additional categories of general phonetic description will certainly be necessary.

The phonetic description of exponents which may be cumulative or discontinuous or both should provide a direct justification of the analysis. It may happen that the exponents of some phonological categories may serve also for syntactical categories. But the exponents of many grammatical categories may require *ad hoc* or direct phonetic description.

If the phonological analysis of longer pieces than the word is to be one of a congruent series at a number of levels of description, there would appear to be no alternative to some form of prosodic approach based on a theory of structures and systems.

The exponents of the phonological elements of structure and of the units or terms of systems are to be abstracted from the phonic material and stated in carefully considered phonetic terms and, if necessary, new ones must be created. The use made of the phonic material in the phonetic description of exponents does not require that the phonic details variously allotted should be mutually exclusive. The description of the phonetic characteristics of elements and categories of structure is relevant to that order, which is a different order from the order of units and terms in systems. It is thus quite likely that certain phonic details may be included in the phonetic characteristics of prosodic elements and structures as well as in those of phonematic units and systems. There are, so to speak, two distinct 'syndromes' and there is no tautology or falsification if there is some overlap in 'symptoms'. There can be no question of 'residue' in the phonic material after any particular abstraction for a specific purpose has been made. All the phonic material is still available for further abstractions for a different order in separate analyses.

The phonetic descriptions of features of the phonic material selected as characteristic exponents of the prosodies and the exponents of the phonematic units need not be mutually exclusive.[51] When they are involved in the interrelations of elements of structure, they are not referred to as exponents of phonematic systems.

Since systems furnish values for elements of structure, and since the ordering of systems depends upon structure, there is always the possibility of some overlap of phonic reference. The exponents of elements of structure and of terms in systems are always consistent and cannot be mutually contradictory.

If pharyngalization were to be abstracted as a prosody of a word or piece, it would not preclude the setting up of a system of pharyngal consonant units in the same piece. Similarly, if 'frontness' or 'backness' were to be set up as word or piece prosodies, it would still be possible to find systemic places for 'front' consonant and vowel units in the pieces characterized by the prosody of frontness, and 'back' consonant and vowel units in the pieces characterized by back prosodies.

This direct and positive phonetic approach avoids a false realism implied in such expressions as 'phonetic implication', 'realization', 'actualization' and 'signal'. While keeping the levels of analysis separate, the introduction of exponents brings the results together and ensures renewal of connection in experience with the language under description.

In the analysis of the nominal phrase in Western European languages, the articles and demonstratives are to be taken with characteristic substantives and adjectives. In German, the statement of the graphic exponents of number, gender and case provides a useful approximation to an analysis. In dealing with the definite article by itself, for example, there are six forms in all as follows:

der	die	das	des	dem	den
a	b	c	d	e	f

If three categories of gender are set up, we get the following distribution forms:

masculine	a, d, e, f
feminine	b, a
neuter	c, d, e

For the two numbers, singular and plural:

singular	a, b, c, d, e, f
plural	b, a, f

If four cases are recognized, the following table shows the mutual exclusiveness of the orthographic exponents:

nominative	*a, b, c*
genitive	*d, a*
dative	*a, e, f*
accusative	*f, c, b*

The tabulation above shows the necessity of considering both the articles and all the demonstratives in colligation with substantives and adjectives in the nominal phrase, and the nominal piece in colligation with the verbal piece. It will be agreed that the individual orthographic forms of the articles do not correlate with the grammatical categories resulting from the analysis of the nominal piece.

VII

The first principle of phonological and grammatical analysis is to distinguish between *structure* and *system*. We have already mentioned the interior phonological relations connected with the text itself: firstly the syntagmatic relations between elements of structure prosodic and phonematic, secondly the paradigmatic relations of the terms or units which commute within systems set up to give values to the elements of structure. The terms *structure* and *elements of structure* are not used to refer to a whole language or even to what may be called portions of a language, but exclusively to categories abstracted from common word form or textual form. And quite similarly, *system, systems, terms* and *units* are restricted to a set or sets of paradigmatic relations between commutable units or terms which provide values for the elements of structure. Though structures are, so to speak, 'horizontal' while systems are 'vertical', neither are to be regarded as segments in any sense. Elements of structure, especially in grammatical relations, share a mutual expectancy in an *order* which is not merely a *sequence*.

Grammatical analysis then deals with texts by setting up structures and systems. The constituent elements of syntactical structures are not words, but generalized classes and categories by means of which the interior relations of the elements may be stated.

The statement of the colligation of a grammatical category deals with a *mutually expectant order* of categories, attention being focused on one category at a time. If two or more categories are in the focus of attention, the study of their colligations is in similar mutually expectant orders.

Such categories are not considered as having *positions* in *sequence*, but can be said to be placed in order.[52]

Many linguists handle these problems of analysis by theories of the morpheme. In the United States, the terms *allomorph, morph* and *empty morph* are found necessary. In this type of analysis also, there are no words as such. The interior relations of the elements of structure are, however, obscured by certain theories of *distribution*,[53] which I held at one time but have since abandoned. The logic of distributional relations, useful as it may be, cannot be the main principle in any theory of the analysis of structures involving the statement of the values of the elements of structure by reference to systems.

Attention must first be paid to the longer elements of text—such as the paragraph, the sentence and its component clauses, phrases, pieces and, lastly, words if they are institutionalized or otherwise established.

In dealing with such longer elements, notional generalizations are admissible in addition to the formal linguistic statements characterizing the categories. Such terms as affirmative, negative, interrogative, exclamatory, emphatic and non-emphatic are applied to sentence types formally established—but there are also notional references summing up certain features of the contexts of situation. References to the non-verbal constituents of the situation are essential to the complete description of the verbal context, i.e. the linguistic text and its elements. This is obvious in describing colloquial speech using such grammatical terms as pronoun, demonstrative, number, numeral, gender (including classifiers) and so-called 'form-words'. Form-words are never empty.

The linguistics of orientation in time and place, of relative position and direction, of deixis, number and numeration, often involving gender and classification, must admit notional generalizations to state what have been described above as 'situational relations',[54] but these are not references to thoughts, ideas or mentalistic content.

References to the non-verbal constituents of situations are admissible in corroboration of formal linguistic characteristics stated as criteria for setting up parts of speech or word-classes. Whatever criteria may have been used to set up, let us say, verbal and nominal categories, it will usually be found that verbal features are distributed over a good deal of the sentence. The statement of a verbal system and the order of its relevant categories leads to the statement of tenses, aspects, operators, auxiliaries, pronouns, negatives, interrogatives and other particles, person, number and gender, to mention only a few. Aspectual auxiliaries and particles necessarily lead to colligation with relevant adverbials and particles suitably grouped and classified, since they corrrelate with the various verbal aspects and will have been noticed at the situational and collocational levels.

The nominal phrase is to be treated similarly and the two sets of categories, nominal and verbal, are themselves mutually expectant in various forms when they are said to be in the same colligation. This leads to the statement of transitive relations by place and order, by particles and by case.

Such verbal pieces as *Je le lui ai donné, il n'y en a pas* at the phonological level must be regarded as prosodic pieces, and the grammatical elements of the whole verbal phrase must be treated in colligation. Such sentences or verbal pieces as *He might have kept on popping in and out all the afternoon* or *He couldn't have kept on running up and down the stairs all morning* must be analysed with reference to periphrastic polynomial verbs, and the characteristic categories of tense, aspect, operators, particles, adverbials state grammatical features abstracted from the whole piece. There can be little profit in any grammatical analysis which deals with the relations of the individual words as such with one another one by one. Surely such 'grammar' is to be abandoned.

The decline of 'grammar' as we have known it, especially of school grammar, is probably due to its naïveté and obvious incompleteness and inadequacy, both in formal description and in dealing with meaning. It has fallen down on the job.

Confining ourselves to English as the language of description, let us face the facts and admit that such words as *time, past, present, future* and all the rest of the 'temporal' nomenclature have been employed with gross carelessness to describe notions supposed to characterize the verb. No attempts seem ever to have been made to distinguish philosophical time (and space), clock time, calendrical time, solar time, personal and situational time from what should properly be called *grammatical time.* Notional time, generally speaking, is a different thing altogether from grammatical time, which differs from language to language. Grammatical time is not limited to or bound by the speaker's temporal world but has an unlimited range, always, however, within the verbal time-resources of the given language. Language itself is timeless, and as an instrument of life, must range over all 'time'. Each language has its own means of handling 'experiential' time, has its own 'time-camera' so to speak, with its own special view-finders, perspectives, filters and lenses. It is childish to draw excessively over-simplified linear diagrams to deal with such linguistic structures and systems. The point is they are not time-systems but linguistic systems.

Similarly, the study of deixis in particular languages is hindered by mentalistic generalizations of orientation.

The system of demonstratives in English is totally different from that of French. The two sets are neither equipollent or equivalent, and there is no general theory of demonstratives universally applicable. Similar puerilities occlude our vision in dealing with number, gender and case in particular languages. The Elizabethan and seventeenth-century grammars of Latin taught seven genders formally, and avoided the sex confusion. There are no 'ideas' of 'singularity' or 'plurality'. It is plainly necessary to distinguish between number, numbers, numerals, figures, the operations of counting and the singulars and plurals of articles and demonstratives where such categories are set up. How can the language *under* description be dealt with clearly if the language *of* description and the language of translation are loose and careless and full of theoretical puerilities condoned by an obsolescent terminological tradition? One fairly obvious course is to try other theories and within the framework of those theories overhaul our descriptive instruments and set up less inadequate languages of description and of translation.

It has been traditional practice to state the structure of the nominal piece and the interrelations of nominal and verbal pieces in terms of gender, number, person and case, and sometimes even to give these categories some sort of conceptualist 'meaning'. Similarly, moods, tenses and aspects have been justified notionally, and in the main at manifest disadvantage both to the linguist and the learner. It would plainly be foolish to abandon all the miscellaneous equipment of two thousand years of linguistic endeavour. But the items and nomenclature are being checked and sorted out and it is suggested that they may be fitted into an entirely serviceable technical apparatus for linguistic analysis and statement, in keeping with the advances in linguistic theory and in harmony with the prevailing intellectual climate.

A necessary preliminary step is to put aside all notional explanations of such categories as gender and case, mood and voice, and also the paradigmatic approach to the morphology of separate words. The paradigmatic hyphenated lists of orthographic forms of individual words can and generally do obscure the analysis of the elements of structure in the syntagmatic interrelations of grammatical categories. These interrelations are not between words as such nor are they properly stated by interrelating the exponents, whether these be graphic or phonetic.

The various structures of sentences in any given language, comprising for example at least two nominal pieces and a verbal piece must be collated, and such categories as voice, mood, affirmative, negative, tense, aspect, gender, number, person and case, if found applicable and valid in descriptive statement, are to be abstracted from, and referred back to, the sentence as a whole. The exponents of the categories may be cumulate or discontinuous or both, and their phonetic description may necessitate the use of terms and notation not based on orthography or, indeed, on any scheme of segmental letters in the tradition of the roman alphabet. Order, place, transposition, commutation within systems, pause, stress or prominence, contonation[55] and intonation are, among others, clearly relevant as possible exponents of grammatical categories.

In Sanskrit, Latin and Greek the categories of case, for example, must be abstracted from the piece or sentence whether nominal or a combination of nominal and verbal, and in renewal of connection by means of further texts, syntactically referred to by description of the exponents of the elements of structure. Voice, mood, tense and aspect would be treated similarly.

In Modern Hindi,[56] the analysis of the nominal phrase and the verbal piece, and both of these in combined structures, involves the description of both discontinuous and cumulate exponents of the necessary categories of gender, number, person, case, voice, mood, aspect and tense, distributed over the whole sentence. Hindi is one of the languages in which the problems of so-called transitive and intransitive verbs, of voice, and of concord and agreement, illustrate the obvious advantages of the present approach.

Linguists are only just beginning to realize the dangers and pitfalls of 'personification' of categories as universal entities.[57] There is a constant need to beware of such bogus philosophizing in linguistics.

There is always the danger that the use of traditional grammatical terms with reference to a wide variety of languages may be taken to imply a secret belief in universal grammar. Every analysis of a particular 'language' must of necessity determine the values of the *ad hoc* categories to which traditional names are given.[58] What is here being sketched is *a general linguistic theory* applicable to *particular linguistic descriptions*, not *a theory of universals* for *general linguistic description*.

Though it is found convenient to employ the words *noun, verb, pronoun, particle*, for example, it must not be assumed that in all languages nouns and verbs *are to be found* as the universalists might express it.

It has been held that in some Melanesian languages the noun-verb distinction is unncessary. The 'universalist' fallacy is constantly with us. It is sometimes said that there are 'no real adjectives' in Swahili, and that 'adjectives are really verbs' in Japanese. The first step towards adequacy in the higher levels of linguistic analysis is the same rigorous control of formal categories set up and of the terms applied to them, as is now the rule in all forms of phonological analysis. This does not mean that the analysis of discourse—of the paragraph and the sentence, for example—can be directly developed from phonemic procedures or even devised by analogy from such procedures.[59] The main criticism to be offered of American structuralist linguistics based on phonemic procedures is that, having attempted just that, it has not furnished any valid grammatical analysis of any language by means of which renewal of connection in experience can be made with systematic certainty. At the present time, descriptive linguistics is suffering from a pre-occupation with phonemics and other forms of segmental phonology, and in the next decade it is probable that linguistic theory and practice will turn to synthesis. The present theory offers, it is submitted, not only a theory of synthesis, but the possibility of a synthesis of the main advances made in the subject during the last thirty years.

Reverting to the discussion of grammatical categories in closed systems for any given language, the 'universalist' is reminded that the grammatical 'meanings' are determined by their interrelations in the systems set up for that language:

A nominative in a four case system would in this sense necessarily have a different 'meaning' from a nominative in a two case or in a fourteen case system, for example. A singular in a two number system has different grammatical meaning from a singular in a three number system or a four number system such as in Fijian which formally distinguishes singular, dual, 'little' plural and 'big' plural. The system of, say, three word classes, noun, verb and particle, is different from the meaning of the category *noun* in a system of five classes in which *adjective* and *pronoun* are formally distinguished from the noun, verb and particle. The application of the word 'meaning' to the function of an element with reference to the specific system of which it is a 'term', 'unit' or 'member' in a given language is an example of a quasi-mathematical theorem.[60]

VIII

Some linguists seem to regard phonemics as a kind of pure mathematics handling ultimate linguistic units, and morphophonemics as a kind of applied mathematics to prove morphemics. Such analysis does not go beyond the basic principle of linear and successive segmentation, and therefore proves inadequate for statements of meaning of such complexes as a sentence or paragraph, or any suitably abstracted longer piece of discourse. From the present point of view such meaningful complexes are described as a relational network of structures and systems at clearly distinguished but congruent levels, converging again in renewal of connection in experience. In attempts to meet such difficulties of analysis from the phonemic point of view, there have arisen involved discussions of theories of juncture and junction. So far none of these juncture theories are satisfactory from the grammatical point of view.

The object of linguistic analysis as here understood is to make statements of meaning so that we may see how we use language to live. In order to do this analysis we must split up the problem and deal with it at a series of levels. Studies at one level must take into account findings at other levels. In all phonological statements, for example, it is always useful, and I would suggest even necessary, to have studied the grammatical meaning of the materials, and even to have some systematic knowledge of the collocations of the words selected from the *corpus inscriptionum* as examples. There are signs of a widespread, though as yet inarticulate, dissatisfaction with the general linguistic results of phonemic analysis 'without meaning', and the pressure of this discontent calls for a new grammatical technique on the one hand, and on the other a greatly developed technique of phonetics and phonetic notation in the service of impressionist description.

To begin with, grammatical classification limits and groups the data in parallel with phonological analysis, for example there is no need for unduly complicated phonetic procedures in order to separate the following pairs: tax (*v.* and *n.s.b. sing.*), tacks (*v.s.* and *n.s.b. pl.*); band (*v.* and *n.s.b.*), banned (*v.p.* and *n. adj.*).[61] Many examples can be given from English to illustrate the difficulties of attempting to build the whole edifice of linguistic analysis exclusively on a phonemic basis. Other levels of analysis are required to deal with such isolates as are lexically represented as follows: heel (*v.* and *n.s.b.*), heal (*v.*), he'll (*v. op. 3rd sing. masc.*); weed (*v.* and *n.s.b.*), we'd (*v. op. 1st. pl.*). The elements of such verbal pieces as *ay ʃl əv siyn im* are prosodically interdependent.[62] If used in easy familiar style and tempo, the structural characteristics must be referred to the whole verbal piece. The elements of the piece structure involve syllabic analysis providing for possible distribution of stress and strength over the five syllables in a mutually expectant order. Only two take the potentialities of stress and length, the first and the fourth. If the fifth be considered for potential stress and length the whole prosodic structure would involve separate statement. Analogous formations would employ such verbal forms as *wiy l əv, yuw l əv, ðey l əv*, and such forms as *ay kəd əv*, etc.

In the phonological analysis of longer pieces with grammatical correlations in mind, it will be found useful to take as first isolates stretches that can be regarded as prosodic groups. In the West Yorkshire sentence *ða d ə dunt 'seem ðy'sen, if ða d ed Pt 't∫əns* (you would have done the same yourself, if you had had the chance), we may recognize two prosodic sub-groups separated by a prosodic comma. There are seven syllabics in the first sub-group and five in the second. It is clear that the first five syllabics of the first group are prosodically interdependent and mutually determined. The value of the first syllabic is dependent on a system of vowel units, the second is the neutral syllabic and a prosodic unit, the third, like the first, one of a system of vowel units, the fourth a prosodic unit being a syllabic stop. The penultimate syllabic in the second sub-group is a glottalized stop.

All these syllabics can be correlated with the syllable structure of the whole group, with the syllabic structure of the nominal and verbal elements and hence with the whole colligation. The grammatical analysis of other verbal pieces can be stated more clearly if the pieces are regarded as prosodic groups for phonological analysis; e.g. (West Yorkshire) *a st ə 'dunˑt if a 'kud, a s∫ 'siy ðə tˑ'mɔɔn tˑ'niyt, a kəd ə 'dunˑt iPtˑ 'mɔɔnyn, a kŋ 'gi ðəˑt wen tə 'kumʒ bak.* The verbal pieces *a st ə 'dunˑt, a kəd ə 'dunˑt, a kŋ 'gi ðəˑt* are prosodically and grammatically holophrastic and once these facts are accepted the phonological analysis can be stated without attempting to justify the joining up of segments or 'words' by theories of juncture. The interrelations of the grammatical categories stated as colligations form the unifying framework, and the phonological categories are limited by the grammatical status of the structures. The linguist can then draw on all the technical resources of phonetics, both descriptive and instrumental, in stating the characteristic prosodic features and giving, whenever possible, phonetic shape to exponents.

The syllable structure of any word or piece is itself to be considered as prosodic, quite apart from other phonetically describable features

13 +

such as length, stress, tone, intonation, the distribution of which is linked with such structures. It is in this connection that one must allot to each syllable a nucleus which may be termed a syllabic. Syllabics need not be considered as co-terminous, and almost any phonetically describable type of feature may be the exponent of such a syllabic. On the other hand, a monosyllable for example may have an added element of structure without that added element being necessarily regarded as a syllabic. For instance, in the examples above quoted *tacks* may be analysed as CVC + the sign of the plural or the 3rd person singular, whereas *tax* carrying a similar addition involves a syllabic. Even if the phrase 'The Society for the Prevention of Cruelty to Animals' in familiar quick tempo style is represented as follows: *ðə sˑˈsaɔty fˑðˑprˑˈvenʃnˑv ˈkruwlty tw ˈanˑmlʂ*, sixteen syllables would have to be reckoned in the structure, only four of which are stressed, the syllabics being vowel units. All other syllabics need not involve any vowel system or vowel units, and might be treated prosodically in relation to the whole title.

The alphabetic representation in the reading transcription given is not intended to represent the results of a phonemic analysis. Prosodically treated, certain features, such as the distribution of stress and intonation, are not segmentable in the phonemic sense. May I remark in passing that phonemic segmentation may find eventual application in the first crude linguistic machines, but by the time the first models are built linguistics may well have abandoned linear units of successive segmentation as a method of handling the mechanism of language.

The prosodic approach to phonological analysis requires a much finer as well as a more extensive range of abstract categories of phonetic observation and several correlated systems of phonetic notation. The single classified phonetic alphabet with supplementary diacritics may have served the earlier stages of one-level-phonemics well enough, but multi-level analysis of longer pieces will necessarily require a considerable development of the phonetic sciences, including the use of instruments and machines.

There are examples in *Studies in Linguistic analysis* of the critical use of phonological and phonetic nomenclature and also of notational invention. Moreover, linguistics has been taken into the laboratory, which is a very different scientific procedure from what is usually called experimental phonetics. The application of instrumental as well as of impressionist phonetics correlates with statements of phonological and grammatical meaning.[63]

IX

In the remaining sections of this synopsis, summary indications are given of the bearing of the theory on stylistics and descriptive lexicography, and attention is drawn to the fundamental problems of translation which are a challenge both to philosophy and linguistics.

The widespread interest in language and the rapid development of general linguistics have affected the study of literature and the practice of literary criticism, and the linguistic trend grows steadily. Even if 'syntax' is said to hold poetry together, in a 'musical' rather than in a 'linguistic' way, the approach is recognizable from the point of view of prosodic linguistics. The careful following of a literary text with painstaking precision requires some sort of linguistic technique, and 'syntactical' concentration does not permit the critic 'to let himself go'.

In a previous essay[64] I have given illustrations of two branches of stylistics, (a) the stylistics of what persists in common usage over long periods, and (b) the stylistics of the idiosyncratic language of such a poet as Swinburne. The suggested stylistic analysis is made at the levels of phonetics (including phonaesthetics), phonology, syntax, word and phrase formation, collocation and vocabulary. In almost any form of English studied from the stylistic point of view, the characteristics of nominal phrases or pieces and the collocations of the key or pivotal words, whether substantives or adjectives, will be found rewarding, and similarly in the complete verbal piece the adverbials and particles will often prove characteristic. The conjunctives, and words with deictic or anaphoric reference are also important features of any given stretch of discourse. The use and distribution of the so-called logical particles are often a marked feature of style and form part of any close syntactical analysis of certain types of discourse.

The elements of style can be stated in linguistic terms. They are formally presented in the text which can be said to have a physiognomy.

X

The application of the theory to lexicography would lead to new types of dictionary, to glossaries of restricted languages and to other specialized studies of vocabulary at several different levels of analysis.

The most productive preliminaries to almost any kind of descriptive dictionary are:

(a) To find criteria for the limitation of the circumscribed field of a restricted language or languages within which selected words or classes or words are to be studied.

(b) The listing or preparation of written materials in the restricted language from which exhaustive collocations of the selected words are to be collected.

(c) It will then be found that meaning by collocation will suggest grouping of the collocations into a manageable number of sets.

(d) Each set of grouped collocations may suggest an arbitrary definition of the word, compound or phrase which is being studied in collocation.

(e) If the materials are being collected from informants, definition texts may be recorded by them in their own language, as their own version of the meanings, group by group. Definition texts provided in this way can be extremely informative but must be critically handled.

Draft entries can now be made, one for each group, definitions can be given and from the *collocations* one or two may be chosen to become *citations* keyed to the definitions.

The use of photographs and diagrams in connection with definition texts often provides the informant with a basis for his statements, and the linguist working in the field will generally know when a photograph or film is perhaps more valuable than a tape recording of the language text.

It is obvious that linguistics today points the way to new types of lexical statement. The day has gone by when lexicographical work must embrace all words just as they come, quite generally from what is called a language or a pair or group of languages, and at the same time follow the order of the alphabet. Dictionaries of the 'bits' which words may comprise and of pieces and phrases are equally necessary. Systems of words and selected groups of words or phrases in the more exotic languages could profitably be presented in dictionaries, always securely based on good descriptive grammar. The lexicographer must always have well-founded grammatical categories for his materials and entries. Indeed, specialist dictionaries restricted to materials of certain grammatical categories might prove of great interest, since in most bi-lingual dictionaries the grammatical categories applicable in the two languages would not be strictly parallel or equivalent, though in some cases a certain common grammatical measure might be established and this would prove useful in the application of machines.

XI

Finally, there are the many theoretical problems raised by the achievements of translation throughout history. There is no point in denying the possibilities of *complete* translation. One of the most important assignments for linguists in the future is the formulation of satisfactory theories of the nature of the translation bridges between languages. Do we really know how we translate or what we translate? What is the 'interlingua'? Are we to accept 'naked ideas' as the means of crossing from one language to another? Are these ideas clothed first in Chinese and afterwards in English? Or does the Chinese clothe a collection of naked ideas from which only a selection may accept English raiment? And do fresh naked ideas come in with the English raiment? There are no clear answers possible to these questions and perhaps the questions themselves are not legitimate. Translators know they cross over but do not know by what sort of bridge. They often re-cross by a different bridge to check up again. Sometimes they fall over the parapet into limbo. There is a good deal of smuggling and surreptitious evasion, and deliberate jettisoning of embarrassing difficulties.

The theory of analysis summarized in this essay suggests that the total meaning complex be split up and that each level of analysis be regarded as dealing with one of a congruent range of modes of meaning. The accumulation of results at various levels adds up to a considerable sum of partial meanings in terms of linguistics without recourse to any underlying ideas, naked or otherwise.

If it be conceded that linguistic analysis at a series of levels produces statements of congruent modes of meaning, then these results must lead to a more critical analysis of congruent modes of translation.[65] If linguistics is to throw any light on the mechanism of translation, it might do worse than to attempt to design interlingual bridges making use of levels of analysis and measuring modes of translation by the theory of modes of meaning.

Nothing of the kind has been attempted yet in linguistic analysis. In structuralist works translation is commonly used almost casually, even when the linguist imagines he has left out 'meaning'. After considerable inquiry it appears evident that the use of all kinds of loose, impressionistic, even casual translation vitiates linguistic analysis. All the discussions on metalanguages are vapid, if slipshod and uncritical translation is not only overlooked but considered legitimate practice.

It has been realized that 'translation meanings' are identification names for language isolates abstracted from the language under description. This is legitimate if the translation procedure has not been surreptitiously used as a criterion for the abstraction. Such translation meanings must be systematic if the isolates from the language under description are systematic. The languages of translation accompanying the presentation of texts may be additional, even parenthetical. Indeed, there is a wide range of languages of translation, from bit-for-bit translations to what are called word-for-word translations, running translations, idiomatic translations and free translations. A careful watch should be kept on all these.

Since the statement of meaning by translation is inevitable in the presentation of ethnographic texts, it is to one of our greatest ethnographers that we must turn for the first organized attempt to face the problem. Malinowski was one of the very few ethnographers to analyse the principles and methods of ethnographic analysis from the linguistic point of view. Though he made contributions to linguistic theory and extended the application of the concept of situational context, his weightiest contribution was the study of the ethnographer's statement of meaning by various forms of translation and definition.[66]

At the phonological level there is no inter-alphabet if symbols are phonemic. In the history of phonetics we have moved from the notion of one sound—one symbol to the principle of one symbol per phoneme. Impressionistic transcriptions in I.P.A. if accompanied by notes and diagrams and statements of correspondences with, and differences from, the language of description comes near to a bridge at the phonetic level. But the phonetic mode is the most intractable in translation.

Between English and French there are some correspondences at the grammatical level, but many more differences. In more exotic languages it is desirable that the grammatical analysis should be keyed to the translations of the texts, and correspondences and differences specifically noted.

In the study of vocabulary there are some cases of parallel lexical systems and parallel lexical fields in cognate and mutually assimilated languages. Generally speaking, however, both in grammar and dictionary there are very few parallel systems or parallel ranges. However that may be, translation meanings and various forms of translation are inevitable and it is suggested that the relations between the language under description and the languages of description and translation should be controlled if not specifically stated.

Finally, the word 'translation' as used in this essay might also be applied to cover statements within any one language following such questions as *Tell me what that means in your own words* or *in other words* or *Give a précis or abstract*. In the interpretation of texts in earlier forms of any language, a translation has to be attempted. In assessing old historical records and documents similar problems of translation are involved. Historians are not the only workers in the other social sciences who would benefit from the advance of linguistics in the theory and practice of translation.

The rise of Asia and Africa and the contraction of Europe make the building of the bridges between languages and cultures an imperative enterprise for all the social sciences. For linguistics there is no better programme than to deepen and extend the description of modes of meaning, with critical reference to modes of translation.

XII

GENERAL CONCLUSIONS

1. Using language is one of the forms of human life, and speech is immersed in the immediacy of social intercourse. The human body is that region of the world which is the primary field of human experience but it is continuous with the rest of the world. We are in the world and world is in us.[67] Voice-produced sound has its origins in the deep experience of organic existence. In terms of living, language activity is meaningful.

2. The meaning of language can be stated in linguistic terms if the problem is dispersed by analysis at a series of congruent levels.

3. It is unnecessary to assume any 'facts' prior to statement. No fact is merely itself so to speak. There are no brute facts. A fact has to be stated in technical language at each level for each technique and for each discipline. An isolate is always an abstraction from the language complex which is itself abstracted from the mush of general goings-on. The notion of a mere fact is the product of the abstractive intellect. It is, however, imperative that we remember what we are doing and how we are doing it, and especially at what level or levels of abstraction and of statement. The various linguistic nets get the materials for the statement of the facts in technical language, with the aid of notations and diagrams of various kinds. We then expect to handle similar relevant events in renewal of connection with experience.

4. Attested language text duly recorded is in the focus of attention for the linguist. In dealing with such texts abstracted from the matrix of experience most of the environmental accompaniment in the mush of

general goings-on must of necessity be suppressed. Nevertheless the linguist must use his nets to catch and retain on his agenda such selected features or elements of the cultural matrix of the texts as may enable formal contexts of situation to be set up, within which interior relations are recognized and stated. Notional terms are permissible at this level. All language pre-supposes other events linguistic and non-linguistic issuing from each other. The abstraction here called context of situation does not deal with mere '*sense*' or with thoughts. It is not a description of the environment. It is a set of categories in ordered relations abstracted from the life of man in the flux of events, from personality in society.

5. The first principle of analysis is to distinguish between *structure* and *system*.

Structure consists of elements in interior syntagmatic relation and these elements have their places in an order of mutual expectancy. The place and order of the categories set up are recognized in structure and find application in renewal of connection with the sources of the abstractions.

Systems of commutable terms or units are set up to state the paradigmatic values of the elements.

The statement of structures and systems provides, so to speak, the anatomy and physiology of the texts. It is unnecessary, indeed perhaps inadvisable, to attempt a structural and systemic account of a language as a whole. Any given or selected restricted language, i.e. the language under description is, from the present point of view, multi-structural and polysystemic. In fact, rather like the human body itself, into which it goes and out of which it comes. As Whitehead said,[68] animals enjoy structure and to be human requires the study of structure.

6. Modes of meaning presuppose modes of experience and when two participants have places in a context of situation, the linguistic statement implies two articulated memories in relation.

It is clear we see structure as well as uniqueness in an *instance*, and an essential relationship to other *instances*. The inclusion of *person* and *personality* recognizes unity, identity, continuity, responsibility and creative effort in communicativeness or diffusion in experience which we may call *vox*. This is a different notion from what is now often called '*communication*'. This leads to a theory of reciprocal comprehension, level by level, stage by stage, in a stated series of contexts of situation. There can be no reciprocal comprehension if there is no situation.

7. The meaning of texts is dealt with by a dispersal of analysis at mutually congruent series of levels, beginning with contexts of situation

and proceeding through *collocation*, syntax (including *colligation*) to phonology and phonetics with or without the use of machines. Stylistics with some notice of the phonaesthetic features, lexicography and the place and use of translation are to be included to complete the spectrum.

8. When an exhaustive scheme of situational contexts cannot be set up, a first approach through a systematic collection of collocations is valuable in both grammatical and lexicographical studies.

9. Every analysis of any particular language must of necessity determine the values of the *ad hoc* categories to which traditional names are given. The meanings of the categories at the grammatical level are stated in terms of structures and systems.

From the point of view of the present theory, it is not considered profitable in linguistics at any rate to regard them as inner language forms, forms of thought or as mental habits or attitudes.

10. Studies of words in attested collocations emphasize the importance of the piece, phrase, clause, sentence, even of a closely knit group of sentences.

11. The statement of the main features of sound, characteristic of such longer pieces as such, makes new and exacting demands on the phonetic sciences. Similarly, phonological statement is not limited to phonemics. Prosodic categories are being developed in addition to the necessary phonematic analysis and both are keyed to the word or piece as a whole.

12. It follows that morphology as a distinct branch of descriptive linguistics has perhaps been overrated, owing to its very different place and value in historical linguistics.

13. A graphic, phonetic or phonological 'shape' or 'form' may be regarded as an exponent of a category at a level other than its own. The exponents of prosodic and of grammatical categories may be continuous or discontinuous, discrete or cumulative. The general idea underlying such analyses is the mutual expectancy of the parts and the whole, rather than an unidirectional sequence of successive linear segments.

The use made of the phonic material in the phonetic description of exponents does not require that the phonic details variously allotted should be mutually exclusive. There may be some overlap of 'symptoms' in different 'syndromes'.

14. All texts are considered to carry the implication of utterance, all utterance is considered among other things to be in terms of syllabic structure, though no general definition of syllable is either implied or indeed possible.

13*

Syllabic structures are prosodic as such, and further prosodic features may be referred to them. The terms *syllabic* and *syllable* can be used as substantives or adjectives if the language of description is English.

15. Both in phonetics and phonology the widest range of notational and formulaic statement is clearly desirable, and so also are experiments with the use of various founts and sorts of type.

16. The use of machines in linguistic analysis is now established. The present approach prefers to take linguistics into the laboratory rather than to look into laboratories for linguistics.

17. The synopsis presents in outline a general linguistic theory applicable to particular linguistic descriptions, *not* a theory of universals for general linguistic description. The main purpose is to guide the descriptive analysis of languages, especially restricted languages, and also to provide the necessary principles of synthesis to deal not only with the longer pieces of language, but also with the results of the linguistic studies of the past.

It is obvious that a theory of analysis dispersed at a series of levels must require synthesis at each level and congruence of levels. Such a theory requires what has been called the prosodic approach in phonology, since this is congruent with studies of the piece and of the longer text in collocation and extended collocation, of colligation, and finally with syntactical analysis. Grammar and lexicography are both keyed to the statement of the meaning of the restricted language under description by the controlled language of description, supplemented by well considered languages of translation.

The business of linguistics is to describe languages, and the main features of the theory, more particularly if applied to restricted languages, should produce the main structural framework for the bridges between different languages and cultures.

Notes

1. *'The technique of semantics.' W. S. Allen, *Phonetics in ancient India*. London: Cumberlege, Oxford University Press, 1953.
2. James B. Conant, *Science and common sense*. London: Cumberlege, Oxford University Press.
3. Richard von Mises, *Positivism—a study in human understanding* (translation), Harvard, 1951, 3, 5, 7, 51, 53.
4. Voegelin, *The new science of politics*. Illinois: University of Chicago Press, 1952.
5. 'Une science n'est qu'une langue bien faite.' Condillac.
6. See also *'General linguistics and descriptive grammar', especially 225–8. 'My own approach to meaning in linguistics has always been independent of

such dualisms as mind and body, language and thought, word and idea, *significant et signifié*, expression and content. These dichotomies are a quite unnecessary nuisance, and in my opinion should be dropped.'

7. *Speech*, 173.
8. *'The technique of semantics', 19.
9. See especially Chapter V, 'The problem of meaning'.
10. *Speech*, 145–6.
11. cf. L. Wittgenstein, *Philosophical investigations*. Oxford: Blackwell, 1953, 53, 61, 80, 81.
12. *Speech*, 150.
13. Ibid., 173.
14. *The tongues of men.*
15. 19–20.
16. 20.
17. cf. Aristotle, *Organon*, Chapter 6.
18. To be sharply distinguished from the interrelations, *not* of words, but of *categories* in syntagmatic relation.
19. *'The technique of semantics', 19–20.
20. Ibid., 21.
21. Ibid., 18–19.
22. Ibid., 33.
21. See *'General linguistics and descriptive grammar', 220.
24. See also *'Personality and language in society', 181–2.
25. *Modes of meaning', 191–2.
26. Gilbert Ryle, *The concept of mind*, London, 1949.
27. *'Modes of meaning,' 192.
28. Ibid., 195.
29. For *context of situation*, see: *Speech*, 173–9; *'The technique of semantics', 27–32; *The tongues of men*, 110–4; *'Modes of meaning', 203; *'General linguistics and descriptive grammar,' 225–7. For *levels of analysis*, see *'Modes of meaning,' 192.
30. Malinowski took the rudimentary notion and the word 'situation' from Dr Ph. Wegener's *Untersuchungen über die Grundfragen des Sprachlebens*, Halle, 1885. Sir Alan Gardiner dedicated his *Theory of speech and language* to Wegener in recognition of the 'Situationstheorie'.
31. See Malinowski's supplement to Ogden and Richards, *The meaning of meaning*, London, Routledge and Kegan Paul, 1949, in which 'meaning' in pragmatic speech is regarded as 'a mode of action' in a 'context of situation'. See also *Coral gardens and their magic*, II, London: Allen and Unwin, 1935.
32. *'The technique of semantics', 24. See also Ogden and Richards, *The meaning of meaning*, 46.
33. *Dunkel war's, der Mond schien helle* . . . edited by Dr Horst Kunze, Munich: Ernst Heimeran Verlag, 1952.
34. See *'General linguistics and descriptive grammar', 219–21, 227–8. The relations between elements of linguistic structures or terms of linguistic systems and non-verbal constituents of the situation are called 'situational relations'.
35. As stated above.
36. See L. Wittgenstein, *Philosophical investigations*, 7–8.
37. See Malinowski's Supplement to Ogden and Richards, *The meaning of meaning*, 315. See also my *'General linguistics and descriptive grammar', 224–6; *'The technique of semantics', 29–33; *The tongues of men*, 110–34.

38. *Philosophical investigations*, 11–2.
39. Ibid., 61 ff.
40. See *'The technique of semantics', 29.
41. Many of Damon Runyon's 'inventions' follow the features of the fable. See especially 'Pick the winner', in *Furthermore*, Constable, 1949.
42. See *'General linguistics and descriptive grammar', 224.
43. *Onomastics* has so far neglected the structural and descriptive study of names in context and collocation.
44. *Philosophical investigations*, 80, 109.
45. See *'Modes of Meaning', 194–5. In this essay, *collocation* is first suggested as a technical term.
46. See *Philosophical investigations*, 181.
47. See *'The technique of semantics', 10, 13, 29, 31.
48. See below.
49. See H. F. Simon, 'Two substantive complexes in standard Chinese,' *BSOAS* 15.2 (1953).
50. See especially 86–7, 101–3.
51. It is also possible to keep such abstractions from the phonic material strictly separate, if an adequate description is thereby achieved [cf. W. S. Allen, 'Retroflexion in Sanskrit: prosodic technique and its relevance to comparative statement', *BSOAS* 16.3 (1954) and 'Aspiration in the Hāṛautī nominal', 68 ff. of *Studies in linguistic analysis*]. Cf. F. R. Palmer, '"Openness" in Tigre: A problem in prosodic statement', *BSOAS* 18.3.576–7. See also para. 17 of Section XII, p. 202, which emphasizes the difference between a general theory for particular application and a theory of Universals for general application.
52. cf. Section II.
53. See *'The use and distribution of certain English sounds', and *'The technique of semantics', especially 20 where 'an exhaustive study of distribution' and 'contextual distribution' are specifically mentioned.
54. See p. 177.
55. See A. E. Sharp, 'A tonal analysis of the disyllabic noun in the Machame dialect of Chaga,' *BSOAS* 16.1 (1954).
56. See W. S. Allen, 'A study in the analysis of Hindi sentence structure', *Acta Linguistica* 6.2–3 (1950–1).
57. A reviewer in a recent well-known linguistic periodical (*Word* 2.1.132–4 (1955)), found it possible to personify the Optative and the Subjunctive and state that 'Apart from Tocharian, Greek is the only IE language with a real opposition between Optative and Subjunctive, all other languages having merged the two', and further that 'the Optative is clearly connected with the preterite tense (aorist or imperfect) and not with the future tense'. From the point of view of the present theory, such personifications or hypostatizations add nothing of value to any type of linguistic statement and only offer short cuts to confusion. To suggest that one can combine '*a preterital element*' with 'a futuristic one' to form an Optative is an abuse of terms in a confusion of grammatical and semantic thinking which can only cloud the precise statement of the facts in terms of linguistic analysis.
58. cf. Frei, 'A note on Bloomfield's limiting adjectives', *English Studies* 36 (1955), also Meillet, *Linguistique historique et linguistique générale* Paris, 1938, 29–35.
59. cf. Zellig S. Harris, *Methods in structural linguistics*. Chicago: University of Chicago Press, 1951, especially 165–71, 197, 213, 218, footnote 48. It will be noticed that from this point onwards, the languages *under* description suffer

from an obsolescent language *of* description and the language of translation · is not as carefully weighed as the language of phonemics, morphemics and morphophonemics. Grammatical 'meaning' is brought in by conceptual terminology, and categories which presumably are abstract and indeed ineffable, 'express what is often called grammatical agreement'. 'A single morphemic segment *l* . . . *l* . . . "the".' 'A morphemic segment consisting of the change . . . and the meaning past.' 'A morphemic segment, meaning noun.' 'Changing the meaning from female to male.' 'Indicating command.' 'With verb meaning.' 'Emphatic meaning.' 'Meaning question.'

60. *'General linguistics and descriptive grammar', 227.
61. See my *'The use and distribution of certain English sounds'.
62. See my *'Sounds and prosodies'.
63. E. J. A. Henderson, 'The main features of Cambodian pronunciation', *BSOAS* 14.1 (1952). W. S. Allen, 'Notes on the phonetics of an Eastern Armenian speaker', *TPS* 1950. J. Carnochan, 'Glottalization in Hausa', *TPS* 1952. 'A study in the phonology of an Igbo speaker', *BSOAS* 12.2 (1948). R. H. Robins and N. Waterson, 'Notes on the phonetics of the Georgian word', *BSOAS* 14.1 (1952). J. R. Firth, 'Word-palatograms and articulation'. *BSOAS* 12. 3–4 (1948). J. R. Firth and H. J. F. Adam, *'Improved techniques in palatography and kymography'. Natalie Waterson, 'Some aspects of the phonology of the nominal forms of the Turkish word', *BSOAS* 18.3.589–91, articles on gemination by J. Carnochan, T. F. Mitchell and F. R. Palmer in *Studies in linguistic analysis*.
64. *'Modes of meaning.' See especially 190, 196–200.
65. See John MacFarlane, 'Modes of translation', *Durham University Journal*, 1953.
66. See **'Ethnographic analysis and language with reference to Malinowski's views'.
67. See A. N. Whitehead, *Modes of thought*, Cambridge University Press, 1938.
68. Ibid., 105, 115, 230.

Twelve

The treatment of language in general linguistics[†]

The treatment of language by general linguistics as understood in London assumes that language is a form of human living, rather than merely a set of arbitrary signs and signals. Moreover, we do not look for an analysis of what is called thought to explain what language means —voice-produced sound is organically rooted in living beings and closely embedded in related events and circumstances. Whatever bits and pieces of language we choose to study are, or should be, functionally engaged in situational contexts. Even in reading and writing a man may be considered as speaking first to himself, and if there is no self-comprehension in this activity, it is unlikely he would be able to share comprehension with anyone else. It is to be noted here that one of the key words is comprehension—not communication.

Self-comprehension and reciprocal comprehension require that language be rooted in the organic basis of life, and necessarily also in appropriateness in situation. We also do not feel at home unless there is a mutual expectancy, not only between the elements of language structures or of the elements of discourse in a conversation for example, or in a description, explanation or argument, but also between spoken or written words and the surrounding living space in which we breathe and move.

General linguistics seeks to make statements about what language means by studying selected forms of speech and writing in actual use by persons, personalities in social life. Once more let me emphasize that this does not mean the study of the use of language as an instrument of thought, as a sort of organ of the mind. We do not deny the concept of

† *The medical press*, 242, 146–7 (1959).

mind, but we have no methodology or techniques for studying it in this way and certainly no technical language for mentalistic treatment. The whole approach could be described as psychosomatic—mind and body taken together and acting in specific living conditions describable in situational contexts.

The human being in society then is not to be regarded as an individual in life, but as a person, and so acting in his many social roles through the seven ages of man, that he conserves both his nature and his nurture in his personality. There are, of course, more than seven ages in a personal biography and many more than seven roles. The relevant forms of language, what we may call the lines of the leading roles or parts accumulate pretty well separately, the interaction of the roles being a conservative force in personality and consequently in society also. As we go through life we have to learn our various forms of language in stages as conditions of our incorporation into our social organizations. We do not mix up our roles and the various forms of language assigned to them in a kind of general mixed stew. Effective action and good manners require appropriateness of language in situational context.

Restricted languages

This leads to the adoption of the notion of *restricted languages*. There are vocational, technical and scientific languages set in a matrix of closely determined sections of what may be called the general language. It is one of the requirements of science that the attention of our scientific equipment should be focused on manageable subjects and hence the importance of the study of restricted languages—restricted by scientific method conforming to functions of language in life. The term 'restricted language' is applied to a scientific fiction required by linguistic analysis. It is not a general term for any actual institutionalized form of language easily recognized by the average man. We have to study the language of babies, or boys, girls and adolescents of different classes and regions, and of all manner of specialized situations determined by manners and customs and recognized institutions. The situationally appropriate forms of language can themselves be regarded as institutionalized.

The social person collects a varied repertory of interlocking roles without conflict or serious disharmony. Such an integrated personality makes for personal and social responsibility and stability.

For the purpose of linguistics such a person would be regarded as being in command of a constellation of restricted languages, satellite languages so to speak, governed by personality in social life and the general language of the community.

Speech and language communities

In this connection it is useful to recognize distinctions between a close *speech fellowship* and a wider *speech community* in what may be called the *language community* comprising both written and spoken forms of the general language. A social personality in any large modern language community has got to be a pluralist in social roles and consequently in varying degrees polydialectal. We may still have among us here in Britain a certain number of U-persons who may be mono-dialectal, almost as unilingual as the ancient Hindu Brahmins or the ancient Athenians. They are linguistically speaking fortunate and probably rather less disposed to split personality than large numbers of our masses being educated upwards. A norm firmly controlled by social sanctions and supported by education saves a good deal of trouble by promoting happiness through good habits. It is the opposite of the go-as-you-please tendencies so common among us and represented by such expressions as 'Why on earth not?' 'I couldn't care less' and 'So what?'

Nevertheless what has been called the escalator personality capable of moving both ways is perhaps functional in Western Europe. If this quality can be referred to as E, then the difficult personalities today are the combinations of U and non-E, and of non-U and non-E. To be both U and E is probably quite a workable formula for general sociability in England. So far we have looked at the treatment of language according to one of the approaches in general linguistics.

Now we may look at the treatment of language by educationists and clinicians. In this therapeutic sense of treatment the psychosomatic approach must again be emphasized. And in order to facilitate the discussion of the treatment of speech defects as distinct from language disorders it might prove useful if we glance at certain technical words and phrases. First of all, levels of analysis or levels of treatment: speech therapists are well aware of the phonetic aspect of language; what they require is, above all, an appreciation of what the phonetic level of treatment means in relation to the other levels such as the phonological and grammatical levels and the semantic level, all three of which are relevant to the treatment of language disorders which are deeply rooted in the person, and clearly so affect the personality in social action that the further development of what might be called 'morbid linguistics' would seem to be indicated by joint research with those concerned in the medical profession.

Idiolect and monolect

Then, in addition to the term *restricted language*, the terms *idiolect* and *monolect* are useful in case description. An *idiolect* is a form of language used between two personalities chiefly in one of their personal roles possibly overlapping with another role. It is possible to imagine two professional men with similar professional training and in the same field who might both lisp or have a similar speech defect and, in the restricted language of professional conversation therefore, share the same idiolect as it would appear at most levels of linguistic description. But a patient with a language disorder as the result, let us say, of a serious injury, would have a patient's form of language with a sufficient number of morbid phonological, grammatical or lexical features to warrant the use of the term *monolect* to refer to it. In works on aphasias and other language disorders which are here clearly differentiated from speech defects, generalizations have quite properly been made from such knowledge as we have of the monolects of patients. But we do not know sufficient about such monolects, and there is a promising field of joint research in linguistic analysis which might lead to a fruitful development of clinical treatment by clinicians with the necessary training in linguistics.

Finally I would like to add a recommendation that more attention might be given to linguistics by psycho-analysts and psychiatrists, whose principal instruments are forms of language operating between therapist and patient in the consulting room.